STILLWATER TROUT FISHERIES

A Guide to Reservoirs,
Lakes and Other Still Waters
in England & Wales

Edited by
H. F. WALLIS

ERNEST BENN LIMITED
LONDON & TONBRIDGE

Published by Ernest Benn Limited
25 New Street Square, London, EC4A 3JA
& Sovereign Way, Tonbridge, Kent, TN9 1RW

First published 1976

© *Ernest Benn Limited 1976*

Printed in Great Britain

ISBN 0 510-21002-3 (lib)
0 510-21005-8 (p/b)

Note by the Editor

This book is divided into ten sections, roughly corresponding to the areas of the new regional water authorities. Waters are listed alphabetically within each section and cross-referenced where necessary. They are also separately listed in the index. Entries have been prepared from personal knowledge, experience and research, and from answers to questions submitted to fishery managers. The shorter entries are for minor fisheries, for those where the data was inadequate for a full-scale entry or for those controlled by clubs and reserved for members only. Some fishery owners have specifically requested that no reference be made to their waters, and this may account for some omissions.

To help anglers assess the quality of a fishery, details have been given on stocking policy, average and record sizes of fish taken, seasonal returns of catches and so on. The figures supplied by fishery managers on average and record sizes are often approximations so should be read with discretion.

An attempt has also been made in most cases to include some advice on fishing the water — best times, conditions, fly patterns and so on. For a selection of notable fisheries we have asked expert anglers with long experience of them to write an appraisal — John Goddard on Blagdon/Chew Valley, Bob Church on Grafham, Dick Shrive on Eye Brook, John Jeffrey on Derwent, Geoffrey Bucknall on Sundridge and F. W. (Ted) Holiday on the Welsh fisheries. These supplement general articles by Dick Walker, Brian Clarke, Dermot Wilson and Conrad Voss Bark which will be found in the opening pages and which make particular reference to some of the well-known private fisheries. They will be found at the start of the book.

Fly-fishermen will find it useful to refer to the detail/contour maps when reading the appraisals. Area maps are also included to help anglers locate the lakes and reservoirs referred to, and further advice will be found in the individual entries.

Wherever possible the permit charges given refer to the 1976 season. Where this data was not available in time, approximate figures are given.

Abbreviations used throughout the book are as follows: st — season ticket; mt — monthly tickets; wt — weekly ticket; and dt — day ticket.

Acknowledgements

In compiling this book I have had to rely heavily on the cooperation of fishery managers and club secretaries, nearly always anonymous but unfailingly helpful. I warmly appreciate the efforts of all those who have supplied information and especially P. J. Parkinson, fisheries scientist of the Welsh National Water Development Authority, Peter A. Cliff, Assistant Press Officer of the Severn-Trent Water Authority, and Peter Muggeridge in the Information Office of the South West Water Authority.

Thanks are also due to Roy Eaton, Production Editor of *Trout and Salmon*, for his valuable help in arranging a trip to Empingham and in supplying illustrations, to my librarian wife, Elizabeth, for aid with the index and to my son, Neil, for his help with proof reading (truly a family concern!). And to Jill Kolat, who typed the manuscript.

But above all I would like to acknowledge the splendid cooperation I have received throughout from the publishers and especially from Michael Gale, whose constant and continuing interest in the guide has been a source of moral as well as practical support.

H.F.W.

Contents

Trout Fishing Transformation

H. F. WALLIS

Gazing into his crystal ball in the mid-1960s, some angling soothsayer might well have prophesied a bleak future for fly-fishermen, especially those based in towns. With the number of anglers fast outstripping the supply of fishable water, and with little immediate prospect of increasing that supply, it seemed then that the chance of finding worthwhile sport within reasonable distance of a suburban home would have been about as great as coming across Dick Walker fishing without that famous hat.

Anglers exiled to Streatham, Selly Oak or Salford faced the daunting prospect of spanning mile after mile of urban sprawl, past the reeking chimneys, the dried-up and poisoned streams and the anarchic mess of traffic roundabouts and petrol stations, and then travelling perhaps a hundred miles and more to cast a fly for trout on some hard-fished river.

The burden of the big town may have been less oppressive in Cardiff, Swansea or Newport, with the beckoning call of those Welsh hills and valleys plainly heard, but if you came from the Rhondda, man, there was a right old battle to be waged against the seepage from the coal mines if you wanted your trout to go on living.

With no sign of a slackening in recruits to the army of anglers, how could anyone at that time dare hope that within ten years there would be such a transformation as we see today?

Yet the solution then was within our grasp. For those with ears to hear, the whispers of it had come drifting across the Atlantic from the USA, where, it was said, hundreds of new trout lakes were being dug and stocked with well-proportioned trout. Although there were scores of trout-holding reservoirs in England and Wales, some of which, like Blagdon and Vyrnwy, had acquired a considerable reputation, the potential was only beginning to be appreciated.

The remarkable returns at Chew Valley in the late 1950s had shown what might be achieved by a forward-looking management and stocking policy. If trout of a quality to make angling dreams come true could be bred here, why not elsewhere?

Anglers were so delighted with Chew and the management so delighted with the response to their efforts that further developments of this kind were inevitable. Ten years later Grafham burst on the scene, to set the seal, as it were, on the new trend.

From all points of view, stocking reservoirs with trout is an eminently sensible thing to do. First, it meets a very real need, as we have seen — and let it not be forgotten that reservoirs cater for other recreational activities, too, such as sailing, canoeing, picnicking and bird-watching. It must have loomed large in the calculations of our legislators that the unpopularity of reservoirs in some quarters might well be due to the fact that, once created, many of them were closed to the public or under-used — since we must have them, it could be argued, why not make the best possible use of them?

Stocking with trout is also biologically desirable, in that trout eat snails, shrimps, insects and other creatures which the water engineer would have to get rid of in some other way and at considerable trouble and expense. Furthermore, there is the economic argument that it provides a substantial source of food and nobody in these days of soaring protein prices needs reminding how valuable a resource that is. Some reservoirs produce over 30,000lb, roughly 15 tons, of trout a year. In addition to this, there must be an economic return for reservoir managements from the sale of fishing permits.

Also, fly-fishing for trout is not subject to the same kind of public prejudice as coarse fishing — people have reacted violently against the idea of 'contaminating' public water supplies by 'lowly' creatures like maggots and worms. Emotional and illogical though such attitudes may be, they nevertheless have to be taken into account.

All these factors have played a part in producing the remarkable situation we have today. How remarkable was revealed by Conrad Voss Bark, a contributor to this book, in an admirable account of the development of stillwater trout fishing in *Trout and Salmon* (July 1974).

His researches showed that by 1969 some 228 reservoirs in England and Wales had been opened for fly-fishing, but that the really big expansion took place between 1945 and 1973. During that period some 75 reservoirs were opened for fly-fishing — thus Chew and Grafham, outstanding though they were, formed only a small part of the revival. What is more, those 75 waters were spread widely throughout the country, so that many could be reached fairly easily from the big conurbations.

Side by side with the opening of reservoirs, Mr Voss Bark pointed out, had come 'an equally astonishing development' — the growth of private commercial lake fisheries, some day-ticket waters, but most operating on a syndicate or subscription basis. Nobody knew how many there were, he stated, though he thought there could be at least 250, even if many were small waters kept for the farmer or estate owner and a few friends.

Two factors are worth noting as having promoted this particular trend. First is the relative decline of traditional agriculture as a profitable enterprise — it became more lucrative in many cases to use the land for a trout fishery than to keep cows or grow corn on it. The other is the introduction of new, low-cost lake construction techniques, details of which can be found in a booklet produced by The Angling Foundation *The Creation of Low-Cost Fisheries*, available for the price of the postage from the Foundation at 145 Oxford Street, London, W1R 3TB.

These private fisheries have made an invaluable contribution to the angling scene, not only by providing more fly-fishing opportunities but by developing skilled management techniques, as at Two Lakes under Alex Behrendt and at Avington, where Sam Holland's 'super trout' have captured world attention.

So rapidly were these developments taking place in both the public and private sectors that Conrad Voss Bark reckoned that from 1945 to 1973 new fisheries had opened at the rate of one a month. And the pace would not seem to have slackened since.

His conclusions: Since 1945 additional fly-fishing facilities have been provided for between 200,000 and 250,000 anglers in England and Wales. Probably more anglers are fishing lakes and reservoirs now than have fished all the rivers of England and Wales before the war. Probably one-third, and possibly half, of the anglers in the country fish still waters either regularly or occasionally. There are four times as many fly-fishermen as there were in the 1930s and nearly all this expansion has been made possible by the provision of reservoirs and lakes. If the present trend continues, by the end of the century most fly-fishermen will be fishing man-made still waters.

Here, then, was the background against which it was decided to produce this book. The aim was to provide as comprehensive and up-to-date a record as possible of the developments referred to. It was a specially formidable task so far as the private fisheries were concerned, because, as Mr Voss Bark said, no proper records covering England and Wales had been kept. This was largely uncharted territory.

What made it even more of a challenge was that the book had to be produced within a strict time scale — between the documenting of returns from one season to the imposition of charges for the next. It was essentially a close-season operation.

It was clearly impossible in these circumstances to register every trout-holding lake and pond in the two countries. One had to be selective — some evidence of quality and availability had to be provided. Though entries have not been restricted to fly-only waters, generally speaking mixed fisheries have been looked at askance. Landing trout on worm or maggot in a water swarming with coarse fish is hardly trout fishing as we know it — however surprised and delighted the captor may be.

So far as private fisheries are concerned, we are aware that there exists a reluctance on the part of some owners to publicise their waters where they already have more than enough regular visitors, and this probably accounts for the non-return of some questionnaires.

For one reason or another, therefore, some waters, and possibly important ones, will have escaped the net, and we would not take it amiss if readers let us know about them so that we can put this right in future editions. The same goes for any inaccuracies.

This has been in many ways an exciting voyage of discovery, especially so far as the private waters are concerned, and we hope anglers will feel some of this excitement as they turn the pages.

Our researches amply confirm the general tenor of Conrad Voss Bark's comments. There now exists a wealth of trout fishing on still waters within easy reach of most big towns. The London fly-fisherman should be specially gratified. Not since the destruction of trout streams like the Wandle, Ravensbourne and Colne has the Londoner had such a variety of trout fishing on his doorstep. When in living memory could he hope to land trout of 3lb and more within half an hour's journey of Central

London? Walthamstow and Kempton Park reservoirs have been joined by Barn Elms and soon the mighty Datchet Reservoir will be opened, even if facilities are restricted. Weir Wood and Bough Beech are not so far away either, and soon Bewl Bridge will be joining them. Study of the Thames section will also reveal a veritable ring of private fisheries in the Home Counties.

Opportunities elsewhere have been similarly reinforced. Overshadowing all the developments referred to will be the opening of the giant 3100-acre Empingham Reservoir in Rutland — projected for 1977. Conceived from the outset as a trout fishery, this water was stocked initially with half a million fish. Although vast, it is so shaped as to be by no means overpowering and our prophecy is that fly-fishermen will be delighted with the facilities available and the quality of the sport.

We are, therefore, on a rapidly rising growth curve so far as still waters are concerned. Even if fewer reservoirs are built in future — and a halt must be called somewhere — there is a vast potential for expanding existing facilities, notably in the county of Yorkshire, where scores of reservoirs are still closed to any form of recreation. The time will come, of course — and some feel it has already arrived — when trout fishermen will be so well catered for that some fisheries will go to the wall. Against this is the argument that the more fly-fishing opportunities you create, the more fly-fishermen will emerge to take advantage of them. Even so, their numbers, too, must be finite.

There are some who find it difficult to be enthusiastic about these changes, who declare their overwhelming preference for wild trout taken from streams or lakes created naturally and not artificially, and who deplore reservoir-fishing innovations such as shooting heads, line trays and 'monstrous' deep-sunk lures.

So be it. Every man to his taste. What we have been considering here is essentially a compromise, dictated by the circumstances of modern life. It is far from ideal — but it clearly meets the needs of thousands of anglers. Nor is only one type of fisherman catered for. There is still a place within the scheme of things for the delicate caster of the dry fly or the expert with a nymph. Very much so, as contributors to our pages demonstrate. The skills required are as varied as the waters listed, and are no less demanding. And with the exercise of these skills in pleasant places comes a special sort of satisfaction; different, perhaps, from that derived from the Test or Tamar, but not to be under-rated, especially when the size of the quarry is taken into account.

And if there are still those who will never on any account be weaned away from rivers, let them take comfort from the fact that the more trout fishing there is to go round, the freer the river banks are likely to be.

H.F.W.

Tackling Up

Fly-fishing for trout in still waters differs in many ways from fly-fishing elsewhere. Traditional river tackle just won't do for most still waters.

Why are stillwater requirements so different? The main reason lies in the wide variety of techniques available to the fisherman — that's what makes stillwater fishing so fascinating. To a far greater extent than on rivers, he can fish his fly at any depth he chooses, from a dry fly on the surface to a lure that 'bumps the bottom'. His tackle must allow him to find the best 'taking depth', which can vary from day to day and hour to hour.

Then again, a stillwater fisherman can 'work' or retrieve his fly at any speed he chooses — from letting it lie motionless to 'stripping' it towards him as fast as he can. His tackle has to permit this versatility, because different rates of retrieve will suit different flies and lures. These in themselves will imitate a greater variety of insects and other trout food than is necessary on any river.

The distance he'll want to cast will also vary enormously. On small still waters, such as Two Lakes or Avington, he may not need much distance. Nor will he need it when fishing the *margins* of larger waters (far too often neglected) or when he's fishing from a boat.

But usually, when he's bank-fishing on medium-sized waters or large reservoirs such as Grafham, he'll need tackle which is at least *capable* of casting a long way out — 30 yards or so. He may not always have to make use of this capability, but he's likely to be handicapped if his tackle doesn't possess it.

Versatility is the keyword, then. Let's consider it in the light of the most common questions asked by fishermen about stillwater tackle. Some will be elementary questions, some more advanced. Experienced fishermen please skip the elementary ones!

Is a good rod the most important item?

It is certainly very important. You won't be able to fish happily without a suitable rod — a rod that's powerful enough to cast a fair distance, light enough for you to use all day without exhausting yourself and also flexible enough to 'present' a fly fairly delicately at short range, without a lot of clumsy splashing.

It's probably your choice of *lines*, however, which will give you the maximum versatility. You can have fast-sinking lines for fishing deep and retrieving quickly, slow-sinking lines for fishing rather less deep, and floating lines for fishing on or near the surface. The lines can also be either heavy or light — and in fact their weight will greatly influence the sort of rod you choose.

How does the weight of the line affect the rod?

A rod works on much the same principle as an archer's bow. It has to be *bent* before it can propel anything. A bow is of course bent by the archer's 'pull'. A rod is bent, as it comes forward, by the weight of line in the air behind it. It takes a heavy line to bend a stiff and powerful rod. But a more flexible rod can obviously be bent by a lighter line.

It is absolutely vital that the rod and line should suit each other. If you use a stiff rod with a light line, the rod won't bend and therefore won't propel the line. Alternatively, if you use a very flexible rod and a heavy line, the rod simply won't be able to cope with the weight. It won't keep the line up in the air, and it may even break. A rod with the right weight of line, however, will cast smoothly and well without any effort or exertion on the part of the caster.

What weight of line should a stillwater rod be able to handle?

Most rod manufacturers nowadays mark on each rod the line weight that is most suitable for it. You'll usually find the symbol #, followed by a number, just above the handle — e.g. #5 or #8. Any fly-line you buy will have a similar number on the package, and this will tell you the weight of the line. As the number increases, so does the line weight.

For instance, a #4 or #5 line, or even a #6 line, is comparatively light and therefore suitable for a fairly flexible rod. This rod-and-line combination won't enable you to cast immense distances but it will be ideal for delicate fishing on small ponds, or from a boat, or for fishing the margins of larger waters, or on calm evenings. Never underestimate the value of a light line when distance isn't essential, because there will be less splash to frighten fish, and less line-shadow too.

For most stillwater fishing, however, you will want to be able to make longer casts. So you'll need a heavier line — say a #8 or #9.

Does this mean I ought to have more than one rod?

Don't worry, most of us can't afford it. Although a number of devoted stillwater fly-fishermen sometimes carry as many as three or four rods, it's perfectly possible to have a 'compromise' rod which will serve you *almost* as well. One reason for this is that many good stillwater rods will handle not only the weight of line they're recommended for, but also a line one size lighter and one size heavier.

For large, still waters, therefore, you might choose a rod designed for a #8 line. When you don't need maximum distance, you can use a #7 with it — and fish fairly delicately. And on the occasions when you do need distance, you can use a #8 or even a #9.

If you normally fish small still waters, however, you may prefer a rod marked #6 or #7 — to allow you just a little extra finesse.

When you get a rod, ask your dealer about its 'tolerance' for different line weights.

What's the ideal length?

The most popular length for a stillwater fly-rod it about 9ft 3in; at any rate so far as large still waters are concerned. And it's a good length too. It is long enough for power and distance and also for fishing from a boat (remember that length comes in handy when you're sitting down), but it isn't so long that it's too heavy or cumbersome.

Most fishermen find that a rod of over 9ft 6in is rather unwieldy — unless it is made of graphite. But more of that later.

For boat fishing a rod should be at least 8ft 9in.

Is a glass rod as good for still water as a cane rod?

Usually it is far better. Cane can be an excellent material for river and brook rods up to 9ft long — because it normally requires less 'line-pull' than glass before it begins flexing. So it lends itself well to delicate fishing with a light line and to casting accurately at short range as well as at medium range. But many glass rods aren't very far behind in these respects, and for still water they have the overwhelming advantage of being appreciably lighter.

Generally speaking, a rod which weighs more than about 5½oz is likely to prove tiring before the end of the day, particularly since the average stillwater fisherman puts in more casts per day than the average river fisherman. Only a cane rod which is 9ft long or less can keep within this weight. Fishermen on small still waters, therefore, can certainly use such a rod if they wish.

But most stillwater fishermen want a slightly longer rod — and if this is made of cane it will need a lot of effort to use it. A glass rod will give the necessary length *and* lightness. Furthermore, glass is a powerful material with a 'fast' action. It is therefore good for building up line-velocity and for casting a long way. Glass is a highly suitable material for a stillwater rod.

How about the new material, 'graphite'?

You'll be hearing a lot about graphite, which is sometimes also known as 'carbon-fibre'.*
It's a new synthetic material which was actually first invented in Britain in 1965. But the USA then took the lead in developing it for fly-fishermen, and graphite fly-rods were marketed there in 1974. They have only recently begun to be manufactured in this country

Good graphite fly-rods are at present very expensive. This is partly because the raw material costs far more than glass, and partly because graphite rods have to be made to more critical tolerances. Another fact to bear in mind is that as with any other material, there are some very good graphite rods and also some very bad ones. The material itself doesn't guarantee a good rod.

But these points having been made, there's no doubt at all that graphite represents a tremendously significant development in rod-making. And it has a number of special advantages for stillwater fishermen.

---

*Terminology is not yet settled. 'Graphite' is the term used here, although 'carbon fibre' might be a more accurate name for the material.

What does graphite actually do?

First of all, graphite is an even lighter and 'faster' material than glass. To be more exact, a graphite rod can be some 25 per cent lighter than an equivalent glass rod — and can develop even more line velocity.

This has important implications for rod length. Suppose you are accustomed to a 9ft 6in glass rod. If you change to graphite instead, you could: (a) use a 9ft rod and achieve the same distance with far less weight in your hand: or (b) continue with a 9ft 6in rod and achieve greater distance with rather *less* effort than at present: or (c) use a 10ft rod and achieve considerably greater distance with no more effort. Graphite reservoir rods 10ft long and weighing less than 3½ ounces are now being produced in Britain.

Graphite has other technical advantages too — including an absence of 'quiver' and the ability to cast a very tight loop, which makes it excellent for casting into a wind. Graphite will also handle an exceptionally wide range of line-weights. It is now very possible that a stillwater fisherman may be able to use #5, #6, #7 and #8 lines on the self-same graphite rod. And although several early graphite rods proved rather fragile, the best models nowadays are just as tough and durable as glass.

But there's no 'magic' about graphite. It won't turn a bad caster into a good one or compensate in any way for lack of skill. For many people a graphite rod could simply be an extravagant luxury, since they'll catch just as many trout on a glass rod. Glass will probably continue to be the most popular material for a long time to come.

What sort of reel is the best?

You can choose from a wide variety of reels. Broadly speaking, any reliable fly-reel will serve you well — provided that it's not altogether too heavy, and provided always that it has sufficient capacity to hold your line, plus 60—100yd of thinner 'backing' behind it. If you hook a big trout in still water, you may well need this much.

The simplest type of reel — a single-action reel — is the lightest. Many fishermen prefer it. Alternatively, you can have a multiplying fly-reel. Each turn of the handle will then make the drum revolve two or more times, so that you can wind line on to the reel more quickly. This type is also in common use, though it's usually a trifle heavier.

A third fairly widely-used type of reel is an 'automatic'. This has a clockwork mechanism which winds itself up as you strip line off the reel for casting (or when a fish takes out line). Then, to wind in, you simply press a lever and the drum revolves of its own accord. Automatic reels are a little heavier still. But they'll prevent your having loose line lying around.

Reels are very much a matter of personal preference. You can use an extremely light and simple reel — or you can have added refinements at the cost of a little extra weight (and money). Nearly all reels are now available with interchangeable spools. This means that you can carry additional fly-lines on spare spools, rather than having to take more than one reel with you.

Are floating lines for dry-fly fishing?

Yes, but they have many other uses. If you're to be a serious stillwater fisherman, you'll certainly need more than one type of line. But at the beginning you'll probably find that a 'floater' is the most useful single type.

This is partly because you can fish some way below the surface. The weight of a wet fly or nymph will draw your nylon leader under (though only gradually) and usually a foot or two of fly-line as well. Theoretically you can fish almost as deep as your leader is long, if you retrieve very slowly indeed.

If you wish, you can make your fly sink a little faster by putting a small split shot on the leader, six inches or so above the fly. Often you won't want it to do this, however, because many nymphs and pupae work best when they're fished slowly only just below the surface. Then you may need to grease your leader — up to the point where you wish it to sink. And, of course, you can always fish a dry fly with a floating line.

Finally, anyone who's still learning how to cast will get on best with a floating line. This is because he'll be able to lift it cleanly and directly from the surface each time he recasts, rather than having to extract it from the depths. Once he's put in a little practice, he'll be ready to add sinking lines to his armoury.

Is a fast-sinking line better than a slow-sinking line?

Not necessarily. It depends on the depth at which the trout are taking — and also on the rate at which you want to retrieve. Any sinking fly-line of a given weight can be made in different 'densities'. As a result, it can be 'slow-sinking' or 'fast-sinking' or 'extra-fast-sinking'.

You can fish deepest with an extra-fast-sinking line and a slow retrieve. As you speed up your retrieve, of course, you'll fish less and less deep. At each speed a 'standard' fast-sinking line will fish slightly less deep than an extra-fast-sinking line. And a slow-sinking line will fish even nearer the surface.

The combinations are virtually endless. But if you're getting just one sinking line in addition to a floater, you may well find that a fast-sinking one or an extra-fast-sinking one will indeed be the most useful. You'll be able to get down to trout without wasting time, if they're feeding deep. And by varying your rate of retrieve, you'll have as much versatility as two lines can give you. If you can afford a third line, get a slow-sinker too.

Should I have a 'sink-tip' line?

You may find it useful on some waters. But normally it will only be a fourth choice. A sink-tip line is a floating line with 3 or 4yd of sinking line at the very end. It will therefore fish deeper than an ordinary floating line, but not so deep as a sinking line.

If you don't wish to go to the expense of a sink-tip line, you can quite easily make up your own — so long as you can get the necessary three or four yards of sinking line. Simply attach it to the end of your floating line with a 'cast connector' (ask your tackle-dealer about this useful device.)

Your home-made sink-tip line won't cast quite so smoothly as a regular one, but it will have compensating advantages. You can add as long or as short a sink-tip as you wish. Then you can attach or detach it very easily, without changing your whole line. And it's also economical.

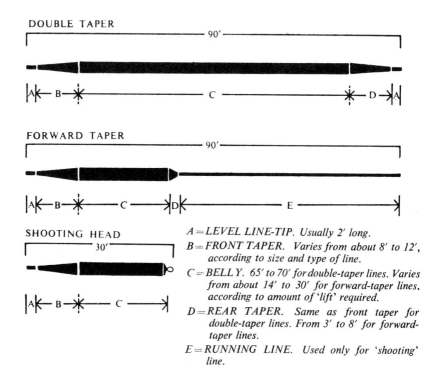

DOUBLE TAPER

FORWARD TAPER

SHOOTING HEAD

A = *LEVEL LINE-TIP. Usually 2' long.*
B = *FRONT TAPER. Varies from about 8' to 12', according to size and type of line.*
C = *BELLY. 65' to 70' for double-taper lines. Varies from about 14' to 30' for forward-taper lines, according to amount of 'lift' required.*
D = *REAR TAPER. Same as front taper for double-taper lines. From 3' to 8' for forward-taper lines.*
E = *RUNNING LINE. Used only for 'shooting' line.*

One final type of sinking line should perhaps be mentioned, though its use isn't always very desirable. Some stillwater fishermen find that they can reach the depths very quickly if they cast out a short length of the lead-core type of line commonly sold for deep trolling.

Are double-taper lines as useful as forward-taper lines?

Double-taper lines are just a little easier than forward-taper lines to cast with, and they'll also present a fly very delicately — but forward-taper lines are better for casting a good distance.

Both types of line are normally about 30yd long. But otherwise they're fairly different. A double-taper line has a long and thickish 'belly' in the middle — some 23 to 24yd of it. On either side of the belly the line tapers down to a fine level tip about 2ft long. So you can use either end for casting. When one end is worn out, you can reverse the line and use the other.

Only one end of a forward-taper line, however, is intended for casting. This again has a level tip which tapers up towards a 'belly' — but the belly is always far shorter, from about 5 to 10 yards according to the make of line. Thereafter all the remaining line becomes fine and level and is called 'running line'.

The big difference in actual use consists of the amount of line you can 'aerialize' when false-casting. You can only aerialize as much of a forward-taper line as will bring you to the beginning of the 'running line'. This is important — because if you aerialize any more, the thick part of the line will be too far beyond the rod-tip to be properly controlled and propelled. But once this amount has been aerialized, you can then 'shoot' a great deal more line on your final cast and achieve a very good distance, because the thin 'running line' slips easily through the rod-rings, without too much friction.

With a double-taper line you don't have to be nearly as careful about the amount you're aerializing, because after the first few yards you'll always have some of the thickish belly-line at your rod-tip. This not only makes casting very simple, but also helps the line to 'turn over' smoothly and present a fly delicately. Nevertheless, it's impossible to 'shoot' so much of a double-taper line, since its thick belly won't pass through the rod-rings nearly so easily.

So a double-taper line is excellent for casting at short range, while a forward-taper line is better for long-range work. It also takes up less room on a spool, allowing either more backing or a lighter reel to be used. Stillwater fishermen often solve the dilemma by using a double-taper *floating* line, when presentation may be more important than distance — and a forward-taper *sinking* line, when distance may possibly be vital.

Many stillwater fishermen, however, prefer a shooting head to either.

What are the advantages of a shooting head?

Most people find that shooting heads need a little more practice to use successfully than do full-length fly-lines, and beginners may be wise to stick to the latter. But for sheer efficiency, shooting heads are the best lines of all on the majority of still waters — and casting with them can soon be mastered by proficient fishermen. A 'standard' shooting head consists of only 10yd of fly-line (virtually the same as the first 10yd of a double-taper line) and to the rear end of this is attached a hundred yards or so of monofilament (20lb or 25lb test).

When being cast, the 'head' is aerialized till the monofilament is reached, in much the same way as a forward-taper line is aerialized till the running line is reached. Then the monofilament is 'shot' on the final cast. But because the monofilament is even finer and smoother than running line, even greater distances are possible.

How about delicacy and good presentation? They're no problem when you're making very short casts, because the join between the shooting head and the nylon won't yet have reached the tip-ring. So you might just as well be casting with a double-taper line.

But when you're casting farther, and when the join does go out beyond the tip-ring, good presentation is undoubtedly a little more difficult — because the line tends to 'turn over' less smoothly. A reasonably good caster, however, will always be able to present his fly well with a shooting head, even at long range.

Good presentation is usually more important with a floating line than with a sinking line. A number of people, therefore, use a full-length line as a floater — but change to a shooting head when they need maximum distance with a sinking line.

Why not have a longer shooting head?

It's a very good idea — particularly for a floater. All you have to do is to acquire a 'half-line' (sometimes called 'single-taper line') of the right weight for your rod. These half-lines are in fact half a normal double-taper line, and are 15yd long. Many tackle dealers sell them.

Then trim the line (from the thick end) till you have exactly the length of shooting head you want. Attach this to your monofilament with a needle-knot. The right length will be the precise yardage that you can aerialize easily, without too much effort and without straining your rod. Usually a length of some 12 yd (rather than the standard 10yd) proves to be best.

This made-to-measure shooting head gives you several advantages. You can use it for distance, just as you'd use a normal shooting head. But the extra length will also allow you to cover more fish at closer range (using the 'head' just as you'd use a double-taper line) *before* you come to the monofilament. If the head is 12yd long, and if you then add another 5yd for the combined lengths of your rod and leader, you'll see that you can cast in this manner for trout up to 17yd away.

Half-lines and shooting heads take up even less room on a spool than forward-taper lines do, so that you can use smaller and lighter reels if you wish. One final point is that longer-than-usual shooting heads are better suited to floating lines than to sinking lines, because it's difficult to lift a lot of sinking line from the water for recasting.

What's the best colour for fly-lines?

It is generally accepted that a trout will be least suspicious of a line when its colour matches the tone of the background. A sinking line should therefore always have a dark tone (green or brown) because trout will normally see it against dark backgrounds.

The ideal colour for a floating line isn't so easy to lay down. Light-coloured lines (white or pale-blue or peach) are by far the most popular, since it's assumed that they'll usually be seen against the background of the sky. On a number of waters, however, a floating line may be seen against a background of trees — and then a green or brown line will be less visible.

Still, the dilemma isn't so important as perhaps it sounds. If a fairly shy trout is feeding on or near the surface (particularly in calm water) he's likely to be frightened by any line that lands near him — *whatever* its colour. For one thing, it will always cast the same amount of shadow. So it's far better if he sees just the leader and fly. Plenty of fish can be caught on either light-coloured *or* dark-coloured floating lines.

Is one sort of leader better than another?

For good casting, it's vital that your leader should have a fattish butt (thick end). Otherwise there'll be too big a difference in diameter between line-tip and leader-butt, resulting in an abrupt interruption in the taper from line to fly. Then the leader's less likely to straighten out properly.

So a good leader should start off with nylon at least 0.45mm or 0.50mm in diameter (some 23lb to 26lb test). Thereafter it should taper gradually down to the size of tip you want. For large trout you may need a tip of 7lb breaking-strain or more, particularly if you're fishing fast and deep. But for smaller trout on a floating line, a 4lb tip may be enough.

You can either make up your own leaders by knotting together several lengths of nylon with differing diameters (the cheapest way) or you can buy your leaders ready-made. In the latter case they can be either 'knotted' or 'knotless' (with the taper already incorporated in a single length of nylon).

Knotted leaders are marginally superior to knotless leaders so far as casting qualities are concerned. They 'turn over' and straighten out very well, especially into a wind. They do, however, have just one disadvantage — in that the knots create little wakes when you're retrieving near the surface in calm water. So knotless leaders are often preferable. (But you can't avoid knots in a leader if you want to have 'droppers' and to use more than one fly.)

How long should a leader be?

The 'standard' ready-made leader is normally 9ft long — and this is perfectly adequate for a great deal of stillwater fishing. It's unwise to use a shorter leader, and a slightly longer one is often a good idea when the weather's bright or the water calm. A skilful fisherman can sometimes handle an 18ft or 20ft leader — but it's difficult to cast out well in a tricky wind.

To have a leader a little longer than 9ft, and also to make sure that it begins with a suitably thick butt, simply keep a 3ft or 4ft length of 23lb or 26lb nylon permanently needle-knotted to your fly-line. Then attach it to the butt of a 'standard' knotless leader (having cut off the loop) with a blood-knot. When you want to renew the leader, do so at the blood-knot. It's a very satisfactory way of making certain of a good leader.

* * *

This by no means covers all the tackle that stillwater fly-fishermen find useful. One glaring gap is any account of the flies themselves. Other contributors to these pages, however, will be offering their own opinions on this large subject. Then there are scores of necessary and not-so-necessary accessories to be seen in shops and in catalogues. A pair of thigh-boots and a landing-net are of course among the more essential of them.

But on the whole there's no lack of good advice to be had about these. And the tackle itself isn't difficult to find. I've simply tried here to describe some of the more important aspects of stillwater tackle, aspects over which some expensive mistakes can be made, and to explain a few underlying principles. The most important principle of all, however, is to realize that no amount of good tackle can be any substitute whatsoever for knowledge and skill. Knowledgeable and skilful fishermen will always catch more trout than other people, even if their tackle is a good deal worse.

Big Fish from Small Waters

DICK WALKER

A recent development in trout fishing is the production, by selective breeding, of very large trout, fish running from 6lb up to 14lb or more. It seems certain that this process will continue and that fish upwards of 20lb in weight will be produced.

So far, most of these big fish have been artificially fed in stewponds, to the size at which they were eventually caught, but there is already evidence that with increased inherited growth potential, better growth rates can also be obtained with rich natural feeding. Trout released into big lowland reservoirs have grown from under 1lb to over 9lb, in the case of rainbow trout, and to even greater weights in the case of brown trout, though these take longer to grow.

The angler who wishes to catch an exceptionally large trout is most likely to do so by visiting small man-made trout lakes, where large fish are released regularly. This is not, as so many anglers suppose, because these fish are rather stupid, or poor fighters, or both. It is simply because in such waters there is a good chance of actually seeing the fish.

There may be many big fish in a reservoir several hundred acres in extent, but the chances that an angler will actually see one, in circumstances where he can spend an hour or more trying to catch it, are almost negligible. If he casts at random, the odds are that any fish he catches will be smaller than the size at which his ambition is set.

Of course, some of our big reservoirs produce several trout of 6lb and more each season, but the vast majority of anglers who fish such waters never even see a six-pounder, and there is little or nothing that they can do to improve their chances of catching one.

On the smaller lakes, an angler can move quietly along the banks, often behind reeds or other cover, pausing at intervals and looking carefully into the water, until he spots an outsize fish.

Contrary to common supposition, such fish are far from tame. They are very easily alarmed and extreme care must be taken not to frighten them. The bigger they are, the longer they take to recover from being alarmed. If the angler can see the fish, the fish may all too easily see the angler.

The angler wading in a reservoir is usually covering fish that are prevented from seeing him by the laws of light refraction. On relatively small lakes, this is not so. To see fish, you have to be quite near, and to avoid being seen means taking advantage of available cover, dressing drably, and even using rods and lines that don't flash.

Looking into the water and seeing fish whenever possible needs practice, but is helped by polarized glasses and a hat with a really wide brim or peak, to minimise the extraneous light that reaches the eyes. The larger the aperture at which the pupil of the eye is operating, the deeper you can see into the water. The broad-brimmed Australian bush hat that I wear for fishing provokes some jocular comment, but it isn't just for ornament or affectation. It allows me to see a fish three or four feet deeper in the water than most other anglers can see.

I cannot over-emphasize the importance of actually seeing the fish. Time after time I have watched anglers who are highly competent on larger waters, standing upright and double-haul-casting great distances on the smaller lakes, with the result that they go home with limit bags of one to three-pound fish, often complaining that the lakes concerned are over-rated and do not hold the big fish that their managements claim. The chances of catching the big ones, if this course is adopted, are poorer than the ratio of large to smaller fish would indicate. The smaller fish are more active, and likely to beat the larger ones in a race for the fly; the disturbance caused by catching small fish scares the big ones out of the area; and the angler's movements, with those of the rod and line, also play their part in driving the larger fish away.

Let us assume that you have spent a couple of hours investigating a lake of a few acres and have spotted one or two big fish. You can be reasonably sure that, even if a big fish has gone away from where you saw it, it will come back. The big fish tend to cruise on well-defined beats or circuits. The time taken by a big fish to return to where you first saw it varies considerably; it may be as short as five minutes or as long as half an hour.

Thus you position yourself so as to be able to offer the fish a suitable fly when it reappears. Depending on the nature of the banks and available cover, you can sit on a folding stool or a piece of foam plastic inside a polythene bag. It pays to have both kinds of seat with you.

Having taken up position, you attach a fly to your leader. Never more than one. Which fly you choose will depend on what you expect the fish to be doing when it reappears. If it were cruising just below the surface, perhaps rising to surface insects at intervals, you will choose a floating fly; more commonly you will be expecting the fish to be several feet below the surface, and then you will usually need a leaded pattern, such as a shrimp, damsel nymph, mayfly nymph or a leadhead of one colour or another. In any case, cast the fly out, on a very short line. If you are using a leaded fly, let it sink to the bottom and lie there, as nearly as possible situated so that if you lift the rod, the fly will come up right in front of the fish.

Then you wait.

When the fish reappears, you pull up your sinking fly, or agitate your floater, unless this is a pattern that should be left floating without movement. In general, you agitate sedge flies and imitations of terrestial insects, except the Daddy-longlegs, but imitations of ephemerid species are left immobile.

One of four reactions by the trout will occur.

1. He ignores your fly;
2. he departs in haste;

3.   he examines but refuses the fly;

4.   he takes the fly.

If the fly is ignored, and you are sure the trout must have seen it, change it.

If the fish hurries away, the probability is that he was scared by seeing you or your rod move. Try to work out how to avoid it happening next time he comes round.

If the fly is examined and refused, try him again with the same fly. He will then usually either take it or ignore it. If the latter, change it.

Before you act on a take you have to know the fly has indeed been taken. There is no doubt in the case of a floating fly but with a leaded, sunk fly, you cannot always see the fly. So watch the trout, and if he opens and closes his mouth, tighten at once. Don't wait for a pull. You can see the white flash of a mouth opening and closing even when it is difficult to see the fish.

If you have had little experience of this kind of fishing, you will find under-water observation difficult at first, but in time you will find you are seeing more and more, provided you take full advantage of cover, limit your movements as much as possible, and do not allow your attention to be distracted. A big trout can arrive and depart while your eyes are fixed on an angler opposite, or while you watch a pair of dabchicks.

Don't be impatient if your fly is refused; once you have found a big fish, keep after him as long as he keeps reappearing at intervals. At a guess, I would say that you will probably have one take out of every four or five of your tries. I have yet to succeed in catching more than three really big trout in a day's fishing of this kind, and more often I catch only one. A lot of time is used in finding the big fish, and even more in trying to catch each one.

A good deal of self-discipline is usually necessary, because you will be tempted often to catch a smaller trout, many of which will move through the area of water that you are watching. It isn't too difficult to restrain yourself from trying to tempt one and two-pounders when you are lying in wait for a seven or eight-pounder, but when a five or six-pounder comes into view, you may find it much more difficult to pass up the chance you are offered.

Catching a lesser fish may destroy your chance to catch the big one for the rest of the day; but sometimes your restraint avails you nothing, because a small fish may snatch your fly almost from the jaws of the big one, or a smaller fish than you want may pick up your fly as it lies inert on the bottom, perhaps when you aren't looking. These hazards have to be accepted philosophically, together with the handicap imposed by the fellow-angler who tramps along the bank, peers over your shoulder and says 'I say — there's a huge fish . . . oh, it's gone now!'

Let us consider dealing with hooked fish. A big trout is a powerful beast and on the tackle you have to use, he can put 70 or 80 yards between himself and you in a very short time. In open water that would matter little, but in small trout lakes there are usually weed-beds, reeds, mats of floating algae, tree branches or angles in the bank, that can lose you fish. The secret is to stay concealed after the fish is hooked. Don't jump up; stay put, and pray that nobody comes pounding down the bank with a landing net in a misguided attempt to assist you. Slide your own net into the water stealthily, while your fish isn't looking, and keep pressure as light as circumstances allow. If your fish doesn't see you, he won't usually make long dangerous runs, or indulge in acrobatics. Steer him rather than pull him.

We are dealing with salmon-size trout on trout tackle. We have to, because a rainbow trout of 10lb or more is still a comparatively young fish, feeding almost entirely on relatively small food items. The large 2 or 3-hook lures that are often successful in reservoir fishing are not usually nearly as effective on small trout lakes, even where their use is allowed, and this means using single hook flies in the size range 8 to 14 or thereabouts. It is unwise to fish a finer leader point than 6lb b/s, though where it is clear that a very small fly is the only thing that will be accepted, one has to risk 4½ to 5lb b/s.

Anglers accustomed to river fishing for trout of modest size find it hard to accept the need for leaders as strong as 6lb b/s (about 1×), but I do not find big trout much worried by nylon of that strength, used with flies of size 12 or larger. It is seeing the angler, or the flash of his rod or line, that frightens them. I may say at this stage that I know, beyond any doubt, that white or very light-coloured fly lines being false-cast in the air can often scare fish badly, especially in sunshine or against dark backgrounds, and all my fly lines are brown, olive or green.

Among the more important items of tackle is a capacious landing net. Ninety per cent of the anglers I see carry short-handled folding tea-strainers, suitable for trout up to 2lb or thereabouts. A 10lb trout is about 30 inches long, so my net has 26-inch arms, non-folding, and a five-foot handle. The mesh is dark green. If a tiring trout mistakes it for a weed bed, I do not complain.

You may decide to have your first big trout set up. If you do, you'll catch an even bigger one quite soon, so where do you stop? And what do you do with eight-pounders if they are not to become trophies? The answer is, have them smoked, just like salmon. Many think they taste even better.

When the Dry Fly can Save the Day

CONRAD VOSS BARK

Dry-fly fishing on still waters is similar in many ways to fishing rivers with the dry fly. It is, at times, surprisingly successful. Surprisingly, because not many lake trout are found with winged flies in their stomachs. Not at all. They feed almost entirely on underwater creatures and so, very naturally, most of us fish for them below the surface.

So do I. My father taught me, at Blagdon in the 1930s, and I don't remember anyone there fishing the surface fly, in spite of Sheringham's enthusiasm for it. And after the war writers like Ivens and others have spread the impression that the surface fly is more or less a waste of time. So I grew up in the underwater school. In the 50s and 60s most of my fish were taken on a small nymph, lightly and slowly fished in the surface film or just under it. Most of my fish still are. But in spite of this I have come to the conclusion — indeed experience has forced it upon me — that there are times when the dry fly on still water is very deadly indeed.

How did this happen? Well, to begin with, it was an accident. I was fishing a lake in France. All I had with me were some small dry flies for river fishing. But I had the chance to fish this lake and when I got there I found the trout rising all over the place to a hatch of small black midge. It was a terrific rise and one I would normally have fished with a small black midge pupa. I hadn't got one so I put up a small black dry fly, a hawthorn, and greased my cast. But I made a mess of it, as I often do, and got grease all over my fingers and all over the fly. I had no way of cleaning it off so I cast out the hawthorn to the fish in the hope that even though it was floating they would take it off the surface. Indeed they did. Wallop! And again! Twelve fish in an hour!

That was lesson number one.

Lesson number two came at Weir Wood, in Sussex, in the late 1950s. Daddy-longlegs were hatching in the grass and being blown over the lake. Again I did not have the right pattern but I did some scissor work on a Red Palmer and floated it out to the fish. Bang! Bang! Bang! Terribly exciting. Why hadn't I thought of this before?

But by then I was obsessed with nymph fishing and in the late 60s was fortunate enough to get a rod at Two Lakes, in Hampshire, where I fished the nymph practically all the time. Two Lakes — it was originally two but by then there were five — is a beautiful fishery with small two- and three-acre lakes set with lawns amid pinewoods and rhododendrons. There I was fortunate enough to have a rod on the same day as a real dry-fly addict, William Nicholson. He taught me a great deal.

Nicholson rarely fished anything but small dry flies, sometimes very small, 16s and 18s, on gossamer-like nylon. With these he would take fish whose average weight was over 2¼lb. Imagine the delicate touch needed to deal with a big rainbow of 3lb or more on an 18 hook with nylon whose breaking strain was between 2½ to 3¼lb! It was fantastic. One season he took some 60 to 70 fish, all on the dry fly, sometimes in the most dour and impossible conditions. These results stood up very well to anything the lure or wet-fly men could produce. At the same time I heard how another dry-fly addict, John Henderson, using similar delicate methods, had startled more conventional fishermen at Blagdon and Weir Wood.

Well, I was fascinated. Here were these chaps bringing up trout to take a surface fly, very often when there was no general rise at all and no trout seemed to be moving anywhere. Not only on small lakes but on big reservoirs. They magicked them to rise. Or so it seemed. I simply had to try and see if I could do the same.

I remember one day at Two Lakes very vividly. A blank calm. Nothing moving. Dour fishing. The lure men scraping the bottom with sinking lines and big flies and getting not much or nothing at all. That sort of a day. I changed from a nymph — not doing anything, why shouldn't I change? — to a small Greenwell, about a 14 or 15.

After about half an hour, I was retrieving it slowly towards the bank over the mirror-like surface of the water and getting rather fed up with my fishless day. The fly was moving gently towards me and I was getting ready to recast. It was about four or five yards away from the shore when I was aware of a grey shape rising from the obscurity of the weeds on the bottom, moving upwards towards the fly. The sight of that fish rising slowly and purposefully upwards sent my nerves cracking like whips. It was so slow, so deliberate, so — inevitable. Up he came. He had a long way to come. Eight or nine feet or more. But up he came, never hesitating, and took the fly from the surface, quietly and gently, and when he turned down again I tightened on him and all hell broke loose. He was a good three pounds.

My golly, but that was exciting!

But the point is: what on earth made that big fish, a very lustful rainbow, rise all that way to the surface to take a tiny little fly? Well, do you know, I haven't the least idea. But very definitely he did. He saw that fly, he wanted it and he rose to take it. That is the answer. It is in the nature of trout, at times, even when there is no general rise, to rise to the surface to take a fly they have seen and like the look of. Nor does this apply only to surface fly in a dead calm when they are clearly visible.

Take my experience at Stafford Moor. This is a 14-acre lake fishery in Devon — the first of its kind in the south-west — which is already making a reputation for good fishing and also for some big fish. I went there on a day I shouldn't. Heavy rain and cold wind and waves rolling like a sea. Dreadful conditions.

But there were, inexplicably, some fish out there rising in the waves. I found out later that their stomachs were crammed with midge pupae. But at the time I had no idea what they could be taking. Anyway, they were not taking my nymph. So, in desperation, I put on a golden-olive Palmer — of all things! — on a number 10 hook, and cast it wildly into the gale, greased to float, if anything could float in that wild weather. It drifted down in the waves. Bang! Bang! Bang! Three or four rises in rapid succession. I missed most of them from excitement and astonishment. But there you are. That's how it happens. When you least expect it.

And — for heaven's sake — this isn't only my own experience. Even while I was writing this article I had a letter from a dear old friend of mine in Dublin telling how he and a companion went fishing in wild wild weather on one of those vast Irish loughs. Underwater flies caught nothing so the companion put up a dry fly, a large Irish sedge pattern, predominantly grey in colour, known as the Grey Flag. The letter goes on: 'I thought he was mad to fish dry fly in such rough and blustery conditions but he quickly took three fine trout of between two and three pounds each.'

But do not, please, imagine that dry fly is always the answer. Do not be conned into it. It is not always successful. Nothing in lake fishing, or any other kind of fishing for that matter, is always successful. How terrible to find an infallible method or an infallible fly. How insufferable are those who pretend there are such things. But do not be conned, either, into thinking the dry fly is no good on lakes and reservoirs. It can be superlatively good.

But what kind of fly? Ah! — that is the problem. At the risk of being torn apart for heresy by flyologists and entomologists I do not think the pattern matters very much. A sedge — any sedge — is a great fly and so is a Red Palmer or a dry Invicta or one of Kingsmill Moore's bumble patterns. All fine on a blustery day or when the sedge are hatching. Drift the fly. Give it a bit of movement. Bobble it like a dropper. Be careful on the take or you can be smashed.

For rippling or calm days you can experiment with smaller flies, even very small flies indeed, 16 or 18 Greenwells, Black Gnats, Pheasant Tails, Badger Hackles, Blue Duns. Cast to rising fish. Let them float or give them a bit of movement. Give the fish time to take the fly and turn down or you won't set the hook. Wait for it — if your nerves can stand the strain.

Only addicts or masters of the dry fly will fish it all the time on still water. I am not yet an addict, though I may become one, and far from being a master. I muddle my way through. Besides, I have a deep love for nymph fishing which I cannot lightly abandon. All the same, if the nymph is dour and dull, and nothing moving I am no longer tempted to put on a sinking line and a Holy Terror, or some other monstrous lure, and drag the bottom. Nor do I like bottom fishing a nymph.

Instead I change to the lightest possible cast — gossamer nylon can land big fish, you know — and I try the surface fly and hope that I can wheedle a fish up from the depths. It is so nice to see your fly. And I experiment. Sometimes small, sometimes medium, sometimes large. I like them floating, really floating, not half sunk. Then, sometimes, it happens. Splosh. The fly vanishes in a rise. Nothing — I assure you nothing — is quite so exciting. You need a good strong heart to stand it. How on earth does it happen? Why do they come up like that? There is a sense of mystery about it that appeals to my primitive nature.

But it is true — isn't it? — that this sense of mystery, this sudden magical appearance of the trout on the surface of the lake, is one of the greatest and deepest delights of all fly fishing. If it is not so I will be dumb. I will never write another word.

Give the Nymph a Go First

suggests BRIAN CLARKE

Far and away the most fascinating way of catching trout that I know is on the nymph.

I have, as I have said many times elsewhere, nothing against lures and the traditional flasher patterns. It is simply that hauling tinsel through water until it stops gives me no satisfaction, and less pleasure.

There are times — many times — when lures and flashers will produce more trout; in particular, of course, when the fish are not feeding, and so cannot be expected to take patterns suggesting food. At times like these, it is essential if fish are to be caught, to fish for them in ways which appeal to instincts or sensations other than hunger.

Consistently, however, what the nymph occasionally lacks in sheer numerical success (and very often it has the advantage!) it makes up a thousandfold in interest.

I do most of my own stillwater nymphing with AFTM-6 and AFTM-7 rods of 9ft and under, even on the big lakes. For most of my fishing on smaller lakes, I have for some time used an AFTM-6 in conjunction with an AFTM-7 line. I prefer the heavier line because the extra weight gives substantial advantage when very short casting is needed, by flexing the rod more easily. The other side of the coin is that the extra weight of line takes the backbone out of the rod rather quickly, too; twice in two years I have had to replace the design of rod I use most. Fortunately, however, I buy it as a kit for less than £9 a time (expensive equipment by no means ensures more fish) so the cost isn't enormously prohibitive.

Given a fast action, which any nymph rod needs to have, I believe the rod to be the least important piece of equipment the angler carries, provided it will put out 20 yards when circumstances demand it.

Far and away the most important is the leader. I can count on the fingers of one hand the number of times in a year when I use the 'conventional' 9-foot leader while nymphing on still water. It is rare indeed for me to use anything under 14ft. More often still, my leader runs between 14ft and 20ft — and occasionally it goes even more. Almost invariably, the point length consists of level monofilament of between 4lb and 6lb varying only with the size of hook; and it tapers down in three or four steps from a butt-piece of 20-25lb.

Leaders of such comparatively great length are necessary because of the conditions in which nymph fishing is practised.

In fishing the nymph, we are trying to make the acquaintance of feeding fish. Fish which are feeding as a rule travel no more quickly than is absolutely necessary to enable them to catch their prey. Most of the creatures on which trout feed are small, and swim comparatively slowly. So in imitating them, the man who fishes the nymph usually retrieves his line only slowly. And the trout which wants the fly on the end of it only needs to swim slowly in order to catch it.

So one of the most fundamental differences between nymph fishing and lure fishing is that the take is recorded only gently. It is recorded so, because the fish has not steamed up to a fly being rapidly hauled back through the water and hit it with a bang at the moment of contact. It has simply, in a leisurely way, swum up to the fly, and absorbed it, *en passant.*

Because the take is so gentle and cannot be felt as it can with a lure, it is essential if one is to be aware of the offer at all, that it be seen. And if it is to be seen — that is, if the gentle movement of the leader responding to the gentle take of a trout is to be seen — then the water must be calm enough for the leader to be clearly visible; and very often indeed that means flat calm.

That is why the leader has to be long; because we build it in response to a remorseless sequence of parameters that say we will often find ourselves fishing the nymph in flat calm water, and in flat-calm conditions the long leader is needed, of course, to assist in an unalarming presentation.

And what fly should we attach to this long and delicate leader, when we have decided that we really do need it?

Increasingly, I find myself concentrating on just a handful of patterns, all of which, of course, either imitate or suggest creatures of the kinds upon which trout feed. My most effective patterns are Sawyer's Pheasant-tail Nymph; midge pupae in various sizes and colours; the White Chomper; Conrad Voss Bark's Palmer Nymph; and the Invicta, which performs marvellously well when sedge are hatching. For deep-nymph fishing, I use either my own Ombudsman pattern, on sizes 12, 10 and 8; or Cove's Pheasant-Tail Nymph, which differs from Frank Sawyer's in everything but the material used. Sawyer's nymph is dressed to imitate the ephemerid nymphs; Arthur Cove's is dressed to the profile of a large midge pupa, but on hook sizes 8 and 6, using hare's body fur to suggest the thorax.

I have settled on these, and a few others, not because I am some casual, one-fly man — or, more accurately, a few-flies man — but because with this handful of patterns I can suggest pretty well everything the fish normally expects to see; and I have flies of different shapes, colours, densities and fishing characteristics which enable me to ring the changes sensibly, when I need to. Everything else, pretty well, is then literally in the hands of the fisherman himself, the way he handles his equipment and presents and fishes his fly.

I have used this combination of equipment and philosophy with some success, on a wide variety of stillwaters.

Some of the most fascinating nymph fishing I have had has been at Peckham's Copse, the well-known day-ticket water at Chichester. Peckham's Copse produces some of the most freely-rising trout of any day-ticket water I know, and I have two favourite ways of going after them. One is in the early evening and morning from the bank on Lake No. 1. The other is during the evening rise from a boat (Peckham's Copse is one of the few places where I ever fish the nymph from a boat) on Lake No. 2.

The most interesting bank fishing on either lake is along the very stretch of water that is most rarely fished — the bank on Lake No. 1 which lies directly opposite the fishing hut. The reason why this bank is so little fished is not because it is overlooked, but because it is shunned: and the reason it is shunned is because there is a long line of high bushes and trees little more than a rod's length back from the water's edge.

Fish which come into the shallow, clear water along this bank, between and on either side of the jetties, are rarely disturbed and so they not only come inshore in large numbers — in ones and twos, but many ones and twos — but they come in very closely indeed, and they stay in; establishing regular beats for themselves, swimming so languidly and slowly that every spot on their sides can be counted.

So close inshore do they come that I have had fish without ever casting at all, doing little more than lowering the nymph in front of a day-dreaming trout and giving the line a tweak or two.

There are some particularly good browns along this bank, which provide a challenge to any man's angling skills; and some hefty rainbows as well.

The over-riding requirements are an unobtrusive approach, a longish leader (longish, that is, for the circumstances), a delicate forward throw when one needs to be made and fervent prayer on the backcast.

The plan I most often adopt is to get myself in the path of a specific fish, to put the nymph out and to wait until the trout is as near as it's going to get. Then I gently tweak the line or lift the end of the rod. Most often the fish will ignore the rising nymph, sometimes it will even sheer away, if it has become particularly well educated and something isn't quite right. But on other occasions it will turn towards the fly and sometimes (just sometimes, do not let me mislead you), quietly suck it in. It is tantalising, frustrating and often heart-stopping work, and it is immensely satisfying when it succeeds.

From a boat on Lake No. 2, I am not conscious of having fished many rises to sedge, but I have fished many rises to midge pupae and many rises to caenis. If there are a lot of fish on the move, I anchor at both ends and stay put. If the rise is spasmodic or (as it quite often is) the fuss is being created by a handful of regular risers, I get great satisfaction from positioning the boat carefully and then sitting quite still, allowing myself to drift softly down into the beat of a feeding fish.

Almost always the individual fish rising late in the evening is sipping down spent flies and nymphs which have failed to break through the surface film with a distinct and audible 'kissing' noise; and it is marvellously fulfilling to deliver a nymph with great precision, to see and hear that punctilious acceptance, and then to watch the leader move positively away before making spectacular contact.

The big lakes which have given me my most memorable sport are Draycote, Grafham and Sutton Bingham; and Draycote it was, indeed, that delivered me my first fish on an imitative fly. Far and away my most successful fly on this water has been the size 12 midge pupa, and one early-season afternoon there, gave me my fastest reservoir limit — eight fish in just over an hour, on an olive pupa that the fish left as little more than a hook with a wisp of floss hanging from it. That incident was interesting because it is so often argued that lures are the only way of taking early-season fish on the big reservoirs. They are not.

During those few minutes the field closed cannily in from either side, one sidling step at a time; and yet, while my pupa was doing so well, on all the lures cast I saw only one other fish come to the bank. And by the time that was taken, the angler on either side was casting almost into my wader-tops.

A great deal of Draycote is dam-face, but because I have an intense dislike of fishing from the stones, whenever conditions allow I head for the natural bank which runs away from the deeps beside the water tower.

It is on the deep water at Draycote and Grafham that Cove's Pheasant Tail nymph comes into its own. This pattern was designed for getting down to bottom-feeding fish and also, I'm sure, to exaggerate and so represent a particularly appealing example of the most popular item of trout food, when retrieved very slowly indeed.

It is essential when fishing this pattern in deep water to watch the leader carefully from the moment the fly has cut through the surface film. I shudder to think of the fish which I must have lost before I realised that large numbers of takes — indeed most takes — come not when a nymph is being retrieved, but when it is 'on the drop'.

At Grafham when nothing is rising and the wind is right, I take this deep-water pattern to the Savage's Creek/Church Cove/dam bank, opposite the fishing lodge, because that is where most deep water can be fished from the bank. And it is where a lot of fish are, too. Their presence results from a particular advantage of deep water, which is that fish cannot so easily be frightened off or discouraged by wading anglers in the way they so often are in shallow water; and so they come close in, just as they do at Peckham's and will anywhere else when they are not disturbed.

The pattern which has taken most fish for me on the really small fisheries — waters of the Avington/Damerham type — has undoubtedly been the White Chomper (white ostrich herl body, ribbed with silver tinsel, with a brown raffine shell-like back tied in at front and rear). The White Chomper is at its best when fished close to the surface, when either thrown to specific fish which can be seen and twitched back beneath the surface film, or retrieved gently in long, slow draws.

A slight variation on this pattern which I tie with an orange head and three or four turns of lead wire under the dressing has proved itself deadly when cast out among rising fish and simply allowed to sink, without being retrieved at all.

In fishing this pattern the fly should be on a long leader and delivered with a controlled 'plop' to send out tiny rings when it enters the water. The 'plop' and the ebbing rings are sufficient to attract from yards away to investigate, fish which may not have seen the fly itself go in.

In defining some of the compass points in my own approach to nymph fishing, I would not like to have created the impression that I have never, ever, used anything else. As I said at the beginning, nymph fishing is the most absorbing way I know of catching trout. Like everything else in fishing, however, it is not infallible. There are times when to persist with the nymph will catch no trout at all (just as there are many times when to persist with lures will catch nothing, either).

At times such as these — when you are convinced that you are getting nothing with a nymph simply because the fish are not feeding — turn to other methods within the rules if you decide you want to, and feel the need to apologise to no man.

As I am at pains to say in my book, *The Pursuit of Stillwater Trout*, the plain fact is that fishing is about pleasure. Some days, trout in the bag will mean everything and on other days they will mean rather less or nothing at all. So in seeking pleasure from the day, do not feel constrained by prejudice, whichever side of the line it falls (I have seen nymphs fished every bit as mindlessly as lures) and prejudice against the nymph festers along the banks of Grafham, among men stripping back multiple hooks.

Ignore it all, and go your own way. But give the nymph its opportunity, first.

Fishing in the Regions

The ten regional areas into which this guide has been divided broadly embrace those of the new, all-purpose regional water authorities, nine in England and one in Wales. These authorities are responsible for water supplies and sewage disposal, involving the functions of water conservation, quality control and recreation. They are thus very closely concerned with still waters.

Although the future pattern has still to be established, certain trends have become clear. For instance, the old river authorities have, for the most part, become subdivisions of the new RWAs — though the precise structure and terminology vary. Many have appointed fishery officers, whose names and addresses are given at the beginning of each section, along with information as to licences, close seasons and so on.

As was widely anticipated, one beneficial effect of the changed system has been the introduction of a single licence for each RWA area. Although this had not been fully implemented when we went to press, it was hoped the proliferation of licences would soon be a thing of the past.

So far as close seasons are concerned, the position is that standard periods are laid down by Parliament, but these can be varied by the water authorities under local by-laws. Anglers should consult the individual entries for guidance here — always bearing in mind that the statutory close season for brown trout is 1 October to the last day of February. There is no statutory close season for rainbows, although a close season is often enforced under by-laws.

1 The Anglian Region

ANGLIAN WATER AUTHORITY
Diploma House, Grammar School Walk, Huntingdon, PE18 6NZ (tel. 0480 56181).
Fisheries Officer: A. J. Miller.

Essex River Division
Fisheries Officer: E. Pearson, Rivers House, 129 Springfield Road, Chelmsford,
Essex, CM2 6JN (tel. 0245 64721).
Close season: 1 October to 28 February

Great Ouse River Division
Fisheries Officer: C. H. A. Fennell, Great Ouse House, Clarendon Road, Cambridge
(tel. 0223 61561).
Close season: 14 October to 31 March

Lincolnshire River Division
Fisheries Officer: P. Kalinowski, 50 Wide Bargate, Boston, Lincs. (tel. 0205 65661).
Close season: 1 October to 28 February

Norfolk and Suffolk River Division
Fisheries Officer: C. K. Jones, Yare House, 62–64 Thorpe Road, Norwich NR1 1SA
(tel. 0603 61561).
Close season: 1 October to 31 March

Welland and Nene River Division
Fisheries Officer: D. Moore, North Street, Oundle, Peterborough, PE8 4PS
(tel. 08322 3701).
Close season: 30 September to 25 March

Trout licences: For fishing throughout the region, annual charge is £2.75 (OAPs 70p,
juveniles (12 to 15 years inclusive) £1.40). The equivalent cost of fishing in just one
division of the region for a year is £1.00 (OAPs 25p, juniors 50p). In addition, a
licence to fish for trout anywhere in the region for any period of seven days costs 40p.

(The licence structure was under review as we went to press.)

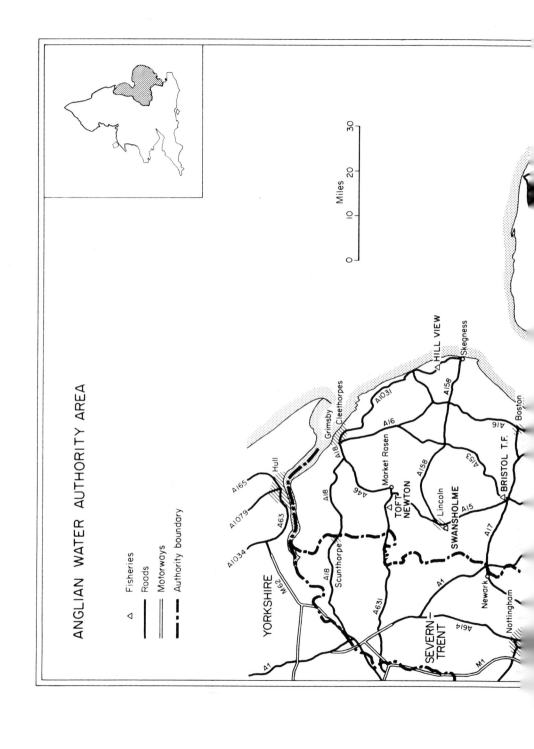

ANGLIAN WATER AUTHORITY AREA

△ Fisheries

— Roads

‖ Motorways

–·–·– Authority boundary

Miles
0   10   20   30

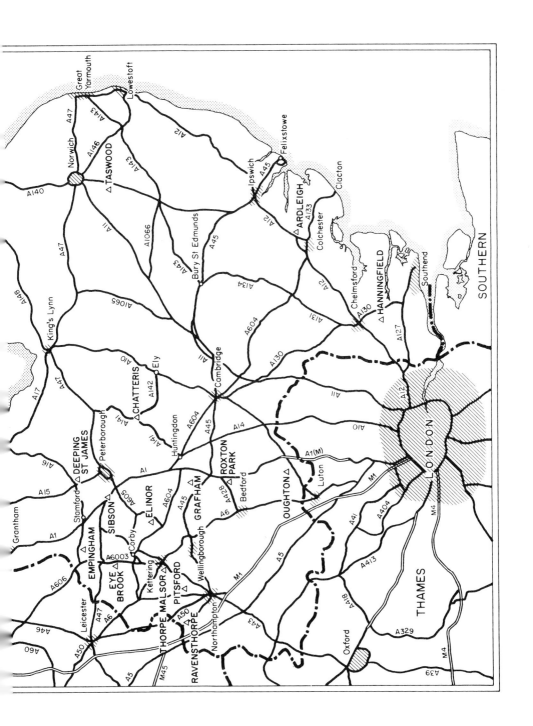

Grafham — Britain's Greatest

says BOB CHURCH

As I write, the 1975 trout season has just drawn to a close and it has proved a record-breaking year for my favourite Grafham Water (1600 acres). Not only did the reservoir produce its record 'brownie' — a fish of 11lb 5½oz — but a record rainbow of 9lb as well!

That isn't the end of Grafham records this past season, for the grand catch total sailed well beyond the previous highest (32,029 in 1967) and finished in excess of 35,000. The top limit bag of eight fish went 34¼lb. Not bad for a water that some critics classed as nothing more than a pike fishery in the seasons '71 and '72.

Through my *Angling Times* weekly column I have always sung the praises of Grafham as Britain's top trout fishery, and I should be a fair judge because I have fished most of the recognized stillwaters in this country. Grafham is unique simply because of its ability to produce a fantastically fast growth rate in both rainbows and browns. This has now been maintained for ten years since the water first opened. One of the reasons for this fast growth is the high alkaline quality of the water. The ph reading is 8.43, which is very high by comparison with other waters. Certainly all aquatic life grows big in Grafham, from tiny insects, shrimps, snails, etc., right through to the coarse fish, of which there are national records present in numbers; here I refer to bream and rudd, possibly roach and pike too.

The stocking policy is very much in favour of rainbows and works out at approximately 6000 browns to 45,000 rainbows. These are planted systematically from April until late July, a practice which has proved the best so far for giving consistent sport. A one-pound stock fish can become a two-pounder in a couple of months and by September it will be 3lb of shining silver that fights like a fresh-run salmon.

Grafham's regular trout fishers are very good and it is here that many new methods are being developed. Some of these were at first scoffed at by the old traditionalists, but now these modern techniques are accepted by anglers and management alike, and they help to catch a lot of trout even on difficult days. All this is far removed from the old chalk-stream approach which is so unsuitable and unrealistic when fishing the large new reservoirs.

Probably the greatest modern invention of all is the drift control rudder device. This was the brainchild of my genial old friend, Dick Shrive. The rudder allows a boat to be drifted bow-first down the wind instead of the traditional broadside drift. The rudder is

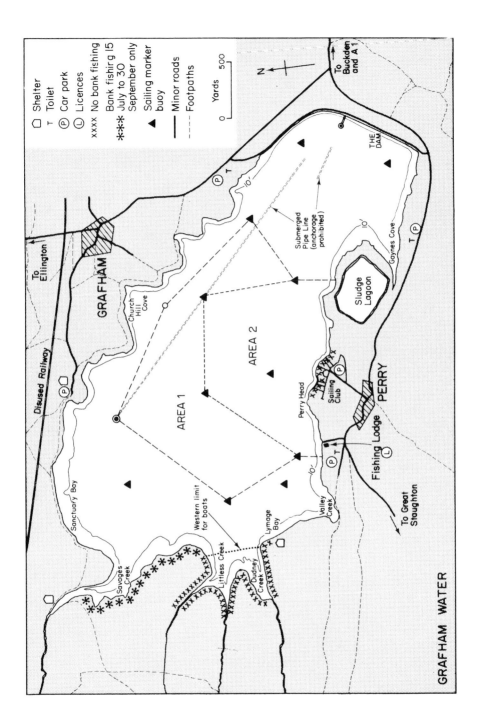

GRAFHAM WATER

Legend:
- ⌂ Shelter
- T Toilet
- Ⓟ Car park
- Ⓛ Licences
- xxxx No bank fishing
- *-*-* Bank fishing 15 July to 30 September only
- ▲ Sailing marker buoy
- —— Minor roads
- --- Footpaths

Yards 0 ____ 500

N

To Ellington

Disused Railway

GRAFHAM

Church Hill Cove

Sanctuary Bay

Western limit for boats

Savages Creek

Littless Creek

Dudney Creek

Lymage Bay

Valley Creek

AREA 1

AREA 2

Perry Head

Sailing Club

PERRY

Fishing Lodge

To Great Staughton

Submerged Pipe Line (anchorage prohibited)

Sludge Lagoon

Gaynes Cove

THE DAM

To Buckden and A1

10'

a simple affair which is G-clamped to the centre of the transom. The angler in the stern position operates the tiller to point the boat virtually in any downwind direction. This operation does not interfere with his fishing.

The method is obviously ideal for sinking-line fishing with a lure. Instead of continuously running your fly-line over and ending up with nothing but slack as in traditional drifting sinking-line methods, now you can fish properly. Each angler casts out from different sides of the boat. At 30yd each, a 60yd strip of water is being covered right down to the bottom for the entire drift. Naturally this searching technique catches fish, especially as the rudder takes you where you want to go and not merely where the wind blows you. For example, you can go in and out of bays keeping 60 to 70yd from the bank. This method has really caught on at Grafham since I first wrote about it in 1973, and the catch rate has improved with it.

When the same drifting is required in very strong winds, naturally the boat travels too fast, so I then use a large 48in square drogue. This has four strong cords attached to each corner of the rot-proof, heavy duty nylon material. These corners are reinforced with leather and punched with sail eyelets. The four cords are of equal length, about 1yd each, and these are collectively tied to a large sea swivel. Finally, a 3yd length of much stronger nylon rope is tied from the other eye of the swivel to the boat. This drogue is lowered from the central stern position and secured by a 4in G clamp.

While other boats drift too fast, and out of control as far as sensible fishing is concerned, my drogue allows me to continue to fish deep and slow. This style of drifting does not have to be sinking-line fishing and, in fact, some of my best results come when fishing for rainbows with a sink-tip fly-line.

As the fish cruise upwind just a few feet or so down, feeding on daphnia, they appear to become reckless and to attack almost any lure if it is pulled 'across' their path. Lures like Black Chenille, Missionary, Appetizer, Church Fry, Whisky Fly, Leprechaun, Sweeney Todd and Jack Frost catch a lot of fish at these times.

A large proportion of the trout caught from the bank during late May through to July fell to some kind of nymph. The normal Buzzer patterns in black, green, orange, brown, claret, grey and red catch plenty of fish. These are fished on hook sizes 14, 12 and 10.

Another type of nymph fishing has really begun to catch on this season. This can be described as the 'Cove' style. Arthur Cove, from Wellingborough, is known as the Pheasant Tail nymph man. He likes to use them large on No 8 or 10 long-shank hooks. These give him a very consistent catch rate. He uses a variation with a grey wool thorax which I feel is even more of a killer.

Arthur always uses a full double-tapered floating fly-line to get a perfect presenta-tion. His line is coloured white so he can see the slightest movement at the tip. He strikes early, long before the take is felt at the hand. I caught a number of good fish on Cove Pheasant Tail variations, using thorax colours of yellow, green and orange, as well as the grey and original.

During mid-July fish come well to the sedge in calm evenings — the calmer the better. For the past two seasons I have really taken advantage of this fishing and have caught some large fish on sedge pupa patterns. Fish that can be seen rising and boiling near the surface are rarely taking the adult sedge; more often than not they will be on pupa in the surface film, taking it just prior to emergence.

At this time my favourite fly is a Brown and Yellow Seal's Fur nymph. This has a couple of turns of yellow hackle at the head too. It can be fished as a centre dropper with an Invicta or Standard Sedge on the top. The Standard Sedge, by the way, is a very effective deer-hair pattern invented by Terry Thomas. I have witnessed take after take coming to it when anglers nearby using Invictas have failed to get any, so bear this in mind. The Brown and Green nymph, also in seal's fur, and the Amber nymph are certainly worth trying at this time.

During the daytime period when nothing is showing, try a No 8 Stick Fly on the point and fish it very slowly on a long leader. This represents the caddis grub which is the larval form of the sedge.

A word about bank fishing: for the occasional visitor to Grafham the large expanse of water can be a frightening sight for decision-making. Where to fish the bank for the best? you say to yourself as you purchase your permit. At this point I suggest you seek the advice of recreations officer, David Fleming-Jones, who is usually on duty from 9am. Failing this, the head bailiff, Haydn Jones, or one of the other bailiffs will tip you off as to where it's all happening.

The north shoreline produces some first-class bank fishing each year, with the Church Cove area very consistent throughout. With the south-west summer winds blowing from right to left, casting can at times be awkward, but never mind this, for the fish will be in close. If you can get one of the points of the bays, better still. These positions certainly give you an advantage to intercept cruising rainbows.

Savages Creek area usually fishes well at the back-end when the fry of coarse fish accumulate there. The bigger fish come on to feed at this time and browns in the 4lb to 6lb class are not uncommon.

I suppose the favourite spot of all for the general bank angler is the Dam Wall. There is a chance of getting fish here at all times of the day no matter what the conditions.

Watch out for the quite large areas of shallow, barren water which occur at Grafham early in the season. Fish seldom come in close at these places, especially in calm, or gin-clear and sunny conditions. By late summer, when there is a thick weed growth in these same shallow margins, the story can be so different. Try them at dawn. You will find a lot of shallow water along the west and south banks.

In general the best tip I can give is to fish in a crosswind, concentrating in May and June on Buzzer Nymph patterns. In July and August try the sedge pupa or larvae imitations, and in September and October perch and bream fry imitations like my Appetizer Lure. A bright attractor lure is also good for Grafham rainbows and must always be tried. Keep this versatile approach and you won't go far wrong.

Eye Brook Tactics

Fishing the season through with

DICK SHRIVE

My early visits to Eye Brook, well over 20 years ago, produced big trout, big chub and, with no perimeter road, more than a fair share of walking. Facilities have improved since then and the fishing has remained consistently good.

Where is the water which can furnish 20,000 trout averaging 1lb 2oz year in and year out?

Thanks to an abundance of natural food, of which roach fry form a considerable proportion, the fish grow fast. Besides good stocks of rainbows, this extensive lake holds beautifully marked brown trout, all bred and reared in the reservoir hatcheries.

The record fish, one of 10lb 4oz, was taken by my friend, the late Cyril Inwood, while bank fishing.

To get the best out of this water the whole season through one must adapt one's tactics to the prevailing conditions. Fishing Eye Brook in April and early May, for instance, with the water temperature well down, concentrate on the deeper spots near the dam and elsewhere, especially when they are found along the banks and in the bays. During this period the trout feed extensively on shrimps, snails and, most important, roach fry.

For tackle I would use a 9ft or 9ft 6in tip-actioned fibreglass rod (10ft if you can handle it), a plastic-dressed forward-tapered slow-sinking line (size 7 or 8), and a 5lb b/s cast 6 to 12ft long depending on wind speed; the stronger the wind the shorter the cast.

Flies should be semi-buoyant, dressed on long-shank hooks and with fine wire to aid sinking, in sizes 6—8, and should be fished very slowly about six inches above the reservoir bed. Recommended patterns include: White Marabous, Black Lure, White Lure, Black and Peacock Spider, Polystickle, Teal Blue and Silver, Sinfoil Fly, Mylar Redthroat, Whisky Fly, etc.

The long-shanked hooks are required to provide sufficient room for the body dressing, so helping to make the fly more buoyant. Long experience shows that a single fly on the cast kills best.

The area around the dam is, as I have said, a good place to try early, but a few words of advice on fishing off the dam may be appropriate here. For instance, dropping the retrieved line on to the concrete is not advised — nor do the hobs on your boots do

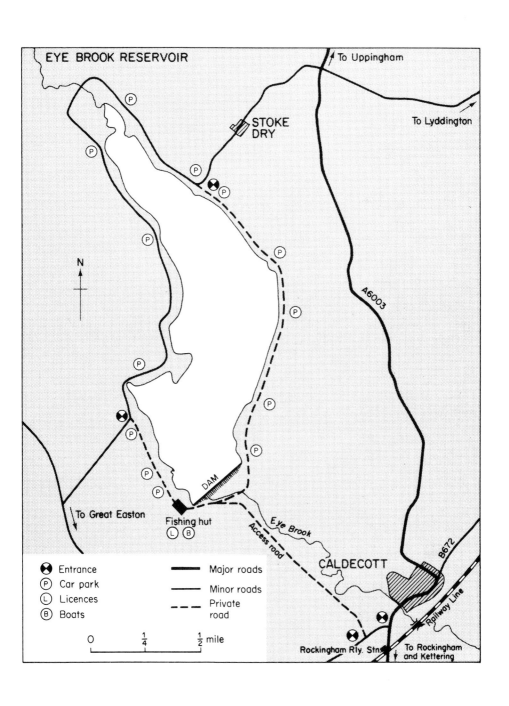

EYE BROOK RESERVOIR

To Uppingham

STOKE DRY

To Lyddington

N

A6003

DAM

To Great Easton

Eye Brook

Fishing hut
Ⓛ Ⓑ

Access road

CALDECOTT

B672

Railway Line

Entrance
Ⓟ Car park
Ⓛ Licences
Ⓑ Boats

Major roads
Minor roads
Private road

0   ¼   ½ mile

Rockingham Rly. Stns

To Rockingham and Kettering

the dressing much good. It is better, when retrieving in such situations, to walk slowly sideways and backwards a few steps, so leaving the line clear of the feet. This means that you are not standing at the water's edge when lifting the fly off — thus putting down any fish which might follow the fly in — and, on recasting, your first back cast, which is always the lowest, will easily clear the dam wall. But walking the few steps backwards down the dam, while casting, does take a bit of practice.

Watch the dam surface, too. If wet with spray or rain, this can become very slimy and many a good angler has taken a long, slow, silent slide into the depths.

Although small chironimids hatch out early in the season, the first sizeable flies to emerge are the lake olives, which usually appear during the milder days of May. In cold, squally weather the hatch may be intermittent or concentrated into an hour or two. Localized hatches may also occur on sheltered bays.

At this time of year fish a 9ft or 9ft 6in butt-actioned fibreglass rod, a long-belly floating line with a tapered cast 9—12ft long and 5lb b/s. The Olive Dun and Nymph, Brown Nymph, Invicta, Hardy's Gold Butcher, Grouse and Claret, and Amber Nymph do well.

As June comes to an end, shoals of tiny roach fry, hatched from eggs deposited in late May, engage the attention of the trout — often for a time to the exclusion of every other type of food. The trout feed in short bursts and are easily satiated. Trying to catch them can be very frustrating. They seem to know all the answers, rising under your feet and between you and the bank.

Find a good clump of marginal weed, well within casting distance and occupied by a shoal of roach fry. Measure off the line and drop the fly two or three feet from the edge of the weed. When the trout appears, you will see the tightly packed fry fan out and bolt into the weeds. With luck a well-timed cast will place your lure in the path of the fish.

Fish a floating or sink-tip line and a single fly size 6, 8 or 10. Peter Ross, Missionary, Jersey Herd, Polystickle, Dunkeld and Muddler Minnow are recommended.

From late July onwards on calm, mild evenings there are usually large numbers of sedges on the water, especially in the vicinity of the pine-tree plantation along the east shore. They will often consist of small and medium-sized Silverhorns and red-brown Cinnamon Sedges. A good rise usually occurs on the upwind shore.

Fish a floating line 9—12ft long and a tapered cast of 5lb b/s with the point greased to the last 18in. Cast out to the edge of the ripple, draw the line in for about a foot, which tends to bring the flies upwards in the water, and pause briefly before the next draw to allow them to sink again. Flies: Greenwell's Glory, Ginger Quill, Tups Indispensable, Wickham's Fancy and Sherry Spinner.

Dry-fly fishing can be successful at these times, as the trout often rise well to sedges. A large, dark, dry sedge, dragged across the surface to form a wake, will often be taken by a big fish with a terrific slash. The biggest brown trout I ever netted from Eye Brook (for an old friend) weighed 7lb 12oz and was taken on the dry sedge.

Boat fishing

Many anglers seem to believe that the boat can provide a substitute for skill and experience. Many boats set out for a day's fishing with the wrong tackle and equipment.

Warm protective clothing is essential and a waterproof cushion helps when sitting on the hard thwarts all day. A good anchor with 30 yards of rope, a long-handled landing net and a large robust drogue are also required.

One further item is essential — a No 7 or 8 weight-forward, fast-sinking line for fishing water up to 30ft deep. With this line, by carefully controlling the speed of the retrieve it is possible to fish the flies inches off the bottom at such depths.

For water up to 15ft deep, a slow-sinking line is best. Smaller flies and nymphs can be used and the rate of retrieve can be much slower.

As the water temperature rises, the floating line with a team of wet flies fished very slowly and quietly just under the surface comes into its own. If fish are seen cruising along a regular beat, it pays to anchor the boat and wait for them to come within casting distance.

The orthodox loch method — that is, drifting the boat beam on to the wind with the drogue trailing behind — can be very productive at Eye Brook when the fish are rising. Fish a team of wet flies on a short cast, just keeping the bob fly dancing on the surface. Very small flies and nymphs can be used, down to size 16.

On very windy days a fairly fast retrieve is necessary to ensure the proper movement of the flies and to take up the slack caused by the boat drifting.

During the big chironomid hatch which occurs at Eye Brook, the fish rise very freely, but are sometimes extremely difficult to catch. Try them with representations of chironomid pupae, and with a Brown and Green Nymph, Brown and Orange Nymph, Yellow Shellback and Amber Nymph, on size 10, 12 and 14 hooks.

In September numbers of Daddy-longlegs usually find their way at intervals on to the water and can cause some excitement among the trout. The artificial can be deadly at such times.

At this time of year the roach fry have become bigger and faster, and the shoals reduced and scattered by predation, with few fish still working the weed bed.

But chironomids still hatch out in great quantity in the deeper parts of the lake, and on calm evenings for the last few weeks of the season night flying moths fall on to the water in considerable numbers and bring on a rise until well after dark.

With the last sparse hatches of pond olives coming off the water most days around mid-day, there ends what I hope has been another enjoyable and productive season at Eye Brook.

ARDLEIGH

nr Colchester, Essex

Off A137 Colchester to Manningtree road, to Clover Way, private road to reservoir. 57m from London via A12.

Controller: Ardleigh Reservoir Committee — formed jointly from Anglian Water Authority and the Tendring Hundred Waterworks Company.

Description: Natural landscaped reservoir covering 130 acres, giving about 5m of bank.

Species/sizes: Brown and rainbow.

	Brown	Rainbow
Average	1lb 2oz	1lb 3oz
Record	4lb 15oz	4lb 3oz

Stocking: Back-end and pre-season stocking, regularly supplemented from rearing ponds during season. Some 30,000 fish (20,000 brown trout) were introduced during 1975. Plans for 1976 involved stocking with 7000 brown trout more than three years old, some over 2lb. In addition 12,000 rainbows were being reared and 18,000 brown trout of two years old and more.

Rules: Fly only. No visitors or dogs on bank, but one non-permit-holder allowed in boat. Fishing 8am to one hour after sunset, when gates are locked. Limit: 4 brace over 12in.

Season: 27 March to 31 October (fishing for rainbows only in October).

Permits: Full st £79; Mon — Fri £59; dt (week-ends and Bank Holidays) £2.95; Mon — Fri £1.95. Juniors (18 and under) 90p. Boats (12) £3.60 full day, £2.30 half-day.

Permits from: Fishing Lodge at reservoir or write to Richard Connell, Fisheries and Estate Officer, Administration Block, Ardleigh Treatment Works, Colchester, Essex (tel. 230642).

Comments: Ardleigh is especially noted for its brown trout. The reservoir fishes particularly well early in the season, with dependable evening rises when conditions are right, and can also be good in September and October. From 7088 returns submitted by 10,352 anglers who fished the water in 1975, it emerges that 12,850 trout were taken averaging 1lb 2oz. The reservoir is an excellent small-nymph and dry-fly water. Recommended patterns include the Ardleigh Nymph, Greenwell Nymph, Mallard and Claret Nymph, Wickham's Fancy, Dunkeld, Dry Greenwell, and Baby Doll, Black Lure and Muddler types.

Note: Angling tuition is available from Richard Connell, who will also be pleased to advise anglers on other matters. Fly-tying classes are arranged locally during the season.

BRISTOL TROUT FISHERY

Sleaford, Lincs.

A15 Lincoln to Sleaford Road; fishery lies in Mareham Lane, Sleaford.

Owner: Marquis of Bristol.

Description: Natural lake.

Species/sizes: Mainly brown trout, some rainbow.

	Brown	Rainbow
Average	1lb 4oz	1lb 4oz
Record	3lb 12oz	3lb

Stocking: One big stocking, then smaller 'booster'.

Rules: Fly only.

Season: 15 March to 30 September.

Permits: st only, £35, plus boat (2 available) at 50p day, £5 season, plus VAT.

Permits from:
The Manager, Bristol Trout Fishery, Bristol House, Northgate Street, Bury St Edmunds.

Comments: The nymph accounts for most fish on this water.

CHATTERIS

Block Fen, Mepal, Cambs.

2m S of Chatteris, ½m off A142, March 8m N.

Controller: Chatteris Aqua Sports Ltd.

Description: 35-acre gravel pit, well landscaped.

Species/Sizes: Brown and rainbow averaging about 1lb.

Stocking: In March and June up to 1200 rainbows and 300 browns, plus several 5lb or 6lb fish.

Rules: Fly only. Limit: 4 brace.

Season: 1 April to 14 October.

Permits: full st £65; weekday season £50; dt £2.75. Reduced rates for pensioners. Boats (3): £5.50 day (motor) £3 (oars).

Permits from:
secretary: T. F. Fensome, Greenridge, Bury Road, Ramsey, Cambs.

Comments: A new lake. Vegetation is well established, all banks graded and no obstacles present. During a trial run, from July to October in 1975, excellent sport was obtained, the biggest fish taken weighing 3lb 2oz.

DEEPING ST JAMES LAKES

West Deeping, Lincs.

Two former gravel pits of 4½ and 9 acres, holding brown and rainbow trout averaging about 2lb (biggest brown 2lb 12½oz, biggest rainbow 3lb 10oz). Stocked at intervals. Fly only. Deeping St James AC members only (sub £35, 15m radius for membership, guests of members £1.50 per day). Full details from hon sec (trout section): A. Beels, 23 Suttons Lane, Deeping Gate, Peterborough.

ELINOR TROUT FISHERIES

Aldwincle,
nr Thrapston, Northants.

Off A605 from Oundle about 3m N of Thrapston.

Owner: Joan Popplewell.

Description: Former gravel pits covering 40 acres.

Species/sizes: Rainbow trout averaging 2½lb, biggest 4½lb.

Stocking: Start of season, then at intervals based on returns. 1000 large 'steelhead' rainbows put in for 1976.

Rules: Fly only. No dogs.

Season: 1 April to 24 October.

Permits: st £50; dt £2.50 (limited to 30 rods). Five punts available at £3 day.

Permits from:
Joan Popplewell, 40 North Street, Oundle (tel. 3671, evenings).

Comments: Chance of 12lb-plus fish. Bailiffs will give angling advice on request, also free tuition at weekends.

EMPINGHAM (projected 1977)

Empingham, Leics.

Approached via A1 to Stamford, turning along A600 Oakham road to W of town. Empingham village lies about 6m along it, some 20m from Peterborough and 95m from London. See map on page 49.

Controller: Anglian Water Authority, Welland and Nene River Division.

Description: Due to open around Easter 1977, this will be the biggest trout reservoir in Europe, rivalled only by some in the USA. It is located in the valley of the Guash, itself a trout stream, and extends over some 6 per cent of the area of the former county of Rutland. Water for it is being pumped from the Nene at Wansford and the Welland at Tinwell. The reservoir is as large as Lake Windermere and twice the size of Grafham. Relevant figures are: length of bank, 24m; surface area, 3100 acres; capacity, 27,300 million gallons; maximum depth 110ft; average depth 35ft; cost £29 million. Its U shape tends to conceal this vast size. The reservoir is divided into long narrow arms by the Hambleton Peninsula, so that a surprising degree of intimacy is attained. The irregular contours of the bank, forming innumerable inlets and bays, and the careful landscaping of the surrounding area (by Dame Sylvia Crowe) help to present the appearance of a natural rather than man-made water.

Species/sizes: Brown and rainbow, expected to reach the 3lb–4lb mark at least by the time the reservoir opens.

Stocking: Water was rotenoned to kill coarse fish and stocked initially with half a million trout around 5–6in at a ratio of 2–1 in favour of rainbows. These have been introduced well in advance of the opening date to ensure that they will reach a good size by the time the reservoir is open for fishing. With the abundance of food, the growth rate is reported to be remarkable. Stocking is being continued with 70,000 to 80,000 bigger fish a season. All the stock fish are being reared at the authority's own hatchery at Horn Mill, 2m NE of Empingham.

Comments: Opening of this huge new reservoir is the most exciting event in the history of stillwater trout fishing in Britain since the inception of Grafham Water. Situated amid a growth area of some 7½ million people, and with excellent communications, the fishery seems destined to become a real angling mecca. All the signs are that it will provide sport of the highest quality amid the most delightful surroundings. Large numbers of anglers will be able to enjoy their fishing without any fear of overcrowding.

Planned from the outset as a recreation centre by the former Welland and Nene River Authority, Empingham will not only cater for fishing, but for sailing and, on a smaller scale, rowing and canoeing. Part of it will be set aside as a nature reserve and there will be picnic areas and facilities for rambling. Excellent parking for 3000 cars is being provided, and it is planned that anglers will be able to drive around the perimeter path to reach their fishing spots. Boats will be allowed into the nature

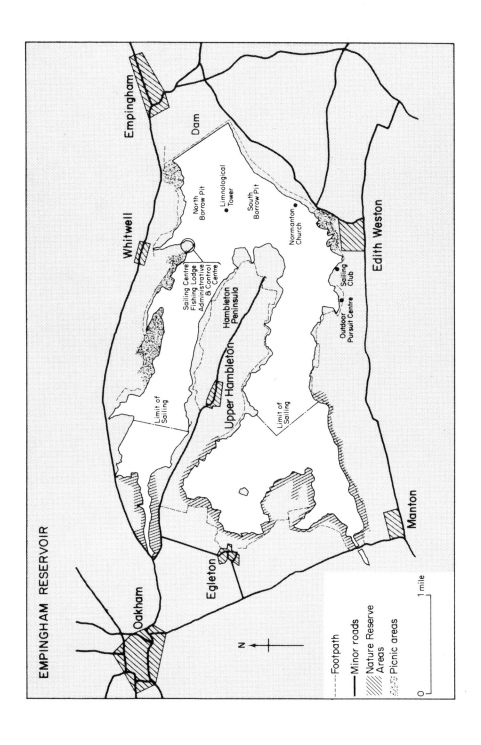

EMPINGHAM RESERVOIR

Oakham

Egleton

Manton

Upper Hambleton

Whitwell

Empingham

Edith Weston

Dam

North Borrow Pit

Limnological Tower

South Borrow Pit

Normanton Church

Sailing Centre
Fishing Lodge
Administrative & Control Centre

Hambleton Peninsula

Sailing Club

Outdoor Pursuit Centre

Limit of Sailing

Limit of Sailing

N

- - - Footpath
——— Minor roads
Nature Reserve Areas
Picnic areas

0   1 mile

reserve, but no bank fishermen. About 60 boats will be available and it is expected that they will all be powered, because of the size of the reservoir. Special safety precautions are likely to be taken, such as the provision of life jackets.

No details were available when we went to press on the rules or permit arrangements, but it is understood that anglers will be fully catered for at a fishing lodge at Whitwell on the north bank and that facilities for obtaining tickets and boats will be available on both arms of the reservoir. As to the likely opening date, the one being most widely canvassed is 1 April 1977 — truly a day to be entered in every stillwater trout fisherman's diary.

EYE BROOK

Caldecott, Leics.

From Northampton (19m) on A43 and A6003 via Kettering or from Peterborough (20m) on A47 to Uppingham. London 85m.

Controller: Corby (Northants) and District Water Co., Stanion Lane, Corby, Northants, NN1 8ES (tel. Corby 2331).

Description: 400-acre landscaped reservoir.

Species/sizes: Brown and rainbow.

	Brown	Rainbow
Average	11lb 10oz	11lb 2oz
Record	10lb 4oz	—

Stocking: Regular stocking with 12in browns and rainbows, based on returns. About half raised from own hatchery.

Rules: Fly only. Shooting heads prohibited. No bag limit.

Season: 1 April to 30 September.

Permits: dt £2. Boats (24 all rowing): £3

extra, £1.50 after 5pm. Available from 8.30am.

Comments: A real value-for-money reservoir with a more intimate atmosphere than some of its neighbours. *See Dick Shrive's appraisal on page 42.* *See Dick Shrive's appraisal on page 42.*

GRAFHAM WATER

West Perry, Huntingdon

Lies between St Neots and Huntingdon, 2m W from A1 at Buckden Roundabout. About 62m from London. See map on page 39. See map on page 39.

Controller: Anglian Water Authority, Grafham Water Area.

Description: Cleverly landscaped 1670-acre reservoir fed by water pumped from the Great Ouse at Offord. Max. capacity: 13,000 million gallons. Max. depth: 70ft.

Species/sizes: Brown and rainbow.

	Brown	Rainbow
Average	2lb plus	2lb
Record	11lb 5½oz	9lb
	(1975)	(1975)

Stocking: At start of season and at intervals until end of July. Rate — two fish to each one caught in previous season (i.e. for 1976, 70,000 fish). Policy favours rainbows in 7:1 ratio.

Rules: Fly only. Limit: 4 brace. All wading from water face of dam prohibited, as are trouser waders. Trolling (oars only) in restricted area.

Season: 1 May to 13 October.

Permits: st £75; dt £2.50 (pensioners, juveniles and disabled £1). Boats (32): motor £8 day; rowing £4 day (half-price after 5 pm).

Permits from:
Area Manager, Anglian Water Authority, West Perry, Huntingdon PE18 0BW (st); dt from fishing lodge (tel. Huntingdon 810531).

Comments: When Grafham was opened in 1966, it was hailed as the greatest trout fishery in Europe. Certainly the figures were impressive — over 10,000 trout landed in three months from July to September, including 15 of 7lb and over. Subsequently it suffered a decline, with catches slumping from 32,029 in 1967 to 16,671 in 1972. Whatever the causes, and many explanations were proffered, those early claims seemed unwarranted.

Skilled management has more than restored the situation, however, and 1975 was Grafham's finest, with catches soaring way beyond the previous highest of 32,029 in 1967 to reach 36,431. Not only that, but the season also saw new records established for both brown and rainbow trout. The capture of an 11lb 5½oz brown was a particularly fine achievement — it was taken in torrential rain on an Esmond Drury 3in Flexi-fly from a boat drifting near the dam.

No fewer than 506 fish of over 4lb were taken, 134 over 5lb, 26 over 6lb, 6 over 7lb 4 over 8lb and 1 of 9lb. The best limit catch of 34lb 4oz was also the best so far. Over the 5½-month period, no fewer than 22,890 bank permits at £2 were issued, an increase of 31 per cent on the previous season and just over the previous record total of 22,861 in 1967, the first full season on the reservoir when the cost was £1 per permit. A record number of season tickets were also sold — 140 against 115 in 1974.

Had it not been for the hot summer the catches would have been much higher; more than 20,000 trout were taken in May and June. Truly a most remarkable year for Grafham and one, moreover, which confirmed previous evidence that predation by pike was not increasing.

The management are not resting on their laurels, however. Plans for 1976 include the construction of a fish barrier at Savages Creek and the provision of five new boats and outboards.

For an appraisal on the water see Bob Church's article on page 38.

HANNINGFIELD

South Hanningfield, nr Chelmsford, Essex

Just W of A130 about 6m SE of Chelmsford and 33m from London.

Owner: Essex Water Company.

Description: 900-acre landscaped reservoir, of which 600 acres are fishable.

Species/sizes: Brown and rainbow.

	Brown	Rainbow
Average	2lb	1lb 8oz
Record	8lb 3oz	7lb 1oz

Stocking: From own hatchery, mainly in spring, followed by staggered stocking.

Rules: Fly only, limit 3 brace. Boat anglers must give way to bank anglers — boats not permitted within 100yd of any bank open to fishing, except for landing purposes. Waders or studded footwear not to be worn in boats.

Season: 1 May to 31 October.

Permits: st only, limited to 250 full season and 100 (Mon–Fri) — waiting list for both; full st £80 approx, weekdays £60. Permit holder may take one guest at £2.20 day or one non-fishing guest free. Boats (25): £3.20 day, £1.60 half-day and 80p evening.

Permits from:
Fisheries Officer, Essex Water Company,
Hanningfield Works, South Hanningfield,
Chelmsford, Essex, CM3 5HS.

Comments: Despite permit restrictions,
this water is fished by nearly 13,000 rods
who in 1975 captured a record 30,887
trout; giving a very respectable average of
2.47 fish per rod visit. No fewer than 907
fish over the 3lb mark were taken; a
striking tribute to the quality of the sport.
A vigorous stocking and management
policy is bringing results. Fishing is best
from boats, sport from the bank being
limited to 1¼ miles of dam wall and 1¼
miles of wading. But boat anglers are
warned to take care, as the reservoir can
become very rough. Muddler Minnow and
other sunk lures are most popular, though
nymphing around the margins brings
good results at times.

HARTSHOLME LAKES

Hartsholme, Lincoln

Located within Lincoln City boundary, to
S, on Doddington road.

Controller: Lincoln (Angling) Fisheries
Ltd.

Description: Two 8-acre lakes, part of
complex of gravel workings.

Species: Brown and rainbow trout.

Stocking: With equal numbers of browns
and rainbows at intervals.

Rules: Fly only. Boat fishing only.

Season: 1 April to 30 September.

Permits: dt £5 (with boat) for two
anglers.

Permits from:
Lincoln Fisheries by telephone: Lincoln
20618 or 63175.

HILL VIEW TROUT LAKE

*Hogsthorpe,
nr Skegness, Lincs.*

Off Willoughby Road (A52), 7m SE of
Alford.

Owners: K. & M. R. Raynor, 19 St
Leonards Drive, Chapel St Leonards, nr
Skegness, Lincs., PE24 5RP
(tel. Skegness 72979).

Description: Natural lake covering 1½
acres in 6½ acres of grounds.

Species/sizes: Rainbows only, averaging
1lb 3oz, biggest 4lb.

Stocking: Weekly.

Rules: Fly only, and only one fly. No
wading.

Season: 3 April to 30 September.

Permits: dt £2.75; evenings £2.00.

Permits from: Warden's caravan at
lakeside.

Comments: Good evening rises in 1975
season. Recommended flies; Teal and
Green, Hare's Ear, Grey Duster. Nymphs:
Green and Black Buzzers, Pheasant Tail.

PITSFORD

Brixworth,
nr Northampton

A508 from Northampton towards Market Harborough — turn off at Brixworth (about 5m) for reservoir. 70m from London via M1.

Controller: Anglian Water Authority, Northants Water Division.

Description: 739-acre landscaped reservoir, 279 acres available for fishing — large sailing area.

Species/sizes: Brown and rainbow.

	Brown	Rainbow
Average	1lb 8oz	1lb 8oz
Record	5lb 10oz	6lb 4oz
	(1970)	(1963)

Stocking: At intervals throughout season. 1975 figures: 1500 2½lb rainbows in March, further 16,000 rainbows and 5750 brown trout (10 to 12in) in nine deliveries.

Rules: Fly only. Limit: 8 fish over 12in.

Season: 1 April to 30 September.

Permits: st £42.50; dt £1.40 (evenings 90p). Boats, £5.80 for two rods (evenings £3.60). Reductions for pensioners and juniors.

Permits from:
Head Office AWA, Cliftonville, Northampton (st); dt from Fishing Lodge (tel. Walgrave St Peter 350).

Comments: This very popular fishery has had its ups and downs. It began well, fell away, had trouble with coarse fish, but appears to have settled down now to producing trout of good average size with a fair number over the 3lb mark. There is plenty of room for the bank angler as a rule, but space is sometimes a little restricted for boat fishing when sailing races are on. Most Grafham-type flies and lures do well here.

RAVENSTHORPE

Ravensthorpe,
nr Northampton

A50 to Spratton from Northampton, and left towards Teeton — reservoir is about 2m along, 70m from London via M1.

Controller: Anglian Water Authority, Northampton Water Division.

Description: 114-acre landscaped reservoir.

Species/sizes: Brown and rainbow.

	Brown	Rainbow
Average	1lb	1lb
Record	8lb 7½oz	4lb 6oz
	(1965)	

Stocking: At intervals throughout season. 1975 stocking: 750 2½lb rainbows early March, then 8500 rainbows and 4250 browns (10–12in) in nine deliveries.

Rules: Fly only. Limit 8 fish 12in and over.

Season: 1 April to 30 September.

Permits: st £42.50; dt £1.40 (evenings 90p). Boats (8): £5.80 for two rods, £3.60 evenings. Reductions for pensioners and juniors.

Permits from:
Head Office, Anglian Water Authority, Cliftonville, Northampton (st); dt from Fishing Lodge (tel. East Haddon 2108).

Comments: One of the noted Northampton reservoirs and only six miles or so from Pitsford, Ravensthorpe is a small secluded water holding some very good fish. Comfortable access is provided by a perimeter path. The water also holds coarse fish, especially rudd, but a deeply worked fly or lure can escape their attention. Incidentally, the record 8lb 7½oz brown trout was taken by Dick Shrive of Northampton on a rudd fry lure.
Dick contributes an article on Eye Brook on page 42.

SIBSON FISHERIES

Stibbington,
nr Wansford, Cambs.

½m off A1 at Wansford, 8m from Peterborough.

Owners: Sibson Fisheries.

Description: Five-acre natural lake with three man-made 'backwaters' 20 yards wide, 500 yards long.

Species/sizes: Rainbow, with some brown trout.

	Brown	Rainbow
Average	1lb 8oz	3lb
Record	2lb 4oz	8lb 4oz

Stocking: Restocked as soon as fish population declines to 60 per cent of fish stocked, based on returns.

Rules: Fly only. Limit: one brace.

Season: 1 April to 31 October.

Permits: st £60; dt £3.50.

Permits from:
Owners at New Lane, Stibbington, Wansford, Cambs., PE8 6LW (tel. Stamford (0780) 782621), or head bailiff (V. H. Bettinson) on Stamford 782733 (dt).

TASWOOD TROUT FISHERY

Flordon,
nr Norwich, Norfolk

From Norwich turn right off A140 at Newton Florman (6m).

Owner: Ken Smith.

Description: 4 lakes and 2m stretch of water.

Species/sizes: Brown and rainbow.

	Brown	Rainbow
Average	1lb 8oz	1lb 8oz
Record	3lb 8oz	5lb 9oz

Stocking: At regular intervals throughout season.

Rules: Fly only. Limit 5 fish. All trout taken to be killed.

Season: 1 April to 30 September.

Permits: st £105 approx, guests of members, £5 day.

Permits from:
Ken Smith, Taswood Trout Fishery, Flordon, Norfolk (tel. Swainsthorpe 818).

Comments: Returns for 1975, the second full season at this fishery, showed that 2301 trout were taken, including 235 over 2lb, 24 over 3lb and five over 4lb. Early on, members averaged three trout per visit.

THORPE MALSOR RESERVOIR

nr Kettering, Northants

Fishing controlled by a private syndicate. Hon sec: J. B. Mumford, c/o 17 Wellington Street, Leicester.

Comments: This water has been fished for one season only during which 2317 anglers caught 4057 trout. The bailiffs are keen fly-fishermen and are always willing to give advice and tuition (tel. Normanby-Spital 433).

TOFT NEWTON

Toft, nr Market Rasen, Lincs.

Located 15m NE of Lincoln. Turn off A631 at West Rasen, or 5m E of Caenby Corner (A15) turn off to Normanby.

Controller: Anglian Water Authority, Lincolnshire River Division.

Description: 40-acre concrete bowl.

Species/sizes: Brown and rainbow.

	Brown	Rainbow
Average	14oz	1lb 2oz
Record	1lb 8oz	3lb 4oz

Stocking: Weekly or fortnightly, depending on angling pressure. Initial stocking was with 5000 trout mostly rainbows weighing at least 1lb.

Rules: Fly only. Limit: 2 brace. Trouser waders prohibited.

Season: 9 April to 30 September.

Permits: dt £3 (restricted to 40). Also special permit at £1.80 (one brace limit). No boats.

Permits from: Self-service unit at fishing lodge or in advance from Lincolnshire River Division, 50 Wide Bargate, Boston, Lincs., PE21 6SA (tel. Boston 65661).

LATE ENTRIES

ROXTON PARK TROUT FISHERY

Roxton, nr Bedford

At Roxton (on A428), 7m NE of Bedford, 1m W of A1.

Owner: P. C. Bath Ltd.

Description: Landscaped reservoir of 15 acres.

Species/sizes: Stocked with rainbows/browns in ratio 85/15%. Average fish 1lb 8oz, rainbows growing up to 6lb.

Stocking: Main (70%) restocking at start of season, mid-season booster of 30%. See *Comments* below.

Rules: No Tuesday fishing. All fish to be killed. Fly only, no spinning, trolling or wading. No fly hooks larger than size 10. Fishing from 9.30am to 1hr after sunset.

Season: 1 May to 31 October.

Permits: st £100 plus VAT. Two rowing boats: free, on rota.

Permits from: P. C. Bath Ltd., Roxton Park, Roxton, Beds. (tel. Bedford 870385).

Comments: A new (1976) fishery, in which the initial stocking was 700 rainbows and 100 browns averaging 1lb 8oz, plus 20 specimen rainbows averaging 5lb. Stocking and restocking rates calculated on 25 rods let, and will be stepped up to cater for additional lettings. Excellent lodge facilities.

SWANSHOLME PARK

Hartsholme, Lincoln

Two ten-acre lakes holding large browns and rainbows (up to 7lb); regularly stocked with both species; dt £5.52 (£1.50 evenings). Boat for two at £5.50, including permit (£3.30 after 7pm). Tickets from Jim Wainwright, resident manager, Lincoln Fisheries, The Bungalow, Doddington Road, Lincoln (tel. 63175).

EAST HANNINGFIELD HALL

East Hanningfield,
nr Chelmsford, Essex

Located about 1m from village along Pan Lane. This 16th century trout lake became dried up and was then restored as a 'natural' fishery of about one acre. Recently restocked with browns and rainbows. Full st £135 (limit: 3 brace); weekly st (Mon-Fri) £110 (limit 2½ brace); dt (Mon-Fri) £5; week-ends £6 (limit 2½ brace). Tickets from D. F. Benson, East Hanningfield Hall (tel. Chelmsford (0245) 400269). Furnished cottage available for letting at lakeside.

REMINDER

We have not as a rule mentioned in the individual entries the need for a regional water authority licence as well as a permit, but this is usually necessary, except for the relatively few cases where the fishery holds a general licence.

---

2 The North West

NORTH WEST WATER AUTHORITY
Dawson House, Great Sankey, Warrington, WA5 3LW (tel. Penketh (092572) 4321).
Regional Fisheries Officer: J. D. Kelsall, Green Bank, Stocks Lane, Penketh,
Warrington (tel. Penketh (092572) 4321 or 3289 (home)).
Trout licences (whole area): season £2 (OAPs, junior £1), week 50p.

Cumberland Area
Fisheries Officer: Norman MacKenzie, Warwick Green, Wetherall, Carlisle, CA4 8PG
(tel. Carlisle (0228) 60249).
Trout close season: 15 September to 19 March.

Lancashire Area
Fisheries Officer: R. D. Parker, Bank Side, Long Preston, Skipton
(tel. Halton-on-Lune (052481) 473 or Long Preston (07294) 353 (home)).
Trout close seasons:
    Northern district — 1 October to 2 March.
    Southern district — 1 October to 14 March.

Mersey and Weaver Area
Water Quality Officer: E. Harper, Microcosm, Hillside Road, Appleton, via Warrington,
WA4 5PZ (tel. Penketh (092572) 5531 or Warrington (0925) 66763 (home)).
Trout close season: 1 October to last day in February.

Note: Licences cover brown and rainbow trout, and char.

REMINDER

Stocking policy depends on returns. Fishery managers have
asked us to stress that whether you catch anything or not, please
remember to fill in the form before leaving the water.

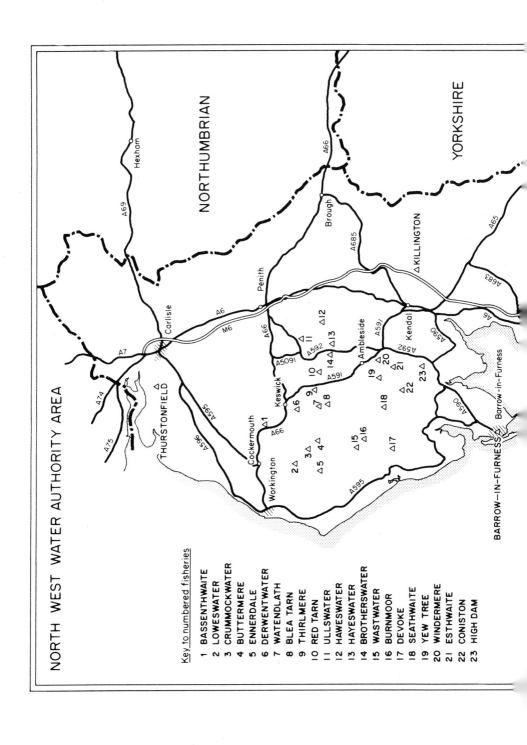

NORTH WEST WATER AUTHORITY AREA

Key to numbered fisheries

1 BASSENTHWAITE
2 LOWESWATER
3 CRUMMOCKWATER
4 BUTTERMERE
5 ENNERDALE
6 DERWENTWATER
7 WATENDLATH
8 BLEA TARN
9 THIRLMERE
10 RED TARN
11 ULLSWATER
12 HAWESWATER
13 HAYESWATER
14 BROTHERSWATER
15 WASTWATER
16 BURNMOOR
17 DEVOKE
18 SEATHWAITE
19 YEW TREE
20 WINDERMERE
21 ESTHWAITE
22 CONISTON
23 HIGH DAM

NORTHUMBRIAN

YORKSHIRE

BARROW-IN-FURNESS

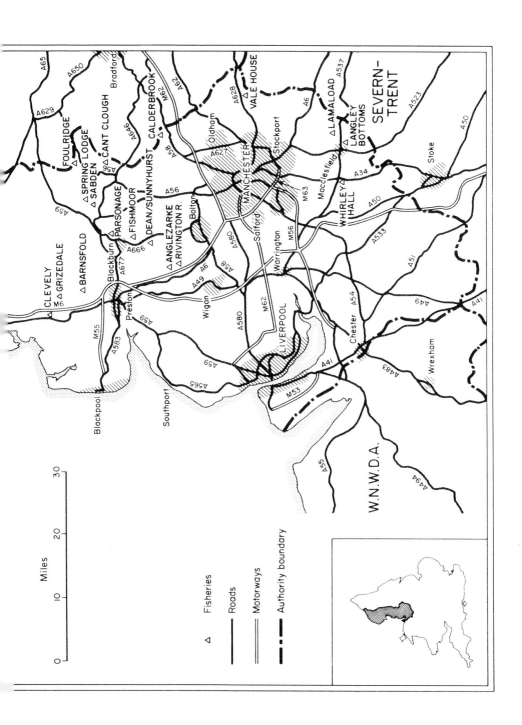

Miles

0   10   20   30

△ Fisheries
— Roads
═ Motorways
–··– Authority boundary

SEVERN–TRENT

W.N.W.D.A.

A65
A650
A629
A59
CLEVELY △ △GRIZEDALE
M6 △BARNSFOLD
FOULRIDGE
△SPRING LODGE
△ SABDEN
△CANT CLOUGH
Bradford
M62
A646
A59
A62
PARSONAGE
△FISHMOOR
DEAN/SUNNYHURST
CALDERBROOK
△
Blackburn
A677
A56
A666
A627
A58
A628
VALE HOUSE
A537
Oldham
MANCHESTER
Stockport
△LAMALOAD
LANGLEY
BOTTOMS
A523
A6
A50
Salford
M63
Macclesfield
WHIRLEY
HALL
A34
Stoke
Warrington
M56
A533
A50
M62
A451
Wigan
A49
A6
A49
A41
A580
A58
Preston
A583
A59
M55
A580
A59
A565
LIVERPOOL
Southport
Blackpool
A55
Chester
A54
A41
M53
A483
Wrexham
A494
△ANGLEZARKE
△RIVINGTON R.
Bolton

ALWEN *see page 163.*

ANGLEZARKE RESERVOIR
see under Rivington Reservoirs

BALLURE
see under Isle of Man Fisheries

BARNSFOLD WATERS

Goosnargh,
nr Preston, Lancs.

7m from junction 32 of M6. Approach from east via Clitheroe or Blackburn towards Longridge, then follow signs to Beacon Fell.

Owner: M. A. Collins, 3 Stanley Road, Hoylake, Wirral, Merseyside.

Description: Two reservoirs of about 10 acres on southerly slopes of Beacon Fell.

Species/sizes: Brown and rainbow.

	Brown	Rainbow
Average	1lb	1lb 8oz
Record	5lb 12oz	7lb

Stocking: At intervals throughout season with fish of 1lb—5lb.

Rules: Fly only. Limit: 2 brace 11in and over. Trolling and wading prohibited.

Season: 1 April to 30 September.

Permits: st vary from £54 (one named day) to £135 (full-rod) (juniors under 16 half-price if accompanied by full subscriber); limited dt £4.86; guests £3.34. Boats (3 on each water) £1 day. Caravans (2) £1 day.

Permits from: Preston 44344 before season opens. Chipping 583 or Ribchester 202 afterwards.

Comments: A well-stocked fishery in open country, easily accessible to Preston anglers. 1975 season's returns: 1346 browns to 5lb 2oz and 1336 rainbows to 5lb 13oz. Further details from P. Jays, 36 Cop Lane, Pentwortham, Preston (tel. 44344).

BARROW-IN-FURNESS RESERVOIRS

Barrow-in-Furness, Lancs.

Five trout reservoirs in area controlled by Barrow A.A. Rainbows in three of them. Limited tickets to friends of members only. For membership inquire hon sec: D. M. Adams, 18 Grantley Road, Barrow-in-Furness, Lancs.

BASSENTHWAITE

nr Cockermouth, Cumbria

Lies alongside A594 Keswick to Cockermouth road.

Owner: Leconfield Estates Co.

Description: 4m long, 1½m wide and up to 68ft deep, in Vale of Keswick.

Species: Brown trout, occasional salmon; pike, perch.

Stocking: None.

Rules: All legal methods allowed.

Season: 20 March to 14 September.

Permits: st £2.31; wt £1.21, dt 33p (reductions for juniors). Boats available.

Permits from: Boatman at Peilwyke Landings, near Cockermouth (he will help visitors). Also from Fishery Manager, Estate Office, Cockermouth.

Comments: Holds some large trout, but they are becoming few and far between. Early season best for fly.

BLEA TARN

Keswick, Cumbria

Six miles from Keswick, at head of Watendlath. Well stocked with trout on small side. Free.

BLOCK EARY
see under Isle of Man Fisheries

BOTTOMS

Tintwistle,
nr Stalybridge, Cheshire

Reached via A628 Manchester to Sheffield road by way of Woodhead.

Controller: North West Water Authority, Eastern Division.

Description: 55-acre reservoir.

Species/sizes: Brown and rainbow.

	Brown	Rainbow
Average	9oz	1½lb
Record	3lb 7oz	4lb 1oz

Stocking: Immediately before season opens, then monthly.

Rules: Bait fishing allowed.

Season: 1 April to 30 September.

Permits: dt approx £1, OAPs approx 75p. No boats.

Permits from:
North West WA, Eastern Division, Bottoms Office, Tintwistle, Hyde, Cheshire.

Comments: Anglers are advised to fish early (before 10am) and late (after 6pm) for best sport on this reservoir.

BROTHERSWATER

Penrith, Cumbria

Linked to Ullswater by The Goldrill, National Trust property. Trout (3 to lb) and perch. Free fishing.

BURNMOOR TARN

Wasdale, via Gosforth, Cumbria

Across country from Wastwater (about 2m SE). Another National Trust lake providing free fishing for small trout.

BUTTERMERE
see Crummockwater, Buttermere and Loweswater

CALDERBROOK DAMS

Littleborough, Lancs.

About 3m NE of Rochdale at summit of Calderbrook Road.

Controller: Todmorden A.S.

Description: Two landscaped reservoirs.

Species/sizes: Brown and rainbow.

	Brown	Rainbow
Average	8oz	8oz
Record	3lb 8oz	2lb 12oz

Stocking: During close season.

Rules: All legal methods allowed. Limit: three fish of 12in and over per week. No keep nets.

Season: 1 April to 30 September.

Permits: st £4 (society sub, plus £2 entry fee); dt 50p.

Permits from:
Steve's Tackle Shop, 204 Yorkshire Street, Rochdale.

Comments: The top dam holds trout only and is suitable for the fly. The bottom dam is a mixed fishery and is open all the year.

CANT CLOUGH

*Hurstwood,
nr Burnley, Lancs.*

Through Hurstwood Village, 3m E of Burnley, then ¾m along private road to car park at dam.

Controller: Mitre Angling Club.

Description: 40-acre reservoir in bleak moorland about 1000ft above sea level.

Species/sizes: Brown trout only, average 12oz (record 3lb 2oz).

Stocking: In December.

Rules: Fly and spinner only; limited to six rods.

Season: 15 March to 30 September.

Permits: Members-only water. Sub £10, entrance £5 (increases expected for 1976). Small waiting list. Cards from hon sec: R. D. Halstead, 32 Parrock Road, Barrowford, Nelson, Lancs.

CLYPSE (and Kerrowdhoo)
see under Isle of Man Fisheries

CONISTON

Coniston, Cumbria

Turn off A593 Broughton to Ambleside road. Or take Hawkshead road just out of Ambleside (B5286).

Owner: National Trust owns most of shore.

Description: Third longest of lakes — 6m long, ¾m wide and up to 184ft deep — at foot of Coniston Fells.

Species/sizes: Trout, char, perch, pike.

Stocking: None.

Rules: All legal methods allowed.

Season: 20 March to 14 September.

Permits: None required, free fishing. Boats available. RD licence for trout and char.

Comments: The trout and char fishing on this lake is disappointing. Trout are plentiful but on the small side. Char fishing reported best in June and July.

CRINGLE
see under Isle of Man Fisheries

CRUMMOCKWATER
BUTTERMERE
LOWESWATER

Buttermere, Cumbria

Reached from Cockermouth via B5292 on minor road from Keswick via Whinlatter (about 14m).

Owner: National Trust.

Description: Chain of lakes along depression between Robinson and Hindscarth Mountains. Buttermere is 1¾m long, ½m wide and up to 90ft deep. Crummock is 3m long, ¾m wide and up to 132 ft deep. Loweswater 1½m long, ½m wide.

Species/sizes: Trout, char, pike and perch.

Stocking: None.

Rules: Any legal method allowed, but fly-only on Loweswater until June 16.

Season: 20 March to 14 September.

Permits: st £5.50; wt £2.20; dt 55p. Boats £1.40, 80p from 2pm.

Permits from:
G. J. Stagg, Croft House Farm, Buttermere, and
Kirkstile Inn, Loweswater.

Comments: Trout (about ¾lb) rise well from May to July and can be caught on local Bustard patterns on summer evenings. Inquire National Trust, Broadlands, Ambleside, for further details.

DEAN (EARNSDALE)

Darwen, Lancs.

From A666 turn left 1m N of Darwen town centre, follow Earnsdale road to Sunnyhurst, turn right at top and follow track — reservoir about two-thirds of a mile down.

Controller: Darwen A.A.

Description: Landscaped reservoir covering 16 acres.

Species/sizes: Brown and rainbow.

	Brown	Rainbow
Average	12oz	1lb
Record	2lb 2oz	1lb 7oz

Stocking: Takeable fish introduced at intervals. Some reared in own hatcheries.

Rules: Adults only (over 18); bait fishing, etc., allowed, but no maggots.

Season: 15 March to 30 September.

Permits: dt 50p. No boats.

Permits from:
County Sports (J. Entwistle), Duckworth Street, Darwen (A666 200yd N of town centre).

Comments: Reservoir fishes best during early part of season — April to July. Further details from club hon sec, J. Priestley, 24 Knowlesly Road, Darwen. Lancs.

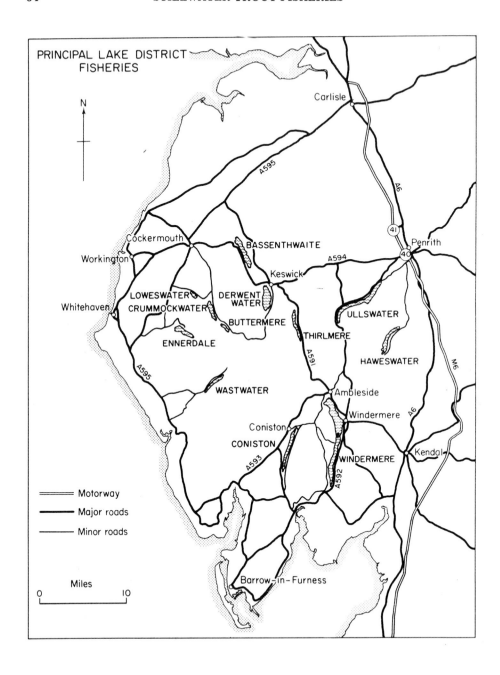

PRINCIPAL LAKE DISTRICT
FISHERIES

N

Carlisle

A595

Cockermouth

Workington

BASSENTHWAITE

Keswick

Penrith

A594

41

40

Whitehaven

LOWESWATER
CRUMMOCKWATER

DERWENT
WATER

BUTTERMERE

ULLSWATER

THIRLMERE

A591

HAWESWATER

ENNERDALE

A595

WASTWATER

Ambleside

A6

Windermere

M6

Coniston

CONISTON

A593

WINDERMERE

A592

Kendal

Motorway

Major roads

Minor roads

Miles

0   10

Barrow-in-Furness

DERWENTWATER

nr Keswick, Cumbria

1m S of Keswick off B5289.

Controller: Keswick A.A.

Description: Island-studded lake in valley of River Derwent, 3m long, 1¼m wide and up to 72ft deep.

Species: Brown trout, perch and pike.

Stocking: None.

Rules: Trout size limit 8in. No ground baiting.

Season: 20 March to 14 September.

Permits: dt 25p; wt £1.25. Boats available at Lodore, Nicoll End and Keswick.

Permits from:
N. Temple, Station Street, Keswick, and hon sec, Keswick A.A.: J. B. Haile, 14 Station Street.

Comments: Sport with fly quite good early in the season. Fish up to 5lb have been taken.

DEVOKE WATER

Woodend,
nr Ulpha, Cumbria

5m E of Ravenglass. Moorland tarn ½m long holding some fair-sized trout, pike and perch. Trout rise well to fly. Access by foot. Millom and District A.A. fishery for members only. Inquire hon sec: J. Coward, 51 Queen's Park, nr Millom, Cumberland.

DRUNKEN DUCK TARN

Ambleside, Cumbria

Brown trout averaging 14oz (biggest 6lb). Stocked annually. Fly only. Grizedale A.C. water (hon sec: W. E. Coates, Grizedale, Hawkshead, Ambleside, Cumbria.).

ENNERDALE LAKE

nr Egremont, Cumbria

Turn left off A5086 on approach to Cleator from Cockermouth.

Controller: Calder A.A., Wath Brow and Ennerdale A.A., Egremont A.A.

Description: Glacial lake beautifully situated in long Ennerdale Valley.

Species/sizes: Brown trout and char.

	Brown	Char
Average	8oz	8oz
Record	2lb	1lb

Stocking: No stocking at present, but clubs are reviewing policies.

Rules: Fly, spinning and worming permitted. No coach parties as lake is supply reservoir.

Season: 19 March to 15 September.

Permits: st £1; wt 50p. No boats.

Permits from:
Hon sec, Calder A.A.: W. N. Nixon, 1 Yottenfews, Calderbridge, Seascale, Cumbria
Hon sec, Wath Brow A.A.: D. F. Whelan, 11 Crossing Close, Cleator Moor, Cumbria

Hon sec, Egremont A.A.: C. Fisher,
69 North Road, Egremont, Cumbria.

Comments: Records dating back many
years show that trout in the region of
6—8lb were caught in Ennerdale and it is
thought that some fish of these
dimensions remain. Best patterns are
silver-bodied flies with red or blue
hackles, or small spinners. Plumb-lining
with small spinners or worm is favoured
technique for the graceful char. Although
no boats are generally available,
arrangements can be made with fishermen
to provide them, but only in very limited
numbers.

ESTHWAITE WATER

Hawkshead, Cumbria

Extends 2m SE from Hawkshead towards
Windermere (3m). Holds good trout (av.
¾lb) as well as pike and perch. Permits: dt
25p; wt 75p, from J. Haselhurst, Post
Office, Hawkshead and W. Rigby,
Hazelseat Lodge, Graythwaite, Ulverston.
Boat and fishing permits from T. Bownass,
Foldgate Cottages, Hawkshead (tel. 442).

FISHMOOR

nr Blackburn, Lancs.

Off Blackamoor road, 2m S of Blackburn.

Controller: Blackburn and District A.A.

Description: 60-acre stone-built basin,
with natural bank on two sides.

Species/sizes: Brown and rainbow.

	Brown	Rainbow
Average	12oz	12oz
Record	2lb 2oz	1lb 7oz

Stocking: Twice, once at start of season
and once during it.

Rules: Fly and spinning.

Season: 1 April to 30 October.

Permits: dt £1. No boats.

Permits from:
J. Hoyle (tackleist), 51 Whalley New
Road, Blackburn.

Comments: Fishes best at dusk with fly
on or just below surface. Further details
from hon sec, Blackburn A.A.: A. Smith,
25 Pickering Fold, Blackamoor,
Blackburn.

FOULRIDGE LOWER RESERVOIR

Colne, Lancs.

Also known as Burwains. British
Waterways feeder for neighbouring Leeds
and Liverpool Canal. Trout, coarse fish;
dt 25p from A. Southworth, Boll Bridge
House, Reedy Moor Lane, Foulbridge
Colne, Lancs. (tel. Colne 6061)

GRIZEDALE LEA RESERVOIR

nr Garstang, Lancs.

Brown trout. Kirkham Fly F.C. issue four
dt at £1 each; boat £1.50. Tickets from
hon sec: J. H. Boulton, 8 Preston Street,
Kirkham, nr Preston, Lancs.

HAWESWATER

nr Penrith or Shap, Cumbria

Take Bampton road from A6 at Shap and turn left at Bampton for lake.

Controller: North West Water Authority.

Description: Natural lake made into reservoir — 2½m long and ½m wide on average.

Species/sizes: Brown trout, char and gwyniad. Trout average 8oz.

Stocking: None.

Rules: Fly, spinner and bait fishing.

Season: 15 March to 30 September.

Permits: Only to guests at Haweswater Hotel.

Comments: When the water warms up sufficiently, the trout rise freely to the fly and char may also be taken on a fly or lure fished deep. Smallwater Tarn, reached from the top end of Haweswater, holds trout, but it is difficult to reach and the fish are on the small side.

HAYESWATER

Hartsop,
nr Patterdale, Cumbria

Small lake on west side of High Street Mountain 8½m WSW of Shap and to south of Ullswater. Good tarn trout (3 to lb) with fair chance of fish around 1lb mark. Controlled by Penrith AA for members only. Inquiries to hon sec: J. N. Norris, 21 Victoria Road, Penrith.

HIGH DAM

Finsthwaite,
nr Newby Bridge, Cumbria

Hill tarn near Finsthwaite, 8m NE of Ulverston necessitating a tough climb but could be worthwhile for the view alone. Holds some good trout. Tickets from bungalow at bottom of track.

INJEBRECK
see under Isle of Man Fisheries

ISLE OF MAN FISHERIES

Eric Horsfall Turner has written: 'If I were asked what areas of Britain contained the best concentration of trout lakes, the Isle of Man would come high on the list. It is true that the island's lakes are called "reservoirs" for the most part; but the distinction between a reservoir and a lake in the hills is one of name rather than appearance or angling quality. If there is a dam at one end, it is forgotten in the natural beauty of the other . . .'

CLYPSE and KERROWDHOO

Onchan

These reservoirs lie, one beyond the other, about 1½m N of Onchan Village and about 1m or so from Douglas. Private road runs to Grange Farm, where there is a box for tickets at attendant's house and where cars may be parked.

Owner: Isle of Man Water and Gas Authority.

Description: Small lakes in picturesque surroundings holding 81 million gallons when full.

Species/sizes: Brown and rainbow.

	Brown	Rainbow
Average	1lb	1lb
Record	6lb 0¾oz	8lb 2¼oz
	(1975)	(1974)

Stocking: By Isle of Man Board of Agriculture and Fisheries at 3-weekly intervals throughout season with fish of over 1lb, mostly rainbows.

Rules: Fly only. Limit: 3 brace. No wading.

Season: 10 March to 30 September.

Permits: st £6; dt 25p (increases likely for 1976). No boats.

Permits from: Attendant's house at reservoirs.

Comments: Although Clypse has a large population of sticklebacks and Kerrowdhoo sticklebacks and perch, the trout, generally speaking, do not feed on these but on aquatic insects which are usually the same as on the mainland; with the notable exception that there is no significant mayfly hatch. The brown trout tend to be bottom feeders, except for the evening rise. The rainbows, which are the predominantly-stocked fish, feed nearer the surface at varying times. Although the rainbows can be taken on lures, the most consistent results come from imitations of natural insects.

INJEBRECK (or West Baldwin)

West Baldwin

Near centre of island. Main road runs past end of dam. Infrequent bus service to West Baldwin village 1m or so from reservoir.

Owner: Isle of Man Water and Gas Authority.

Description: Landscaped reservoir holding 301 million gallons when full.

Species/sizes: Brown and rainbow.

	Brown	Rainbow
Average	12oz	1lb
Record	6lb 12oz	5lb
	(1974)	(1974)

Stocking: As Clypse.

Rules: Fly and spinner only. Limit: 3 brace. No wading.

Season: 10 March to 30 September.

Permits: st £6; dt 25p (increases likely for 1976). No boats.

Permits from: Attendant's house at reservoir.

Comments: Condition similar to Clypse and Kerrowdhoo, except that there are no perch in Injebreck.

Other Water and Gas Authority reservoirs:
BALLURE, just south of Ramsey. Access by private road off main road to Douglas on Douglas side of Manx electric railway crossing near town boundary. Box for fishing tickets at Filter Plant just below dam.

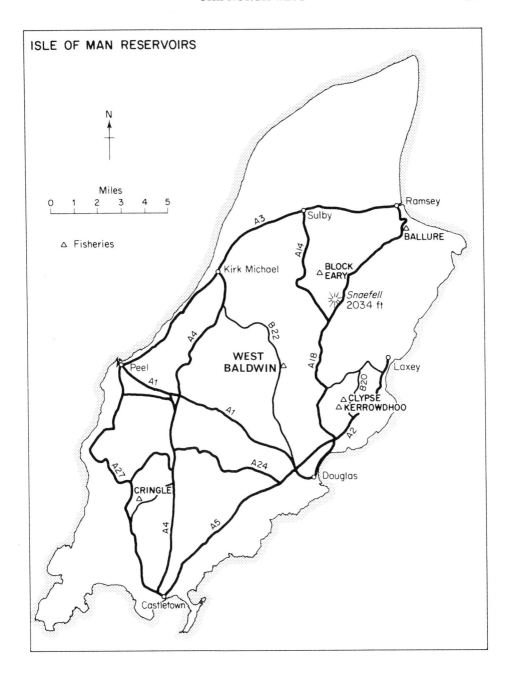

ISLE OF MAN RESERVOIRS

N

Miles
0 1 2 3 4 5

△ Fisheries

Ramsey

A3   Sulby
A14
△ BALLURE

Kirk Michael

BLOCK
△ EARY

Snaefell
2034 ft

B22
A4   WEST
BALDWIN △   A18   Laxey

Peel
A1   B20
△ CLYPSE
A1   △ KERROWDHOO
A2
A27
A24
CRINGLE △   Douglas
A4   A5

Castletown

BLOCK EARY, on tributary of Sulby River on north slopes of Snaefell. Access by private road leaving Sulby to Tholt-y-Will road about ¾m from Tholt-y-Will. Private road too rough for cars. Tickets must be left in box at dam; may be bought at Sulby Glen Filter Station, on Sulby to Tholt-y-Will road about 2½m from Sulby.

CRINGLE, lies just north of road from Ronague to Foxdale and on south slopes of South Barrule. Cars may be parked on reservoir land. Tickets to be put in box at end of dam; may be bought at Ballagawne Filter Plant about 2½m from reservoir on road from Ronague to Colby.

Rules: As Injebreck. Charges same as other reservoirs.

KERROWDHOO

see under Isle of Man Fisheries (Clypse and Kerrowdhoo)

KILLINGTON

New Hutton,
nr Kendal, Cumbria

Turn right off A684 from Kendal (5m).

Controller: Kent A.A.

Description: Landscaped reservoir (canal feeder owned by Bristol Waterways).

Species/sizes: Brown and rainbow, also pike and perch.

	Brown	Rainbow
Average	10oz	9oz
Record	4lb	2lb 8oz

Stocking: Usually in spring and autumn.

Rules: Fly, spinning, bait fishing (but no maggots).

Season: 1 March to 30 September.

Permits: st £3; wt £1.25; dt 40p.

Permits from: Reservoir keeper and T. Atkinson & Sons, Stricklandgate, Kendal. Also from club hon sec: J. C. Parkin, 11a Blea Tarn Road, Kendal, Cumbria.

THE LAKE DISTRICT

Although the widening opportunities for catching gargantuan trout from 'put and take' fisheries has tended to overshadow regions like Lakeland, there are still many anglers who prefer their quarry to be wild fish, and not from the stewpond. Moreover, when they can pursue them amid such a glorious landscape as that of the Lake District, the compensations for indifferent sport — and it can be indifferent at times — are not to be under-estimated. Also, there are still fine fish to be taken by the persistent and dedicated angler, as a five pounder from Derwentwater and an eight-pounder from Ullswater bear witness. If the fisherman is not too much of a stickler for the fine art, even bigger ones may be taken on the troll from Windermere.

An extra attraction is the char, still found in fair numbers in many lakes. Though normally a deep-water species, these can be taken on fly at certain times of the year, especially when they are ascending tributary streams to spawn.

Among the more important lakes from the fishery point of view, apart from those mentioned, are Bassenthwaite, Buttermere, Coniston, Ennerdale, Crummockwater and Wastwater. Most of the bigger lakes can be fished for a small charge. Elsewhere, fishing is often free, though the sport is likely to be variable and the trout no more than herring-size. In this North-West section there are entries for all the important trout waters in the Lake District, as well as shorter references to a number of smaller fisheries in Lakeland.

LAMALOAD

nr Macclesfield, Cheshire

Half a mile off main Macclesfield to Buxton Road, 3m from Macclesfield.

Controller: Prince Albert A.S.

Description: 48-acre landscaped reservoir.

Species/sizes: Brown and rainbow.

	Brown	Rainbow
Average	1lb 8oz	1lb 12oz
Record	5lb 8oz	4lb

Stocking: At intervals throughout season.

Rules: Fly only, no wading. Limit: 1 brace 12in and over.

Season: 1 April to 10 October.

Permits: Available on club ticket: £10pa, plus £5 entrance fee. Also dt £1.10p (five only).

Permits from:
Ray Newton (tackleist), Park Lane, Macclesfield.

Comments: Often 'twinned' with its smaller neighbour, Langley Bottoms, Lamaload holds some fine fish but visitors should note that day tickets are strictly limited.

LANGLEY BOTTOMS

Langley,
nr Macclesfield, Cheshire

1½m SE of Macclesfield. Left off A523 to Langley village; Reservoir on right.

Controller: Prince Albert A.S.

Description: Landscaped reservoir of 10 acres.

Species/sizes: Brown and rainbow.

	Brown	Rainbow
Average	1lb	1lb 3oz
Record	5lb	3lb 8oz

Stocking: At intervals throughout season with brown and rainbow trout.

Rules: Fly only. Limit: 1 brace, min 12in. No wading.

Season: 16 March to 10 October.

Permits: Members only, sub £10pa plus £5 entrance fee. No dt.

Comments: A much smaller water than its neighbour, Lamaload, but provides comparable sport.

LOWESWATER
see Crummockwater, Buttermere and Loweswater

PARSONAGE

nr Blackburn, Lancs.

Lies on northern outskirts of Blackburn along Parsonage Road, about 2m from city.

Controller: Blackburn and District A.A.

Description: 50-acre reservoir.

Species/sizes: Brown and rainbow.

	Brown	Rainbow
Average	12oz	12oz
Record	2½lb	1lb 3oz

Stocking: Twice, once at start of season and once during it.

Rules: Fly only.

Season: 1 April to 30 October.

Permits: dt £1. No boats.

Permits from:
J. Hoyle (tackleist), 51 Whalley New Road, Blackburn.

Comments: Fishes best at dusk with fly on or just below surface. Further details from hon sec, Blackburn A.A.: A. Smith, 25 Pickering Fold, Blackamoor, Blackburn.

RAKE BROOK RESERVOIR
see under Rivington Reservoirs

RED TARN

Glenridding,
nr Patterdale, Cumbria

Situated immediately beneath Helvellyn 2356ft above sea level. Provides free and fair fly fishing for trout late in season, but involves a tough climb from Glenridding (Ullswater).

RIVINGTON RESERVOIRS

nr Bolton, Lancs.

Six waters lying between Bolton and Chorley, and about 30m NE of Liverpool, as follows:
Upper and Lower Rivington, Anglezarke, Upper and Lower Roddlesworth, Rake Brook and Yarrow. Controlled by North West WA, Lancs. River Unit. Trout and coarse fish, some large trout taken; fly and bait; dry-fly only on Upper Roddlesworth and Upper Rivington. Limit = 4 brace. dt 50p; st £5 from: Divisional Manager, Merton House, Stanley Rd, Bootle, Lancs. (tel. 051–922 7260); Victoria Hotel, Tockholes, nr Darwen; and local tackleists.

SABDEN RESERVOIR

Whalley, Lancs.

7½m NE of Blackburn. Trout and carp. Trout averaging ½lb. Accrington and District F.C. water; dt 50p from: T. Little, 2 Pendle Street, West Sabden, Lancs.

SEATHWAITE TARN

Coniston, Cumbria

About 4m WNW of Coniston; drains into R. Duddon; trout and char. Furness F.A. (hon sec: J. W. Ball, 48 Elterwater Crescent, Barrow-in-Furness). Permits for non-members, £1.25. No live minnow fishing or ground-baiting with maggots. Assn also has other trout lakes; inquire hon sec.

SMALLWATER TARN
see under Haweswater

SPRING LODGE

Sabden,
nr Burnley, Lancs.

Lies to right of Whalley road (A671)
about 5m NW of Burnley.

Controller: Accrington and District F.C.

Description: Reservoir formed from
disused mill lodge.

Species/sizes: Brown trout (averaging
10in) and carp.

Rules: Bait fishing permitted, but no
ground-baiting or maggot fishing.

Permits: dt 75p.

Permits from:
Bailiff, T. Littler, 2 Pendle Street West,
Sabden. Further details from club hon
sec: A. Balderstone, 1 Grime Row,
Altham Lane, Huncoat, Lancs.

SUNNYHURST HEY

Darwen, Lancs.

From A666 turn left 1m N of Darwen
town centre, follow Earnsdale road to
Sunnyhurst, then take left fork in
track at bailiff's cottage (right fork leads
to Dean).

Controller: Darwen A.A.

Description: Landscaped reservoir
covering 18 acres.

Species/sizes: Brown and rainbow.

	Brown		Rainbow
Average	12oz		1lb
Record	1lb	7oz	1lb 7oz

Stocking: Takeable fish introduced at
intervals. Some reared in own hatcheries.

Rules: Adults only (over 18), bait fishing,
etc. allowed, but no maggots.

Season: 15 March to 30 September.

Permits: dt £1.

Permits from:
County Sports (J. Entwhistle), Duckworth Street, Darwen (A666 200yd N of
town centre).

Comments: This relatively new fishery
(opened in 1973) is proving particularly
good for fly, although any technique is
permitted. Best times are early morning
or late evening from April to July.
Further details from club hon sec:
J. Priestley, 24 Knowlesly Road, Darwen,
Lancs.

THIRLMERE

nr Keswick, Cumbria

Midway between Grasmere and Keswick
on A591 (road runs alongside lake).

Controller: North West Water Authority.

Description: 3¼m long and ¼m wide,
Thirlmere is natural lake turned into
reservoir. Capacity: 8000 million gallons.

Species/sizes: Brown trout, perch, pike.
Trout average about 1lb, biggest 7lb.

Stocking: None.

Rules: Fly only.

Season: 20 March to 14 September.

Permits: Limited number of tickets issued by North West WA to employees only.

Comments: The trout population is not only large but the size and quality of fish are good. Best months: April, May and June.

THURSTONFIELD LOUGH

*Thurstonfield,
Carlisle, Cumbria*

Reached via lane 100 yards from Carlisle to Anthorn road about 5m W of Carlisle.

Owner: H. G. Stordy.

Description: Shallow lake covering 37 acres fringed with trees and reed-beds. It was first mapped in 1818 and until the beginning of this century provided water power for corn mills.

Species/sizes: Brown and rainbow.

	Brown	Rainbow
Average	1lb 8oz	1lb 4oz
Record	2lb	2lb
	(approx)	(approx)

Stocking: Usually once, at start of season, but sometimes again at end of June.

Rules: Fly only. Limit: 2 brace 12in and over. Gates open 8am, close one hour after sunset.

Season: 1 April to 30 September.

Permits: st £100 (OAPs £60); mt £50 (approx); wt £30 (approx); dt £4.50.

Permits from:
Lough House, Thurstonfield, Carlisle (tel. Burgh-By-Sands 431)

Comments: Fishing normally from boats, to be booked well in advance. Six boats at no extra charge. Best times: April to June all day, early mornings and late evenings July and August. Best conditions: fresh breeze, overcast sky, warm. Most trout are caught drifting across the lake, casting a short line. Try near reed-beds. Nymph patterns do well April—June (up to size 16), then cast with Greenwell's Glory on tail and any other traditional pattern on 'dropper' is recommended. Dry fly best in calm weather, July—September.

ULLSWATER

Penrith, Cumbria

Reached from Penrith (5m) via B592.

Owner: Much of Ullswater is in hands of National Trust.

Description: Drained by the Eamont, an Eden tributary, this is the second largest of the lakes — it covers 2200 acres, is nearly 7½m long, ¾m wide and up to 210ft deep. Road follows north shore from Pooley Bridge to Patterdale.

Species/sizes: Trout (about 3 to lb) and gwyniad.

Stocking: None.

Rules: All legal methods allowed.

Season: 20 March to 14 September.

Permits: Much free fishing though Cumberland RD licence required. Boats available at several places.

Comments: One of the best of the Lakes for trout fishing. The fish do not run large, though an eight-pounder has been taken, but they rise well to fly, especially early on. The best sport is from boats, but fishing from the bank can also be good — wading is allowed.

VALE HOUSE

Tintwistle, Cheshire

From A628 Manchester to Sheffield road via Woodhead.

Controller: North West Water Authority, Eastern Division.

Description: 62-acre reservoir.

Species/sizes: Brown and rainbow.

	Brown	Rainbow
Average	9oz	1lb 8oz
Record	2lb 12oz	4lb 8oz

Stocking: Immediately before season and then monthly throughout.

Rules: Fly and spinner.

Season: 31 March to 30 September.

Permits: dt £1 (approx); OAPs 50p. No boats.

Permits from:
North West WA, Eastern Division, Bottoms Offices, Tintwistle, Hyde, Cheshire.

Comments: Fishing reported best on this reservoir before 10am or after 6pm. For brown trout small surface or sub-surface nymphs are recommended and for rainbows the traditional patterns do well — Zulu, Jersey Herd, Butcher, Teal and Claret, etc.

WASTWATER

Wasdale,
via Gosforth, Cumbria

A5086 from Cockermouth, then A595 from Egremont, left at Gosforth to Wasdale.

Owner: Egremont Estate Office, Cockermouth.

Description: 3m long, ½m wide and up to 270ft deep, this lake presents a somewhat forbidding aspect, being overshadowed by high mountains and barren screes to the south-east.

Species/sizes: Brown trout, char. Also salmon, sea trout, July onwards.

Stocking: None.

Rules: Any legal method allowed.

Season: 20 March to 14 September.

Permits: dt 25p; wt £1.50. No boats.

Permits from:
Fishery Manager, Estate Office, Cockermouth Castle;
Santon Bridge Hotel, Santon Bridge, Holmrook;
Lutwidge Arms Hotel, Holmrook.

Comments: For the trout angler this lake is not particularly rewarding, but the presence of char (and sea trout and salmon from July onwards) are added inducements.

WATENDLATH TARN

Keswick, Cumbria

About 4m due S from Keswick. Trout; free; fish plentiful but on small side. Evenings May and June are best.

WEST BALDWIN

see under Isle of Man Fisheries (Injebreck).

WHIRLEY HALL LAKE

Capesthorne,
nr Macclesfield, Cheshire

Trout. Fly only. Prince Albert A.S. water. Inquiries to hon sec: C. Sparkes, High Lodge, Upton, Macclesfield.

WINDERMERE

Windermere, Cumbria

Reached from Kendal via A591.

Description: Called the 'river lake' on account of its narrowness. Windermere is the largest of the Lakes — 10½m long, 1½m wide and up to 240ft deep.

Species/sizes: Trout and char, pike and perch. Trout run large — fish up to 8lb taken.

Stocking: None.

Rules: All legal methods allowed.

Season: 20 March to 14 September.

Permits: Free fishing but Cumberland RD licence required. Many boats for hire.

Comments: April and May are reported to be the best months for the fly, which should be cast into the margins. A southerly breeze is good. Many large trout (around the 6lb mark) are taken by trolling from a boat and by bait fishing with worms.

YARROW RESERVOIR

see under Rivington Reservoirs

YEW TREE TARN

Coniston, Cumbria

3m from Coniston on Coniston to Ambleside road. Trout. Coniston A.A. fishery (hon sec: N. Dixon, 2 Lake View, Coniston). Permits 60p day, £1.50 week from R. J. Ward, Newsagent, Coniston.

LATE ENTRY

CLEVELEY LODGE

Forton,
nr Preston, Lancs

Well-established 30-acre lake holding brown and rainbow trout up to 6lb and more. Stocked at least four times a year with fish of 14–16in. Full st £225; week-end st £100; weekday st £90; two named days £65 (midweek only). Guest rods permitted. Apply Geoffrey Taylor, Cleveley Lodge (tel. Forton 791702).

3 Northumbria

NORTHUMBRIAN WATER AUTHORITY
Eldon House, Regent Centre, Gosforth, Newcastle upon Tyne, NE3 3PX
(tel. Gosforth (0632) 843151).
Fisheries Manager: D. J. Iremonger, Northumbria House, Regent Centre, Gosforth.
Trout licences (whole area): season £2, month £1 (juniors £1).
Trout close seasons: 1 October to 21 March. Derwent and East and West Hallington
Reservoirs: 1 November to 30 April. Tees Valley Reservoirs: Selset, Grassholme,
Balderhead, Blackton, Hury and Cow Green: 1 October to 23 March. Scaling Dam:
1 October to 31 March.

Note: Licences cover brown and rainbow trout, and char.

REMINDER

Stocking policy depends on returns. Fishery managers have
asked us to stress that whether you catch anything or not, please
remember to fill in the form before leaving the water.

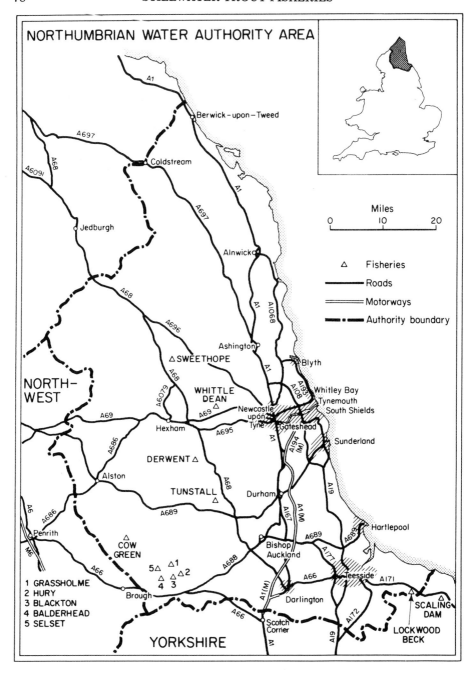

Fancy a day out on Derwent?

asks JOHN JEFFREY

Situated on the Durham/Northumberland border, Derwent Reservoir is now established as a first-class angling water. It is set in magnificent moorland and pasture and, with the scars of bulldozers erased by nature and the selective planting of woodland copses the beauty of a very picturesque Derwent Valley has been enhanced.

During the months of May, June and July there are substantial hatches of chironomids and olives, followed by sedges. There are the usual terrestrial insects and flies one finds drifting on such a vast expanse of water. It is not unusual on a fine summer evening to see the whole area pimpled by rising trout.

Undoubtedly Derwent holds an enormous quantity of rainbow and brown trout, with a few grayling which have survived since the initial flooding of the River Derwent. The only other fish in occupation are minnows; no perch, pike or other coarse fish.

To be successful on this water — as on all reservoirs — one must use tactics to suit the occasion. The angler will find that on most days the wind blows directly or obliquely down the reservoir; from the Nature Reserve at the head directly to the dam wall. This leaves certain sheltered areas, namely the small bays below Hunter House on one side, the Millshield Picnic Area Bay and Cronkley Bay on the other.

When the wind is in this direction, particularly good boat drifts are: across Millshield Bay, usually referred to as 'The Bay of Plenty', from the point below the yacht club, to the old road at the bottom of the picnic area. This follows the approximate route of the submerged road, embankment and hedge.

Drift No 2 is across the bay at Cronkley, about 40yd from the shore. When the water is at high level, a very good place is in the vicinity of the outfall of Cronkley Burn.

The bays at Hunter House are also very productive. On this side of the reservoir the bed is still covered with submerged heather. A fine brown trout of over 3lb 2oz was caught here this season on a red Muddler Minnow. Bank fishing in these areas is also very productive.

When the wind is predominantly blowing across the reservoir, it usually pays to have a drift or two just below the boat limit marker flags. It is also possible to make a good drift right into Millshield Bay (dodging the moored yachts), into the bay at Cronkley and the one below Hunter House.

The visiting bank angler may find that during holiday week-ends the Cronkley and Millshield areas are fished quite heavily. Many of the regulars usually switch to the opposite bank, where there is a superb car park in Pow Hill Country Park, just above Edmundbyers.

From this point one has good, quick access to the water, with enough bank space to suit the most solitary angler. Should your wanderings take you towards the dam, spend some time in the bay opposite the large solitary oak tree.

After the periodic introduction of trout during the season, for quite a few days these fish tend to shoal. Mr. Dennis Forster, the reservoir superintendent, has tried various means of stopping this — placing new arrivals by boat into the middle of the lake or into the 'out of bounds' area at the yacht club, and by prohibiting angling for some days at other points of entry; with occasional success.

Usually the fish (especially the rainbows) tend to congregate at the confluence of the Burnhope Burn, meander along off the stone embankment, continue their tour towards Cronkley and return on the same route. These trout can be caught with almost anything. I have noticed that among the anglers fishing for them the most fortunate are the plyers of Muddler Minnows in all colours and guises and Baby Dolls.

Since the first few years of the impoundment of water in this now-almost-natural lake, the type of angling has changed considerably. Local anglers, most of whom were river men, adapted the techniques with which they were familiar — with modifications to suit this great new expanse of water. With the advent of anglers from the Midlands and farther south, one now finds that most people are equipped with floating lines, sinking lines and other impedimenta advocated by writers and advertisers in the angling press.

Should you not be the possessor of such equipment be not dismayed. The most successful angler on this water fishes with a home-made fibreglass rod, a silk, tapered line of doubtful vintage, a couple of reels of nylon and a varied assortment of two patterns of dry flies, plus a king-size tin of floatant. The method used has been adopted by quite a few anglers on Derwent . . .

Should you have the American type of floating line, this may be utilized, although we find that the English dressed silk line doped with floatant is best. Casting from a lee shore, allow the dry fly (or flies, depending on the quality of eyesight) to drift with the wind, paying out just enough line to permit the minimum of slack. It is possible with the line in good order to drift out the fly for a considerable distance; well past the casting ability of the average angler.

When the fly disappears — strike. This must be quite decisive, not a mere tightening of the line, as rightly advocated for normal angling.

To use nylon under 4lb breaking strain for any form of angling on Derwent seems to me to be pointless. I cannot accept that it is more sporting, having caught numerous trout with all manner of 'ironmongery' attached to far-too-fine line. This is detrimental to the reservoir and usually fatal to the trout concerned.

For lure fishing I would advocate about 8lb breaking strain. Always remember that some of these large fish go very deep, very fast indeed.

During the major part of the season, conditions being normal, there are three distinct feeding periods per day — very early in the morning, late afternoon and the evening before sundown. It is noticeable, except on very few occasions, that the evening rise suddenly terminates and does not continue into darkness.

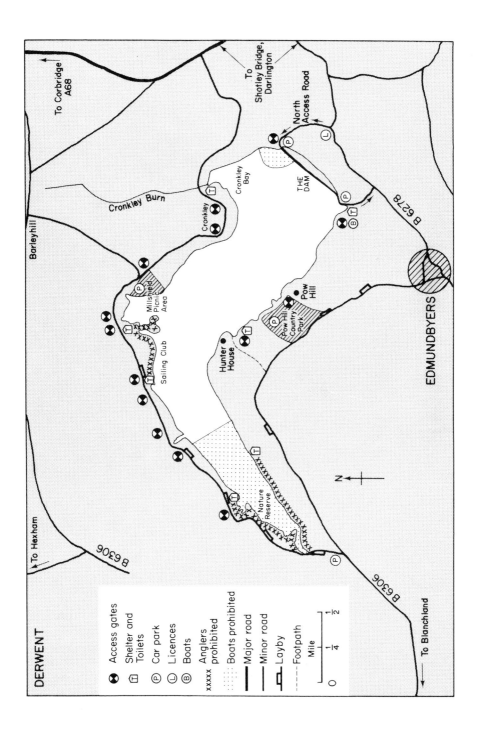

DERWENT

Legend:

- ⊗ Access gates
- 🏠 Shelter and Toilets
- Ⓟ Car park
- Ⓛ Licences
- Ⓑ Boats
- xxxxx Anglers prohibited
- ⋯⋯ Boats prohibited
- ▬▬ Major road
- ─── Minor road
- ▭ Layby
- ─ ─ ─ Footpath

Mile

0   1/4   1/2

Map labels:

To Corbridge A68

To Shotley Bridge, Darlington

North Access Road

Barleyhill

Cronkley Burn

Cronkley Bay

Cronkley

THE DAM

B6278

Millshield Picnic Area

Sailing Club

Pow Hill

Pow Hill Country Park

Hunter House

Nature Reserve

To Hexham

B6306

N

EDMUNDBYERS

To Blanchland

B6306

There are times, of course — should one be fortunate enough to be fishing those days — to find these Derwent trout feeding the whole day. Such a day occurred during June this year . . .

Having booked a boat, my son and I (at precisely 10am) headed straight for Millshield Bay, to do the drift already recommended. It was quite choppy, the usual breeze blowing straight down the reservoir.

Drifting from the lee shore, we noticed an occasional slight disturbance near the surface of the water. We immediately delved into our fly boxes and attached a No 16 chironomid with black body on point, a dark No 14 orange nymph on first dropper and the usual black bushy dry fly (ungreased) on top dropper. (The dressings of these flies are given below.)

We both fished with identical flies. My son was using 6lb b/s nylon, and mine was 4lb b/s. The day was clear with some scattered cloud. On each drift we caught the occasional fish and decided we would not keep anything under 1lb.

The different thickness of nylon made no difference at all. Indeed, I wished on one occasion that I had been using the thicker stuff, especially when a very big rainbow 'went to earth' directly under our boat and it took about ten minutes of concerted effort before it was finally netted.

Moving our venue to the bay below Hunter House, we hit a considerable shoal of rainbows. These were not newly-stocked fish, being larger than any introduced that season. We netted ten over 1½lb in ten drifts. Progressing onwards down the shore (rather too far out), we did not raise another fish before lunch at 2 o'clock.

During the afternoon we fished other favoured places, without success, then returned to our 'Bay of Plenty' at Millshield. Here we had a repeat of the morning's experience, as we did when we revisited Hunter House Bay.

The question arises: Why do rainbow trout shoal in selected places? Is it because of the filtered slight effluent from Hunter House and the small streams at Cronkley and Millshield carrying some nitrates and phosphates to complete the ecological cycle in these areas?

Techniques for Different Times

I feel it might help visitors to the water if I set out suggested procedures for fishing from the bank in varying conditions.

Weather: Cold, blustery

Fish as deep as possible. Lures (size 8 or 10) Muddler Minnow, brown, yellow or red, or Baby Doll. Draw in very slowly, just enough to give 'movement'. Alternatively, use leaded nymphs (size 12 or 14) or chironomid in black or dark orange. Wet flies: Peter Ross, Black and Peacock, Butcher, Teal and Green, Black Pennel. Size 10 or 12.

Warm, blustery

Fish near surface with floating line. Try slow stripping, then fast stripping with lure; preferably Muddler Minnow (original dressing, alternated with yellow Muddler). Use a floating line with nymphs or wet flies as above, slow stripping, with pauses of about one second.

Cold, light wind or no wind
Fish as deep as possible with lures, nymphs and wet flies as before. Strip very slowly.

Warm, slight breeze
Use floating line from lee shore, as explained before, with bushy dry fly, or use a floating line with dry fly on point, nymph on first and second dropper, leader greased to near point. Be sure there is no floatant on droppers or nymphs. Try occasional twitch when retrieving line, very slowly.

Warm or hot, calm
Use dry-fly method described. Cast out as far as possible without undue disturbance. Leave for about a minute and 'twitch' slowly inwards, a few inches, then pause, a few inches again, pause. Nylon leader, about 12ft long, 4lb b/s. Fish lure at various speeds until proper depth of fish has been found. I am informed that Muddler Minnow accounts for more than 40 per cent of fish caught. Alternatively, use nymphs on long leader on floating line, fished very, very slowly.

The value of fishing the margins cannot be emphasized enough. Approach the bank with extreme care and start by fishing a very short line. Most of the better fish have been caught just a few yards out.

Recommended Patterns

Dry flies   Sizes 10, 12 & 14   All season
Double shiny black double hackle, rather 'bushy'. Black fur or wool body, ribbed with white horse hair, white silk or silver wire. Three or four black tails. Double shiny ginger-brown cock hackle. Brown fur or wool body, ribbed with fine gold wire. Three or four brown tails.

Dry flies   Sizes 10 & 12   Middle and late season
Black shiny cock's hackle with one turn of crimson cock hackle. Black silk body, ribbed with three turns of silver wire. Three or four black tails. For the angler who must purchase flies, suitable alternatives would be: Black Pennel, Black Spider, Sedge, Blae and Black.

Wet flies   Sizes 14 & 12   All season
Butcher, Alexandra, Teal & Green, Black Pennel, Black & Peacock. Later in the season, alternate with Invicta, Cinnamon and Gold, and Dunkeld.

Nymphs   Sizes 14 & 16
Chironomid, dressed black body, ribbed fine silver wire or white silk; dark orange body, ribbed gold wire.

It has been noticeable for some years that the Snipe and Purple dressed in North of England style, with very sparse hackle, peacock herl thorax and purple silk body, is equally effective during the hatches of chironomids. With the normal commercial fly, just pull off a few fibres from the hackle and leave the fly a bit 'tattered'.

It is advisable to have a yellow-bodied fly for a few sunny days. Recommended: Snipe and Yellow, or Woodcock and Yellow. Fished as point fly.

Note: The hook sizes given above are 'old numbers'.

BALDERHEAD
BLACKTON and
HURY

nr Barnard Castle, Durham

B6277 out of Barnard Castle, take minor road off to left and to village of Hury. Blackton/Hury Reservoirs are nearby and Balderhead lies beyond them.

Description: Chain of moorland reservoirs lying deep in the Pennines in the valley of the River Balder — Balderhead (289 acres) Blackton (66 acres) Hury (127 acres).

Species/sizes: Native brown trout averaging about 6oz; biggest verified catches; Balderhead 1lb 12oz, Blackton 1lb 10oz, Hury 2lb 10oz.

Stocking: None.

Rules: Fly and worm.

Season: 24 March to 30 September.

Permits: st £30; dt £2 (OAPS, juniors £1).

Permits from: Fishing lodges (dt) or Northumbrian WA (st).

Comments: A two-pounder is a very good fish on these moorland waters. Deep-sunk lures and nymphs take fish until the water warms up, when dry fly can be successful. Balderhead is the deepest of all the Tees Valley group (max. 157ft) and provides more than 5m of bank fishing.

COW GREEN

Upper Teesdale, Durham

Lies off B6277 about 17m from Barnard Castle.

Description: Large relatively new moorland fishery covering 770 acres.

Species/sizes: Native brown trout averaging about 12oz; biggest 3lb 1oz.

Stocking: None.

Rules: Fly and worm.

Season: 24 March to 30 September.

Permits: st £30; dt £2 (OAPS, juniors £1).

Permits from: Fishing lodge (dt) or Northumbrian WA (st).

Comments: Cow Green was not opened for fishing until the 1971 season. Since then it has attracted a growing number of anglers, topping the 1000 mark in 1974. They have caught on average slightly less than one fish apiece, showing that these native brown trout are not easily deceived.

DERWENT

Edmundbyers,
nr Consett, Co. Durham

Lies west of A68 at its junction with B6278.

Owner: Sunderland and South Shields Water Company.

Description: Landscaped reservoir of 1000 acres when full — 7m of bank available to anglers.

Species/sizes: Brown and rainbow.

	Brown	Rainbow
Average	12oz	1lb
Record	3lb 2oz	4lb 1oz

Stocking: At intervals throughout season to produce total of 4000 browns, 10,000 rainbows between 12 and 13in.

Rules: Fly only. Limit: 5 brace, 10in and over. Boat fishing 10am to sunset. Bank fishing mainly 1hr before sunrise to 1hr after sunset. Trolling from rowing boats only.

Season: 1 May to 14 October.

Permits: st £42; dt £1.50 (juniors and pensioners half-price). Boats (7): motor £6; rowing £3 (half-price after 5 pm).

Permits from:
Water Company (st) 29 John Street, Sunderland, SR1 1JU; dt from Utilities Building at reservoir (tel. Edmundbyers 250).

Comments: As a fly-only reservoir in bait-fishing country, Derwent is something of a novelty in the north-east. Its success may be judged from the fact that it has attracted a steadily increasing number of anglers since it was opened in 1967 and currently well over 13,000 rods are taking about the same number of fish, many of them in the 2—3lb range. In fact, the 1975 season produced a record attendance of 13,501 rods who caught a record number of fish — 13,546.
For an appraisal of the water see John Jeffrey's article on page 79.

GRASSHOLME and SELSET

nr Barnard Castle, Durham

Leaving Barnard Castle on B6277, these reservoirs lie in next valley to the Balderhead/Blackton/Hury group.

Description: Grassholme, the first to be reached, is a long, narrow water covering 140 acres. Selset, a short distance away, is bigger (275 acres).

Species/sizes: Brown and rainbow.

	Brown	Rainbow
Average	12oz	12oz
Record		
(Grassholme)	2lb 3oz	3lb 12oz
(Selset)	1lb 11oz	4lb 2oz

Stocking: Fortnightly.

Rules: Fly and worm.

Season: 1 April to 30 September (to 14 October for rainbows).

Permits: st £30; dt £2.
Boats: Grassholme only, £2 day, £1 after 4pm.

Permits from: Fishing lodges (dt) or Northumbrian WA (st).

Comments: These waters were restocked with 8000 fish during the 1975 season and stocking continues. Catches at Grassholme have topped the 5500 mark for about 4200 rods and similar ratios are reported from Selset, which wasn't opened until 1971 — 4400 fish by 3300 rods.

HURY

see Balderhead, Blackton and Hury

SCALING DAM

nr Whitby, N. Yorks.

Conveniently situated close to Guisborough to Whitby road (A171).

Description: Moorland reservoir covering 120 acres.

Species/sizes: Brown and rainbow.

	Brown	Rainbow
Average	12oz	12oz
Record	7lb 3oz	3lb 14oz

Stocking: Fortnightly.

Rules: Fly and worm only.

Season: 1 April to 30 September (to 14 October for rainbows).

Permits: st £30; dt £2.

Permits from: Fishing Lodge (dt); st from Northumbrian WA.

Comments: Perhaps the best known of the Tees Valley group, this reservoir is fed by Scaling Beck and other small streams and trout from them formed the original stock. It has been stocked annually since 1970 and 8000 trout went in during 1975. There has been a remarkable increase in the number of anglers fishing this water — rod days topped the 8000 mark in 1974, when the number of fish taken was a record 6114.

Note: Two islands are planned to be constructed on this reservoir to foster wildlife and especially to assist the breeding of the Great Crested Grebe.

SELSET

see Grassholme and Selset Reservoirs

SWEETHOPE LOUGH

Harle, nr Otterburn, Northumberland

Proceeding N up A68, turn right over cattle grid at Bellingham Knowsgate cross-roads. Entrance to lough signposted on right.

Controller: The Manager, Percy Arms Hotel, Otterburn (Lt. Col. S. P. Wood).

Description: 75-acre natural lake.

Species/sizes: Brown trout only averaging 10—11oz, biggest 1lb 14oz.

Stocking: 1000 9—11in fish put in annually.

Rules: Fly only, 5 rods only. Limit: 4 brace, 10in and over.

Season: 1 April to 30 September.

Permits: dt £3, half-day (before or after 2pm) £1.50. Boats (3) 50p day, 25p half-day. All charges + VAT. Reduced rates to hotel guests. Note: booking advised.

Permits from:
The Manager, Lake House, Sweethope Lough, Harle, Newcastle upon Tyne, NE19 2PN.

Comments: May, June and September are usually best. Black patterns do well — Blae and Black, Pennell, Williams Favourite, etc.

TEES VALLEY RESERVOIRS

Scaling Dam, Grassholme, Selset, Cow
Green, Hury, Blackton, Balderhead,
Lockwood Beck.

All these reservoirs except Lockwood
Beck are controlled by the Northumbrian
Water Authority, Eldon House, Regent
Centre, Gosforth, Newcastle upon Tyne,
NE3 3PX. Fishing rights on Lockwood
Beck are leased to the Association of
Teesside and District Angling Clubs.
Secretary: A. Allen, 1 Scalby Grove,
Fairfield, Stockton-on-Tees, Cleveland
(tel. Stockton (0642) 580251).

The Water Authority reservoirs
produced around 18,000 fish in 1974, of
which Scaling, Grassholme and Selset
between them accounted for about
16,000. Sport was not quite so good last
season, Selset's catches in particular being
well down. Even so, Scaling and
Grassholme still managed to achieve
figures of 5651 and 5209 respectively.
Some of these lakes are deep in the
Pennines and, being sheltered from the
sun, do not warm up sufficiently for the
fish to take surface fly until high summer.

Rules: Worm as well as fly fishing allowed
on all waters. Maggot fishing and
ground-baiting strictly forbidden. Wading
generally permitted, but no chest waders.
Limit bags on Scaling, Selset and
Grassholme are 4 brace. No bag limit on
Cow Green, Balderhead, Blackton or
Hury. Size limit: 9in.

Northumbrian WA rod licence
required for all waters except Scaling
Dam (Yorkshire WA). OAPs, juveniles
(under 16) and disabled persons may fish
for half the normal charge..
*Further details for specific reservoirs
are provided within individual entries.*

TUNSTALL RESERVOIR

Wolsingham, Durham

10m NW of Bishop Auckland. Good trout,
well stocked each season. North-West
Durham A.A. water. Fly and worm fishing
but no maggots. Limit: 5 brace. Sunday
fishing allowed. Limited dt 50p (40p
after 1 June) from Angling Service Ltd.,
Claypath, Durham City, and Mr. Dimambro,
Front Street, Consett. This association
also has fishing on **Hishope, Smiddy Shaw**
and **Waskerley** reservoirs, but no tickets
are issued. Inquiries to hon sec: J. W.
Sanderson, 3 Sherburn Terrace, Low
Westwood, Ebchester, Durham.

WHITTLE DEAN

*Harlow Hill, nr Newcastle
and Wear*

Off B6318 about 11m W of Newcastle.

Controller: Newcastle and Gateshead
Water Company.

Description: Six landscaped reservoirs
known as Great Northern, Northern
Subsiding, Great Southern, Northern,
Lower and Great Western.

Species/sizes: Brown and rainbow.

	Brown	Rainbow
Average	12oz	1lb
Record	3lb	2lb 8oz

Stocking: Once, at start of season.

Rules: Fly only as a rule, but spinning
permitted on Great Southern after 31
May and after 30 June in Lower
Reservoir. No more than 20 rods allowed
on reservoirs simultaneously. Limit: 12
fish over 10in; 2 brace on Great Western,

stocked with rainbows. Fishing 10am to half-hour after sunset.

Season: 1 April to 30 September.

Permits: dt 85p approx. Boats £1 day approx.

Permits from: Reservoir keeper, F. Palmer, between 9am and 12 noon, and 1pm and 5pm (tel. Wylam 3210).

Comments: These somewhat exposed waters react especially badly to north and east winds. At other times, however, they can provide good sport. Mr Palmer, who is always pleased to help anglers, recommends these patterns in order of preference: Greenwell's Glory, Peter Ross, Black Spider, Bluebottle Spider or Black Peacock Spider, Grouse and Claret or Yellow Invicta, March Brown, Butcher, Partridge and Orange or Yellow.

REMINDER

We have not as a rule mentioned in the individual entries the need for a regional water authority licence as well as a permit, but this is usually necessary, except for the relatively few cases where the fishery holds a general licence.

4 The Severn-Trent Region

SEVERN-TRENT WATER AUTHORITY
Abelson House, 2297 Coventry Road, Sheldon, Birmingham, B26 3PR.
Assistant Director (Fisheries, Amenities and Recreation): M. L. Parry (tel. 021 743 4222).
Fisheries Coordinator: Dr P. E. Bottomley.
Trout licences (whole area): Season £1.50, 28 days, 50p. Severn or Trent area only:
Season £1. OAPs (whole area) 20p.
Close seasons: Severn area: 16 September to 14 March. Trent area: 16 October to
17 March. *Dates under review.*

Severn Area
Area Fisheries Manager: Peter Hunt, Severn Area Laboratories, 139 Church Street,
Malvern, Worcs. (tel. 068 45 61511).
District Fisheries Officers: Alan Churchward and John Woolland.

Trent Area
Area Fisheries Manager: Robin Templeton, Trent Area Laboratories, Meadow Lane,
Nottingham (tel. 0602 865007).
District Fishery Officers: North, Michael Cathcart; South, Martin Cooper.

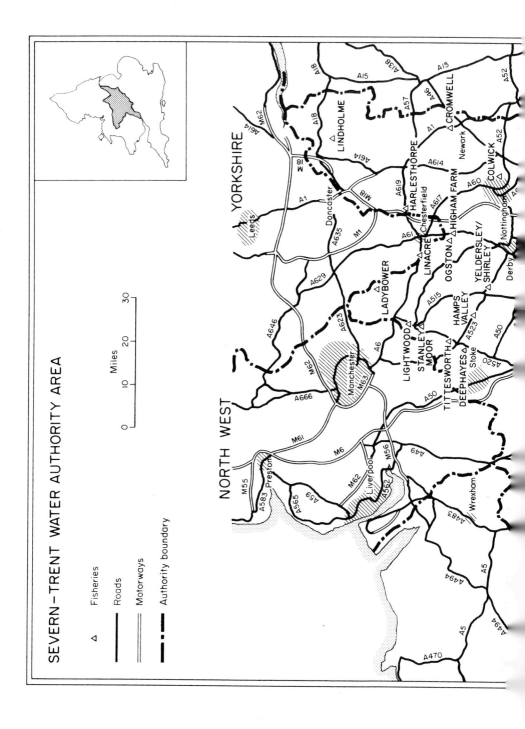

SEVERN–TRENT WATER AUTHORITY AREA

△   Fisheries

────   Roads

═══   Motorways

▪·▪·▪   Authority boundary

Miles

0   10   20   30

NORTH WEST

YORKSHIRE

Preston   M55

A583

A565

A59

M61

M6

M62

Liverpool

A562

A56

A49

A483

Wrexham

A5

A494

A470

A5

A494

M62

A666

M63 Manchester

A6

A623

A646

A629

A635

M1

A1

Leeds

Doncaster

M18

M18

A1(M)

A18

A18

A614

A15

A614

A15

A138

A15

A1

A57

A46

△CROMWELL

A52

Newark

Colwick△ COLWICK

A60

A52

Nottingham

A52

Derby

A617

△HIGHAM FARM

△OGSTON

△LINACRE

Chesterfield

A61

A619

△HARLESTHORPE

LINDHOLME△

A619

M62

A61

A515

YELDERSLEY△

△SHIRLEY

LADYBOWER△

HAMPS VALLEY△

A523

A50

A520

LIGHTWOOD△

△STANLEY MOOR

△TITTESWORTH

DEEPHAYES△

Stoke

A50

A50

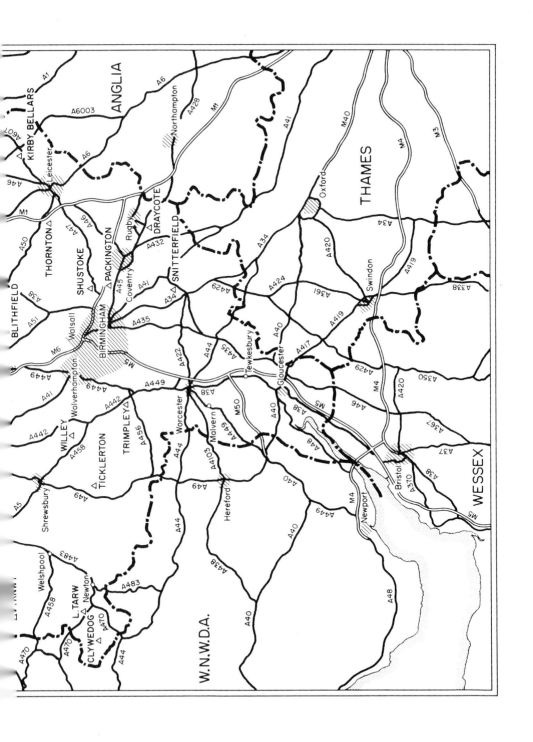

BLITHFIELD

Abbots Bromley, Staffs

Lies about 10m E of M6 motorway. A513 from Stafford to Rugeley; reservoir is 4½m NE.

Owner: South Staffordshire Waterworks Company.

Description: Long, narrow reservoir in valley of R. Blythe.

Species/sizes: Brown and rainbow.

	Brown	Rainbow
Average	1lb 4oz	1lb 3oz
Record	8lb 0½oz	5lb 8oz
	(1975 figures)	

Stocking: About 30,000 browns and rainbows introduced per season, mostly from company's own hatchery.

Rules: Fly only.

Season: 1 April to 30 September.

Permits: Fishing by st only.

Permits from: Recreations Office at reservoir.

Comments: 1975 was a very successful season on this reservoir. 13,799 rainbows were taken and 1,274 browns; total weight of catches was 21,438lb. 26 trout over 5lb were captured. 8241 permit holders visited the reservoir, with 1235 guests.

COLWICK TROUT FISHERY

Colwick,
nr Nottingham

In Southwell Road, Colwick, 3m E of Nottingham town centre.

Controller: Severn-Trent Water Authority, Trent Area.

Description: New fishery created from disused gravel pit and covering 9 acres.

Species/sizes: Brown and rainbow averaging 12oz.

Stocking: 1500 fish introduced over four-monthly period before 1976 season.

Rules: Fly only.

Season: 18 March to 15 October.

Permits: dt £2.

Permits from: Site office.

CROMWELL LAKE

Cromwell,
nr Newark, Notts.

To west of A1 at Cromwell exit just north of Newark.

Controller: Cromwell Fly Fishers, working committee of Doncaster AA.

Description: Old landscaped gravel pit of some 20 acres.

Species/sizes: Brown and rainbow.

	Brown	Rainbow
Average	1lb 2oz	1lb 4oz
Record	3lb 1oz	5lb 12oz

Stocking: About every fortnight.

Rules: Fly only. Limit: 2 brace. No dogs. Access by car park on south shore only.

Season: 18 March to 15 October.

Permits: st £40; dt £2.25. No boats.

Permits from:
F. Gale and Son, 26 Copley Road, Doncaster (tel. 68950) and Mr Stock, Carlton Service Station, Cromwell.

Comments: 1975 returns: 2743 anglers took 2522 trout. Dry-fly and nymph successful. Further details from hon sec, Cromwell Fly Fisheries: J. Mallender, 10 Mill Meadow View, Blyth, Worksop, Notts.

DEEPHAYES RESERVOIR

nr Leek, Staffs.

Water of 20.5 acres, Leek and Moorlands F.C. (hon sec: S. White, 10 Gandry Buildings, Fountain Street, Leek, Staffs.).

DRAYCOTE WATER

Kites Hardwick, nr Rugby, Warks.

Just W of A426 Southam to Rugby road, 1¾m from Dunchurch and 5m SW of Rugby.

Owner: Avon Division, Severn/Trent Water Authority.

Description: Landscaped reservoir covering 600 acres — nearly a square mile — with 5m of banks, and holding 5000 million gallons when full at a maximum depth of 68ft.

Species/sizes: Brown and rainbow.

	Brown	Rainbow
Average	1lb 8oz	1lb 6oz
Record	6lb 15oz	5lb 9oz

Stocking: Operated on a 'put and take' basis. About 23,500 fish in all introduced during autumn and spring, and then further 45,000 throughout season as required.

Rules: Fly only. Limit: 4 brace; all under 12in to be returned. Juniors must be accompanied by adult ticket-holder. No rod licence required.

Season: 16 April to 17 October.

Permits: Full season £65; dt £2.20 (£1.65 after 3 pm); juniors 55p. Boats (24): rowing £2.20; petrol £7.70; electric £5.50 (reductions after 3 pm).

Permits from: Fishing Lodge (dt only) (tel. Rugby 811107 before 10am). Advance bookings from the Warden at Draycote (tel. Rugby 810490).

Comments: Opened to angling in 1970, Draycote has provided consistent, high-quality sport ever since. It has been producing well over 18,000 trout a season, mostly rainbows, the average catch for 1975 (by about 12,800 anglers) being 1.46 fish per visit. There are no coarse fish to speak of, apart from the minnows, sticklebacks and gudgeon which can be classed as trout food. When the water swarms with small black chironimids, as it frequently does, the Black Buzzer nymph and Black Lure do well. As an experiment, spinning was tried at the close of one season but the water is still fly only.

HAMPS VALLEY FISHERY

Winkhill, nr Leek, Staffs.

Adjacent to A523 Derby to Manchester trunk road 6m S of Leek, 9m N of Ashbourne.

Owner: Hamps Valley Fishery (Partners D.R., D.M., R.M. and G.M.L. Boydon).

Description: Two pools of about 1 acre each and half a mile of double-bank river fishing.

Species/sizes: Brown and rainbow.

	Brown	Rainbow
Average	1¼lb	1¾lb
Record	5lb 8oz	3lb 8oz
	(approx)	(approx)

Stocking: Usually twice a year.

Rules: Fly only (no lures). Limit: one brace 10in and over.

Season: 1 April to 31 October.

Permits: st £65; dt £2 (pool 1 only). Boat available but unnecessary.

Permits from:
Hamps Valley Fishery, Winkhill, nr Leek, Staffs.

Comments: Best times: June to September. Best conditions: day or two following river spate. Favourite flies: Copper Nymph, Blue Dun, Red Tag, Derby Beetle.

HARLESTHORPE

Clowne, Derbyshire

8m NE of Chesterfield. Trout and coarse fish; some large trout taken. Mostly worm fishing. Tickets: dt on site (tel. Clowne 810231).

HIGHAM FARM

*Old Higham,
nr Alfreton, Derbys.*

Off B6013 near Alfreton (reached via M1, junction 28).

Owner: Higham Farm Trout Fishery.

Description: Landscaped ponds and lakes and 1½m of River Amber.

Species/sizes: Brown and rainbow.

	Brown	Rainbow
Average	1lb	1lb 8oz
Record	6lb 14oz	8lb 2oz
		(1975)

Stocking: At six-week intervals.

Rules: Fly only.

Season: 1 April to 15 October.

Permits: st £120; (midweek) £90; (weekend) £85; dt £5.

Permits from:
G. H. Collier, Higham Farm Hotel (tel. Alfreton 3812).

Comments: This well-run fishery produced more than 5000 fish in 1975, including the record rainbow for the water. Among the catches were 34 over 3lb, including six over 6lb. An experienced bailiff will advise anglers.

KIRBY BELLARS LAKE

Asfordby,
nr Melton Mowbray, Leics.

Take A607 Leicester to Melton Mowbray road, leave road at Flying Childers Inn, ½m to lake.

Owner: Acresford Sand and Gravel Ltd.

Description: 17-acre gravel pit in beautiful Wreake Valley.

Species/sizes: Brown and rainbow averaging about 1lb 8oz.

Stocking: In March and throughout season to maintain about 100 fish per acre.

Rules: Fly only. Ten day rods only. Limit: 2 brace. All coarse fish taken to be killed.

Season: 1 April to 30 September.

Permits: st £35 (+VAT); dt £2, £1.25 after 5pm. Juniors may fish for 50p day if accompanied by adult ticket holder.

Permits from:
Fishery Manager (R. J. A. Hawksley), Kirby Bellars Pit, Station Lane, Asfordby (tel. East Goscote 3725), or from fishing hut.

Comments: An improving fishery, well stocked with trout around the 1½lb mark.

LADYBOWER

Bamford, Derbyshire

Off A57 Sheffield to Manchester road about 10m W of Sheffield and 25m from Manchester.

Controller: Severn-Trent Water Authority, Derwent Valley Supply Division.

Description: 500-acre landscaped reservoir in R. Derwent valley.

Species/sizes: Brown and rainbow averaging about 12oz.

Stocking: At intervals throughout season. 60–40 in favour of browns.

Rules: Fly only. Limit: 2 brace first 2 months, 3 brace thereafter.

Season: 10 April to 15 October.

Permits: st £30; dt £1.50.

Permits from:
Severn-Trent WA, Bamford office (below dam), tel. Bamford 424; dt at Fishing Lodge.

Comments: Henry Walker, a 'regular' at Ladybower in its early days, from 1945–50, wrote that the reservoir produced magnificent fly fishing the like of which had never before been available to so many fishers from Sheffield and neighbouring towns. He mentioned that a Teal and Green with a gold-ribbed seal's fur body as a tail fly was a deadly pattern when the trout were rising to sedges as darkness set in. This advice from the days before double-haul casting and heavy lures may be worth recalling. If you are seeking more up-to-date information ask at the Fishing Lodge.

LIGHTWOOD
STANLEY MOOR

nr Buxton, Derbys.

Waters of 2.35 and 10 acres, let to Buxton F.F.C. (hon sec: D. Canning, 18 Compton Road, Buxton, Derbys.).

LINACRE

nr Chesterfield, Derbys.

Off B6050 3m W of Chesterfield.

Controller: Severn-Trent Water Authority, North Derbyshire Supply Division.

Description: Three new landscaped reservoirs; fishing restricted to middle and bottom ones.

Species/sizes: Brown and rainbow averaging 12oz.

Stocking: At intervals throughout season.

Rules: Fly only. Limit: 2 brace.

Season: 10 April to 15 October.

Permits: st £30; dt £1.50.

Permits from:
Severn-Trent WA, West Street, Chesterfield S40 4TZ (tel. 0246 75901).

Comments: Fishing only started on this reservoir in 1975, so information is somewhat sparse. The warden on site will give advice on likely places and fly patterns.
Note: Although operated by the Severn-Trent WA, this reservoir lies in the statutory area of Yorkshire WA, so a Yorkshire licence is required.

LINDHOLME

Sandtoft,
nr Epworth, Lincs.

About 3½m NW of Epworth off A18, Doncaster 15m.

Owner: B. Lindley.

Description: 18-acre landscaped spring-fed lake created from 100-year-old quarry workings.

Species/sizes: Brown and rainbow.

	Brown	Rainbow
Average	1lb	1lb
Record	2lb	4lb 14oz

Stocking: At intervals from own floating cage.

Rules: Fly only. Limit: 2 brace. No fish to be returned to water. Juniors must be accompanied by an adult.

Season: 18 March to 16 October.

Permits: st £50; dt £2.50 (juniors 75p).

Permits from:
B. Lindley, Haverthward House, Burnham Road, Epworth (tel. 872015);
F. G. Gale, 26 Copley Road, Doncaster; and
Sportfishers, High Street, Hatfield.
Also from petrol filling station, Sandtoft.

Comments: Lindholme has completed two successful seasons (1974 and 1975). In 1975 2272 trout were taken by 2146 rods, the heaviest a rainbow of 3lb 14oz. Free tuition is available, for which tackle will be lent. Apply to Eric Allen of Sportfishers (tel. Doncaster 840287).

LLYN CLYWEDOG

nr Llanidloes, Powys

From Rhayader turn left off A470 at Llanidloes. Reservoir lies to W of B4518, about 3m from Llanidloes.

Controller: Severn Trent Water Authority, but leased to Llanidloes and District A.A.

Description: 615-acre landscaped reservoir, 12m of bank fishing in heart of lovely mid-Wales scenery.

Species/sizes: Brown and rainbow.

	Brown	Rainbow
Average	1lb 2oz	1lb 5oz
Record	4lb 4oz	6lb 3oz

Stocking: At intervals.

Rules: Fly only. Limit 4 brace over 10in (brown) and over 12in (rainbow).

Season: 18 March to 15 October.

Permits: st £16.50; wt £6.50; dt £1.60 (90p after 5 pm). Pensioners half-price. Boats (5): £1.50 a day (75p after 5 pm).

Permits from:
Powys Sports, Great Oak Street, Llanidloes. Boats from W. J. Vaughan, Penybank, Clywedog (tel. 055 12 2552).

Comments: Clywedog fishes best in a strong south-west wind or a very light breeze. Fish respond well to the dry fly in fine weather from June onwards — early morning or dusk are best in midsummer. Recommended patterns: *Wet:* Mallard and Claret, Zulu, Butcher, Welsh Partridge, Williams Favourite (sizes 10–16). *Dry:* Coch-y-Bonddhu, Greenwell's Glory, Black Gnat, Coachman, Red Tag, Wickhams (sizes 12–16). For further details contact

association hon sec: J. Dallas Davies, Mount Villa, China Street, Llanidloes, SY18 6AB (tel. 055 12 2644 after 6pm).

OGSTON

Alfreton,
nr Chesterfield, Derbys.

On B6014 Matlock to Clay Cross road, about 4m from Matlock.

Controller: Severn Trent Water Authority, Derwent Division. Fishery leased to Derbyshire County Council A.C.

Description: 206-acre reservoir with capacity of 1300 million gallons. Bank fishing (limited).

Species/sizes: Brown and rainbow trout averaging 1lb-plus.

Stocking: Natural stocks of big brown trout supplemented by regular planting of rainbows.

Rules: Fly only. Limit one brace.

Season: 1 April to 15 October (rainbows from 16 May).

Permits: dt £1.50 (limited to 15).

Permits from:
Severn-Trent WA, Derwent Division, West Street, Chesterfield, S40 4TZ (tel. 75901), or
New Napoleon Inn, Woolley Moor on B6014 (adjoining north bank).
Advance booking from STWA recommended for weekends in view of limited number of permits.

Comments: Relatively new water with restricted facilities for public, but promises good sport.

PACKINGTON FISHERIES

Meriden, Warks.

Served by M1, M6, M5 motorway network. Turn off at junction 4, M6 and fishery is 5m away. Can also be reached via A45.

Owner: Packington Fisheries.

Description: Eight lakes—three landscaped gravel pits, rest old-established lakes. Also 4m of River Blythe.

Species/sizes: Brown and rainbow.

	Brown	Rainbow
Average	1–2lb	1–3lb
Record	5lb 1oz	8lb 14oz (1970)

Stocking: Weekly on a 'put and take' basis. Initial stocking is with brown trout only and rainbows are introduced as they regain condition after spawning (usually April/May).

Rules: Fly only.

Season: 18 March to 14 November.

Permits: st £65–£200 (variety of rod options); dt £2.90 (evenings £2). Boats: £1 per rod/day; evening £1 (one or two rods).

Permits from:
Packington Fisheries, Fishery Lodge, Broadwater, Maxstoke Lane, Meriden, CV7 7HR (tel. Meriden (0676) 22754).

Comments: Packington has already become a mecca for Midland anglers, as shown by a rising tally of rods and fish taken. One of the attractions is the wide variety of fishing offered, ranging from small, secluded waters to large expanses of 30–40 acres. Early in the season this fishing is mainly with lures and wet fly patterns, but as the water warms up, nymph and Buzzer come into their own and dry fly can be tried. Stocking continues throughout the season, thus eliminating the normally dour period of midsummer. Water produced record 14,883 fish in 1975.

PRESS RESERVOIR

nr Chesterfield, Derbys.

Three waters of 3.3, 3.1 and 5 acres respectively. Let to Press F.F.A. (hon sec: J. Brearley, 55 Somersall Park Road, Chesterfield, Derbys.).

SHIRLEY LAKES
see Yeldersley and Shirley Lakes

SHUSTOKE

nr Coleshill, Warks.

Reached via A47 to Coleshill (about 10m from Birmingham) then via Reservoir Road, Shustoke.

Owner: Tame Division, Severn/Trent Water Authority.

Description: Two concrete reservoirs built in 1876, one large, one small, covering about 90 acres in all.

Species/sizes: Brown and rainbow.

	Brown	Rainbow
Average	1lb	1¼lb
Record	9lb (1962)	4lb 10oz (1974)

Stocking: Mainly in close season, but 1000 takeable fish introduced around mid-season.

Rules: Reservoirs are both fly only (flies no larger than No 10 permitted in small water). Only two fish to be taken from small reservoir per day, with maximum of four from both. Trout under 12in to be returned.

Season: 12 April to 15 October.

Permits: Full season £45, five-day season (Mon–Fri) £30; five-day season (limited time) £15; dt (large reservoir only) £2 (six only). Boats (10): st holders 40p a session, dt holders 80p a session. Except on the two opening days, subscribers may be accompanied by a fishing companion at an extra daily charge of £1.80.

Permits from:
Tame Valley House, Newhall Street, Birmingham, B3 1DL (tel. 339978). Boat permits only issued from Shustoke. Rod licence required — obtainable from tackleists or Divisional Manager's office (address above).

SNITTERFIELD RESERVOIR

nr Stratford-on-Avon, Warks.

4-acre reservoir let to Leamington Spa A.A. Inquiries to hon sec: E. G. Archer, 9 Southway, Leamington Spa, Warks.

STANLEY MOOR
see Lightwood and Stanley Moor

THORNTON

Thornton,
nr Market Bosworth, Leics.

About 3m south of the junction of M1 (junction 22) and A50, approximately 5m NE of Market Bosworth and 7m W of Leicester.

Controller: Severn Trent Water Authority, Soar Division.

Description: New landscaped reservoir of 76 acres (opened 1975).

Species: Brown and rainbow.

Stocking: At intervals on a 'put and take' basis.

Rules: Fly only. Limit: 2 brace of 10in and over. Fishing 6 am to one hour after sunset.

Season: 1 April to 15 October.

Permits: dt £1.50 (restricted to 20). Limited st (10) for local residents only, £30. Boats (8): £2 day. Charges under review.

Permits from:
Bull's Head, Thornton (dt); st from Severn-Trent WA.

Comments: Few details of the fishing on this new water yet available. Inquiries to Soar Division, Severn-Trent WA, Gorse Hill, Anstey, Leicester, LE7 7GU (tel. 29992). Biggest fish (1975) was 6lb 12oz brown.

TICKLERTON POOLS

nr Bridgnorth, Salop

Also Willey Park Pools. Rainbow, brown and some American brook trout. Salopian Fly F.A. water. Inquiries to hon. sec: Donald Jones, 56 Wrekin View, Madeley, Salop. Club membership limited.

TITTESWORTH

nr Leek, Staffs.

About 2m N of Leek and to west of Leek to Buxton road (A53).

Controller: Severn-Trent Water Authority, Upper Trent Division.

Description: 189-acre landscaped reservoir in the Churnet Valley.

Species/sizes: Brown and rainbow.

	Brown	Rainbow
Average	1lb 3oz	1lb 7oz
Record	9lb 5oz	3lb 8oz
	(1967)	(1971)

Stocking: Some 6000 trout introduced at intervals during season.

Rules: Fly only. Limit: 3 brace 11in and over; fish under 11in to be returned if uninjured. Thigh waders only.

Season: 13 April to 15 October.

Permits: st £40; dt (limited to 80) £1.80. Boats: 12ft £1.40 a day; 15ft £2.50.

Permits from: st from Severn-Trent WA, Upper Trent Division, Albion Street, Hanley, Stoke-on-Trent, Mon–Fri only, 9 am to 4.30 pm; dt from Fishing Lodge near reservoir bridge, off Blackshaw Lane (from 8 am).

Comments: This reservoir holds some very good fish, especially brown trout; a number over the 6lb mark have been recorded in recent years. Size of the rainbows, too, would seem to be increasing. The reservoir was expanded to have its own shop, cafeteria and professional instructor for the 1976 season—believed to be the first public water to offer these facilities.

TRIMPLEY

Trimpley, nr Bewdley, Worcs.

A442 from Kidderminster, turn left after about 2m and proceed through Trimpley village or take B4190 from Bewdley to Wolverley.

Owner: Severn-Trent Water Authority, Tame Division.

Description: 13-acre landscaped reservoir.

Species/sizes: Brown and rainbow trout, coarse fish.

	Brown	Rainbow
Average	12oz	12oz
Record	8lb 12oz	4lb 12oz

Stocking: Initially stocked with over 2000 brown and rainbow trout to supplement natural stocks. Further stocking at intervals.

Rules: Fly only 15 April to 30 June, then until 14 March any legal method permitted. Limit: 2 brace. No trout under 10in to be retained; no trout 10in and over to be returned to water.

Season: 15 April to 14 October.

Permits: st only £25 weekdays, £15 weekends. Friends' dt £1.80. Boats: probably two in 1976 at £2 per day.

Permits from:
Tame Division, Severn-Trent WA, 156/170
Newhall Street, Birmingham, B3 1SE
(tel. 021 236 9888).

Comments: This water was operated as a
trout fishery from 1969–72, then closed.
It reopened as a mixed fishery in 1975.
It then produced 1649 trout weighing
1116lb. The capture of a brown trout of
8lb 12oz indicates its potential. Facilities
are shared with a sailing club. Further
details from Birmingham 338878.

VYRNWY

nr Llanwddyn, Montgomeryshire

A494 to Bala, then about 10m SE along
B4393, or else A490 from Welshpool to
Llanfyllin, then about 7m W along B4393.

Controller: Lake Vyrnwy Hotel.

Description: Long narrow lake 800ft
above sea level covering some 2000 acres
of picturesque Llanwddyn valley. Many
small bays and indentations, and several
larger bays. Peaty water, trout food not
too plentiful. Supply reservoir for Liverpool.

Species/sizes: Brown and rainbow trout,
and fair stock of chub.

	Brown	Rainbow
Average	11oz	14oz
Record	4lb 2oz	3lb 12oz

Stocking: With brown and rainbow trout
at monthly intervals, February to June, to
supplement natural stock of brown trout.

Rules: Fly only. Limit: 10 brace; 10in
brown, 11in rainbow. All fishing from
boats, except for hotel guests.

Season: 1 March to 30 September
(14 October for rainbows).

Permits: dt £1.75 March, July, August,
September; £2 April, May, June.
Boats free to hotel guests; for visitors
80p day low season and £1 high season.

Permits from: Lake Vyrnwy Hotel, via
Oswestry, SY10 0LY (tel. Llanwddyn
244).

Comments: Early in the season most trout
are taken deep down on biggish flies.
Standard patterns and the new breed of
reservoir flies do well. From June onwards
the dry fly often brings results — Coch-y-
Bonddhu and Alder are recommended.
April and May are usually the best months.
Good feeding places are Rhiwargor and
Eunant at the top end, Llwyn Rhiw on
the south bank and Cedig on the north.
The mouths of feeder streams are also
useful places to try, especially at the dam
end around two large tunnels diverting
water from the adjoining valleys of Afon
Conwy and Afon Marchnant.

WILLEY PARK POOLS
see under Ticklerton Pools

YELDERSLEY and SHIRLEY LAKES

nr Ashbourne, Derbys.

Part of Ashbourne Fly Fishers' water.
Small club with restricted membership.
Hon sec: F. W. Mellor, 2 Boothby
Avenue, Ashbourne, Derbys.

5 The South

SOUTHERN WATER AUTHORITY
Guildbourne House, Worthing, Sussex, BN11 1LD.
Principal Fisheries Officer: J. R. Chandler (tel. Worthing 205252).
Trout licences (whole area): Season £2, 14-day 50p, Juniors 50p.
Close season: 29 October to 1 April.

Kent Area
Fisheries Inspector: B. M. Joslin, 78 College Road, Maidstone, Kent
(tel. Maidstone 55211).

Sussex Area
Fisheries Inspector: J. W. Walters, Anston House, 137/139 Preston Road, Brighton
(tel. Brighton 507101).

Hampshire Area
Fisheries Inspector: D. Paterson, Eastleigh House, 2 Market Street, Eastleigh, Hants.,
SO5 5WA (tel. Eastleigh 4622).

REMINDER

Stocking policy depends on returns. Fishery managers have
asked us to stress that whether you catch anything or not, please
remember to fill in the form before leaving the water.

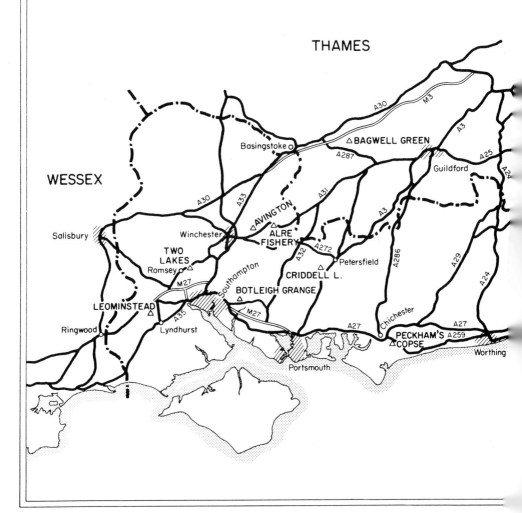

SOUTHERN WATER AUTHORITY AREA

△ Fisheries

— Roads

═ Motorway

▬ ▬ Authority boundary

THAMES

A30   M3

Basingstoke   △ BAGWELL GREEN

A287   A3

WESSEX   A25

Guildford

A30   A33   A24

△ AVINGTON   A31   A3

Salisbury   Winchester   △ ALRE FISHERY

TWO   A32   A272   A286   A29

LAKES   Petersfield   A24

Romsey   CRIDDELL L.

Southampton   △

M27   BOTLEIGH GRANGE   Chichester

LEOMINSTEAD   A27   PECKHAM'S   A259

△   M27   COPS E

Ringwood   A35   Lyndhurst   Worthing

Portsmouth

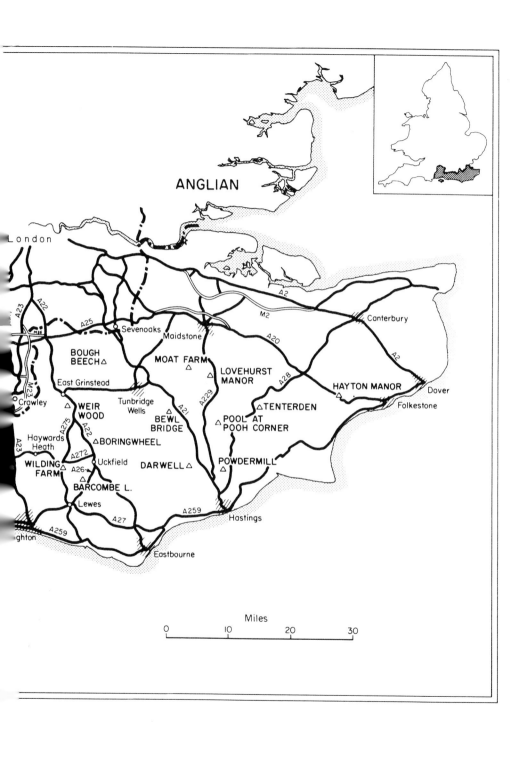

ANGLIAN

London

BOUGH
BEECH△

MOAT FARM
△   △ LOVEHURST
              MANOR

East Grinstead

Sevenoaks
Maidstone

Canterbury

A2

M2

A20

A2

Dover

HAYTON MANOR
△

Folkestone

Crawley

WEIR
WOOD
△

Tunbridge
Wells

BEWL
BRIDGE

A229

A21

A28

△TENTERDEN

POOL AT
△ POOH CORNER

Haywards
Heath

△BORINGWHEEL

A275

A22

WILDING
FARM
△

A272

A26

Uckfield

DARWELL △

POWDERMILL
△

A23

BARCOMBE L.
△

Lewes

A27

A259

Hastings

ghton

A259

Eastbourne

Miles

0   10   20   30

ALRE FISHERY

Alresford, Hants.

Main road from Winchester to New
Alresford (A31) and turn down Drove
Lane. Winchester 9m SW.

Owner: H.R.G. Lane.

Description: Fishery is mainly river but
includes two landscaped lakes of around
one acre apiece.

Species/sizes: Brown and rainbow.

	Brown	Rainbow
Average	2lb	2lb 4oz
Record	3½—4lb	5lb

Stocking: Lakes are stocked on a 'put and
take' basis.

Rules: Fly only, sizes between 10 and 12;
no shooting heads. Six rods only, priority
for members.

Season: 1 April to 30 September.

Permits: Full-season £300, half £170; dt
£12 (by arrangement, at least 24 hours
notice required). No boats.

Permits from:
Fishery Bailiff, Keeper's Cottage, Fob
Down, New England Estate, Alresford,
Hants.

Comments: An exclusive fishery
providing high-quality sport. Recom-
mended dry flies: Beacon and Beige,
Sherry Spinner, Red Spinner, Pheasant
Tail, Ginger Quill. Wet flies: Hare's Ear,
Wickham's Fancy, Tupp Nymph,
Pheasant Tail Nymph, Mallard and Claret.
Further information from Bob Edwards,
bailiff (tel. Alresford 2837).

AVINGTON FISHERY

*Avington,
nr Winchester, Hants.*

Owner: S. Holland.

Description: Three landscaped lakes
totalling eight acres, and ¾m of R. Itchen.

Species/sizes: Brown and rainbow.

	Brown	Rainbow
Average	2lb	4lb
Record	5lb 1oz	14lb 4oz (British record)

Stocking: Regular introductions of large
fish from own stock ponds.

Rules: Fly only. Limit: 2 brace rainbows,
1 brace browns. Non-fishing guests not
allowed.

Season: 2 April to 30 September.

Permits: full-rod £168.48, half-rod
£91.80; few dt at £8.10 by prior arrangement.

Permits from: Owner at fishery
(tel. Itchen Abbas 312).

Comments: Sam Holland's success in
breeding 'super trout' has won him
national and even international acclaim.
During the 1975 season no fewer than
42 rainbows landed were over 10lb!
The fish which broke the British record
was also taken in 1975 — on July 22.
Avington has demonstrated that the
production of salmon-size rainbows over
a relatively short period is possible. For
this alone the fishery is remarkable.

BAGWELL GREEN

Winchfield,
nr Basingstoke, Hants.

At Greenways Farm — off A3016 from M3 at Odiham or A30 at Phoenix Green, Hartley Wintney.

Owner: Mrs. J. K. Marshall.

Description: Two spring-fed lakes of 1-acre and ¾-acre respectively.

Species/sizes: Brown and rainbow.

	Brown	Rainbow
Average	1lb	1lb
Record	5lb	3lb

Stocking: Twice or three times a season.

Rules: Fly only. Limit: one brace. St holders may bring a guest by arrangement. All dt by appointment.

Season: 1 April to 20 October.

Permits: st (two-day) £50; (one-day) £30; half-season from mid-July, £25; dt £2.

Permits from:
Greenways Farm, Winchfield, nr Basingstoke, Hants.

Comments: These ponds, opened in 1965, vary considerably in character. One would appear to have been established in Saxon times. The other was re-excavated some years ago and is considerably deeper. Advice on flies, etc. will be given when booking. A selection is available on the premises.

BARCOMBE LAKE

Barcombe,
nr Lewes, Sussex

½m W of A26 Lewes to Uckfield road, 3½m N of Lewes. Take Barcombe Mills road off A26.

Controller: Ouse Angling Preservation Society.

Description: 40-acre concrete reservoir.

Species/sizes: Brown and rainbow.

	Brown	Rainbow
Average	1lb 4oz	1lb 6oz
Record	2lb 6oz	2lb

Stocking: Main stocking in March, thereafter at six-week intervals; some autumn stocking also.

Rules: Fly only. Limit: 3 fish 12in and over.

Season: 15 April to 29 October.

Permits: dt £2 approx till end of June, £1.75 approx thereafter.

Permits from:
Hon sec: Dr John L. Cotton, Down End, Kingston Road, Lewes, Sussex (till season opens);
then from bailiff at Fishing Hut (tel. Ringmer 815593). Note: dt limited to holders of society season permits (£6, OAPs £4).

BEWL BRIDGE

nr Lamberhurst, Kent

Projected trout reservoir covering 770 acres at top water level, in Teise valley. Access will be by the recently improved Bewl Bridge Lane from the A21. Water is 12m from Tonbridge, 17m from Hastings. Stocking with brown trout aimed at developing water as 'put and take' fishery, had begun as we went to press. At top level the bank would be 15m long, and the water a maximum depth of 95ft, although the water area could drop to 500 acres or less in summer. Part of the reservoir will be designated a nature reserve, and anglers will also have to share the water with sailing/rowing interests. It was reported that the reservoir would become a coarse fishery in two or three seasons.

BORINGWHEEL FISHERY

nr Nutley, Sussex

Off A22 East Grinstead to Eastbourne road about 5m NW of Uckfield.

Owner: C. Impney.

Description: Six-acre landscaped lakes and short stretch of stream.

Species/sizes: Brown and rainbow; best rainbow (1975) 8lb 12oz.

Stocking: Regular stocking includes big fish.

Rules: Fly only.

Season: 1 April to 30 September.

Permits: dt £5 (limited).

Permits from: Owner at Boringwheel House, Cackle Street, nr Nutley, Sussex (tel. Nutley 2629).

BOTLEIGH GRANGE LAKES

Botley, nr Southampton

Off A334 about 1½m W of Botley and 5m E of Southampton.

Controller: D. Plumpton, Botleigh Grange Hotel.

Description: Two lakes in hotel grounds.

Species/sizes: Brown and rainbow averaging 1½lb.

Rules: Fly only, no lures. Limit: 1 brace.

Permits: dt £5; evenings (after 6pm) £2.50. Charges plus VAT.

Permits from:
Botleigh Grange Hotel, Hedge End, Southampton.

Comments: A comparatively new fishery holding some good trout. No Water Authority licence required as hotel has a general licence.

BOUGH BEECH

Chiddingstone, Kent

Off B269 5½m W of Tonbridge. London 33m.

Controller: East Surrey Water Co.

Description: Landscaped reservoir (capacity 2000mg) formed by damming tributary of River Eden. First opened for fishing in 1970.

Species/sizes: Brown and rainbow.

	Brown	Rainbow
Average	1lb 8oz	1lb 8oz
Record	5lb 3oz	—
	(1975)	

Stocking: Periodically, depending on returns. Introduction of larger fish (16in and over) in 1975 may have helped raise average size of trout taken.

Rules: Fly only.

Season: 1 May to 30 September.

Permits: Restricted to 220. Full permit £75.60. Mid-week permit £48.60. Children under 12 may accompany guests for 50p extra provided warden is informed. Boats £2 day (two seats), £1 half-day.

Permits from:
East Surrey Water Co, London Road, Redhill (in advance).

Comments: Catches at Bough Beech have quadrupled since the reservoir opened and topped the 9000 mark in 1974, giving an average of 1.57 fish per visit. Although the weather in 1975 was no help to the angler, more than 8000 fish were taken, including 73 over 3lb, and a record brown trout of 5lb 3oz. There have been some problems with coarse fish, mainly pike and perch. In fact, a pike of 20¼lb was taken on a Black Lure, giving the reservoir the dubious distinction of holding the national record for the largest fly-caught pike! However, fewer problems of that nature were reported last season. Hatches of Pond Olives would seem to be increasing. Greenwell's Glory and Olive Nymphs have proved successful imitations.

BRIMCLOSE FISHERY

Salisbury, Wilts.

This fishery consists of two well-stocked trout lakes and 1¼m of chalk stream. Rods limited to 4 per day. Limit: 2½ brace. Permits: st £100; dt £6.50. Further details from Philip W. Gauntlett Sporting Agency, Waterside Cottage, Micheldever, Hants. (tel. Micheldever 223).

CRIDDELL LAKE

Ramsdean,
nr Petersfield, Hants.

Turn left off A272 at Stroud, about 1m W of Petersfield.

Owner: Butser Turf Co. Ltd.

Description: Landscaped reservoir of 4 acres.

Species/sizes: Brown and rainbow.

	Brown	Rainbow
Average	1lb 4oz	1lb 8oz
Record	4lb	5lb 12oz

Stocking: First stocking six weeks before season opens, then at intervals.

Rules: Fly only. Limit: 2 brace. No fish caught to be returned to water.

Season: 1 April to 15 October.

Permits: st £110 (+VAT) for any one day/week; £170 for any two days/week. Rods limited to five a day.

Permits from:
Butser Turf Co. Ltd., 25 Portsmouth Road, Horndean, Hants. (tel. Horndean 3242).

Comments: An increasingly productive fishery. Criddell is returning totals of around the 1000 mark, including a dozen or so trout over 4lb.

DARWELL

Mountfield,
nr Robertsbridge, Sussex

Off A21 Robertsbridge to Battle road (entrance at Tunstall Farm).

Controller: Hastings Flyfishers Club.

Description: 180-acre landscaped reservoir fringed with fields and woods.

Species/sizes: Brown and rainbow.

	Brown	Rainbow
Average	1lb	1lb
Record	4lb 4oz	8lb 10oz

Stocking: Throughout season as required (mostly rainbows).

Rules: Fly only, no spinning or trolling. Fishing 9am to one hour after sunset.

Season: 1 April to 29 October.

Permits: dt only, £2. Boats (10): £1.10 day; for bookings phone Robertsbridge 880407 between 9 and 10am only.

Permits from: Bailiff 9–10am. Southern WA licence required, obtainable from bailiff.

Comments: Attractors on sunk line effective early on. Otherwise standard wet and dry flies take fish; nymphs should include green patterns. Sedges and daddy-longlegs are good for dry fly. Lines of not less than 6lb b/s recommended.

Further details from hon sec at 2 West Terrace, Eastbourne, Sussex, BN21 4QX (tel. 25211).

GT SANDERS
see Powdermill

HASTINGS
see Darwell, Powdermill

HAYTON MANOR FARM

Sellindge, Kent

1m off A20 Maidstone to Hythe road.

Controller: Mid-Kent Fly Fishers.

Description: Natural lake of about 3½ acres, suitably landscaped.

Species/sizes: Rainbows averaging 1lb 4oz, biggest 3lb 8oz.

Stocking: At intervals.

Rules: Fly only.

Season: 1 May to 31 October.

Permits: st only, £25.

Permits from:
Eric Stratton, 6 Bell Meadow, Sutton Road, Maidstone, Kent (tel. Maidstone 61877).

Comments: One of the fisheries controlled by Mid-Kent Fly Fishers; inquiries to hon sec as above.

LEOMINSTEAD TROUT FISHERY

Emery Down,
Lyndhurst, Hants.

A35 Southampton to Lyndhurst; Emery Down lies about 1m W of village and fishery is 1m N of that.

Owner: Leo Jarmal.

Description: Natural lake in heart of New Forest.

Species/sizes: Brown, rainbow and some brook trout.

	Brown	Rainbow
Average	2lb	2lb 3oz
Record	6lb 2oz	9lb

Stocking: At intervals throughout season.

Rules: Fly only (no tandems or droppers). Limit: 2 brace 12in and over. No fish to be returned to water. Casts should exceed 5lb b/s to prevent injury to stock.

Season: 1 April to 1 November.

Permits: Full rod £140, half rod £75; dt £7. Boat £1 per person.

Permits from:
Leominstead Trout Fishery, Emery Down, Lyndhurst, Hants., SO4 7GA (tel. Lyndhurst 2610).

Comments: A carefully managed and secluded fishery holding large trout, including double-figure rainbows. No WA licence required for season rods.

LOVEHURST MANOR

Staplehurst, Kent

Half a mile off A229 at Staplehurst, 8m SSE of Maidstone.

Controller: Mid-Kent Fly Fishers.

Description: Stream-fed moat in attractive situation.

Species/sizes: Wild brown and rainbow; latter average 1½lb, biggest 4lb 8oz.

Stocking: At intervals.

Rules: Fly only.

Season: 1 April to 15 October.

Permits: st only, £22.

Permits from:
Eric Stratton, 6 Bell Meadow, Sutton Road, Maidstone, Kent (tel. Maidstone 61877).

Comments: One of the fisheries controlled by Mid-Kent Fly Fishers; inquiries to hon sec as above.

MOAT FARM

Collier Street,
nr Maidstone, Kent.

Off A229 between Yalding and Marden, about 7m SW of Maidstone.

Controller: Mid-Kent Fly Fishers.

Description: 2½-acre landscaped reservoir.

Species/sizes: Rainbows averaging 1½lb, biggest 4lb 6oz.

Stocking: At intervals.

Rules: Fly only.

Season: 1 April to 15 October.

Permits: st only, £22.

Permits from:
Eric Stratton, 6 Bell Meadow, Sutton
Road, Maidstone (tel. Maidstone 61877).

Comments: One of the fisheries
controlled by the Mid-Kent Fly Fishers;
inquiries to hon sec as above.

PECKHAMS COPSE

*North Mundham,
Chichester, Sussex*

Off B2166 about 2m SE of Chichester.

Owner: Heaver Estates (Southern) Ltd.

Description: Two landscaped lakes of
about 20 acres apiece.

Species/sizes: Brown and rainbow.

	Brown	Rainbow
Average	1lb 8oz	2lb
Record	4lb	6lb 2oz

Stocking: About every 7-10 days with fish
of 1½-2½lb. Total stock: 4-5000, mostly
rainbows.

Rules: Fly only: no lures: Limit: 2 brace.
All fish caught to be killed.

Season: 1 April to 29 October.

Permits: st rates range from £91.80 (one
named day) to £345.60 (full season);
dt £5.94. Boats (6): £2.16 day.

Permits from:
Manager, Heaver Estates (Southern) Ltd.,
Vinnetrow Road, Chichester, Sussex
(tel. 87715). No ticket guaranteed unless
booked in advance.

Comments: Opened in 1969, these former
gravel workings have settled down to
become one of the most notable of
southern fisheries. The banks have been
graded to a gentle slope and the setting
made so attractive that the fishery
gained an award in a national competition
for restoration and after-use in the gravel
industry. With trout being stocked at
over the 1½lb mark, it is not surprising
that Peckhams Copse should have gained
repute as a big-fish water. Recently the
fishery has been returning over 200
fish per acre, one of the highest for a
trout lake open to the public.
*Some interesting comments on fishing
the water are contained in the article
by Brian Clarke on page 29.*

THE POOL AT POOH CORNER

*Rolvenden,
Cranbrook, Kent*

1m from Rolvenden on B2086 just off
A28. Within easy reach of Ashford,
Maidstone, Tunbridge Wells and Hastings.

Owner: I. A. G. Thomson.

Description: Relatively new landscaped
pool fed by natural springs covering just
under 1½ acres and with depths varying
from 3ft to 18ft.

Species/sizes: Rainbow trout only,
averaging about 2lb, biggest 4lb 12oz.

Stocking: With 1lb-plus fish fortnightly as
a rule, or more frequently at peak of
season.

Rules: Fly only, and only one fly of conventional pattern. No more than 3 rods allowed on fishery at any one time.

Season: 3 April to 31 October.

Permits: dt £6 (£3.50 after 4pm); mt by arrangement.

Permits from:
The owner at Pooh Corner, Rolvenden, Cranbrook, Kent, TN17 4JE (tel. Rolvenden 219). Prior booking recommended.

Comments: The declared object of this small fishery is to give anglers variety in the size of fish they may expect to catch in pleasant, uncrowded rural surroundings where a leisurely approach is the order of things. A fishing hut on the bank is equipped for tea and coffee-making, and furnished with wall charts to help with the identification of fly life. Artificial flies are also available for purchase. The owner or a member of his household is always willing to give advice.

POWDERMILL (GT SANDERS)

*Sedlescombe,
nr Battle, Sussex*

Off A229 Maidstone to Hastings road, Turn left at Sedlescombe on to Brede road.

Controller: Hastings Flyfishers Club.

Description: Attractive tree-fringed reservoir of some 55 acres.

Species/sizes: Brown and rainbow.

	Brown	Rainbow
Average	1lb	1lb
Record	5lb 5oz	4lb 3oz

Stocking: Before opening of season and then periodically as required.

Rules: Fly only, no spinning or trolling. Fishing 9am to one hour after sunset. Bank fishing limited to 10 rods. Southern WA licence required; obtainable from bailiff.

Season: 1 April to 29 October.

Permits: dt only, £2. Boats (6): £1.10 day; phone Sedlescombe 248 for bookings.

Permits from: Bailiff at reservoir 9—10am.

Comments: Although sunk lures are popular, many feel the finest sport is with dry fly and greased line from May onwards, when sedge is being taken, or with nymph patterns during the evening. Lines of at least 6lb b/s recommended. Further details from hon sec at 2 West Terrace, Eastbourne, Sussex, BN21 4QX (tel. 25211).

TENTERDEN TROUT FISHERY

Tenterden, Kent

A28 Ashford to Tenterden road, turn right in St Michael's to Shoreham Lane.

Owner: B. Evans.

Description: Landscaped reservoir.

Species/sizes: Rainbows only averaging 1lb 8oz, biggest 5lb.

Stocking: At start of each month of season.

Rules: Fly only. Limit: one brace. Multi-hook lures and tandems not permitted. Wading not recommended.

Season: 1 April to 31 October.

Permits: dt £4, evenings £3.

Permits from:
Proprietor, Coombe Farm, Tenterden (telephone booking advised: Tenterden 3201).

Comments: Mr Evans is willing to advise and help anglers at any time. A rest room is available on this pleasant and attractive fishery, and flies may be purchased.

TWO LAKES

Crampmoor,
nr Romsey, Hants.

Off A31 Winchester to Romsey road 2m ENE of Romsey.

Owner: Alex Behrendt.

Description: Chain of carefully-landscaped man-made lakes set in delightful grounds.

Species/sizes: Brown and rainbow.

	Brown	Rainbow
Average	not available	2lb 9oz
Record	9lb 11oz	12lb 4oz

Stocking: Several times throughout season.

Rules: Fly only.

Season: 1 April to 30 September.

Permits: st £178.20.

Permits from: Alex Behrendt.

Comments: First-class management has produced one of the most noted big-fish waters in the country. T. C. Ivens has declared that Two Lakes provide 'more good trout fishing for more people than any other similar area of water anywhere in Britain'. It was at Two Lakes that Barrie Welham developed his technique of stalking large fish. But the capture of a Two Lakes trout demands skill and dedication of the highest order.

WEIR WOOD

Forest Row,
East Grinstead, Sussex

33m from London via A22 to East Grinstead, then to Forest Row.

Owner: Southern Water Authority.

Description: 280-acre reservoir attractively situated on fringe of Ashdown Forest — 250 acres available for fishing.

Species/sizes: Brown and rainbow.

	Brown	Rainbow
Average	1lb	1lb
Record	5lb 7oz	4lb 6oz

Stocking: At intervals from Feb to Oct with over 17,000 fish between 12 and 16in.

Rules: Fly only, no trolling, thigh waders only. Fishing prohibited from dam, Valve Tower Bridge and above Admirals Wood. Limit: 3 brace 12in and over (all undersized fish to be returned to water).

Season: 1 April to 30 September.

Permits: dt (bank) £2.00; evening £1.50 wt £13.00; st (whole season) £70; (weekdays) £55. Reduced rates for students and juniors. Southern WA rod licence also required.
Boats (11 double, 7 single), £4 extra for two-seater, £2.50 extra for single-seater.

Permits from: Recreations Officer at Weir Wood in advance or on day at Fishing Lodge (tel. Forest Row 2731). Ticket vending machine available before 7.30am. Permits other than st may, with prior permission, be transferred to another person or day if holder unable to make use of it. Advanced booking essential on opening day.

Comments: Formed by damming the upper Medway, Weir Wood was opened for angling in 1957 and produced 3000 fish in its first season. The fact that returns are now around the 12,500 mark — 1975 actually produced a record total of 12,540 fish — bear witness to the success of its management and stocking policy, and to the popularity of the reservoir. It is fished by around 10,000 rods a season. An encouraging feature is that fish are also breeding naturally. A line of at least 5lb b/s is recommended. Sunk flies and lures on size 12 hooks are most popular, but good sport can be had with the dry fly, especially sedge patterns. There is a tackle shop which holds a good stock of tackle, flies, nymphs and lures.

Note: Anglers share the water with sailing enthusiasts and the reservoir also provides a haven for wildlife. The Recreations Officer, Mr E. C. Crumplin, is available at Weir Wood during the trout season to advise on all recreational matters.

WILDING FARM FISHERY

Chailey, Sussex

Off A272 midway between Haywards Heath and Uckfield.

Owner: J. Usborne.

Description: 3-acre landscaped reservoir.

Species/sizes: Brown and rainbow.

	Brown	Rainbow
Average	1lb 8oz	1lb 8oz
Record	2lb 4oz	2lb

Stocking: At intervals as required.

Rules: Fly only. Limit: 2 brace.

Season: 15 April to 1 October.

Permits: st £80 (two days per week, includes one guest rod).

Permits from:
J. Usborne, Wilding Farm, Chailey, Sussex.

LATE ENTRY

ARLINGTON

nr Berwick, Sussex

Relatively new 120-acre reservoir about 7m SE of Lewes. Well stocked with browns and rainbows. Full st £90; one-day st £45; £50 Sats or Suns (all plus VAT). Boats at small charge. Season: 15 April to 17 October. Further details from bailiff, Mr Evans, Fishing Lodge (tel. Alfreston 815).

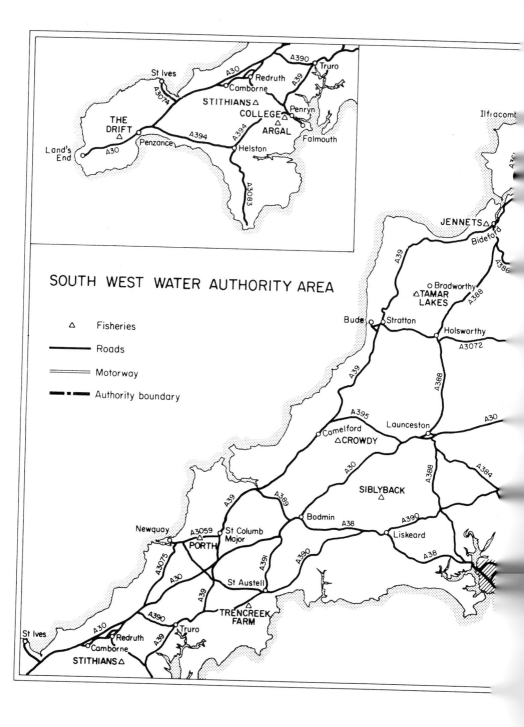

SOUTH WEST WATER AUTHORITY AREA

△   Fisheries

────   Roads

════   Motorway

━·━·   Authority boundary

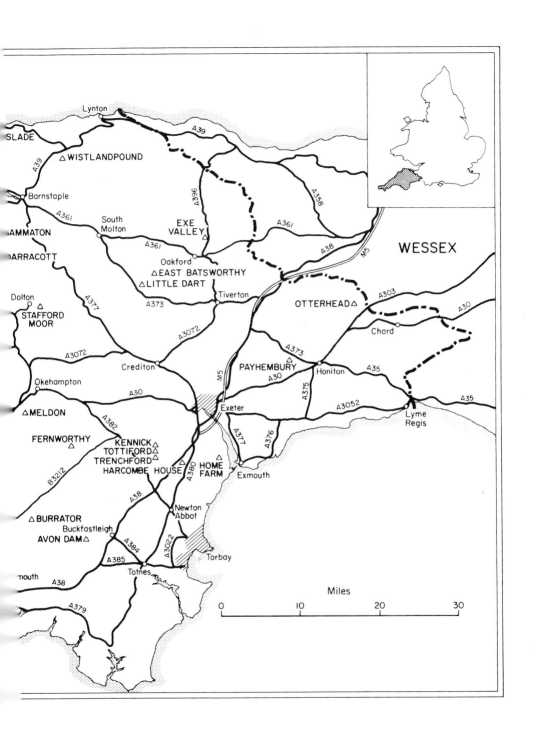

SLADE

Lynton

△ WISTLANDPOUND

A39

Barnstaple

A361

South
Molton

AMMATON

ARRACOTT

A361

EXE
VALLEY

Oakford
△EAST BATSWORTHY
△LITTLE DART

Tiverton

A373

Dolton
STAFFORD
MOOR

A377

A3072

Crediton

A3072

Okehampton

A30

△MELDON

A382

FERNWORTHY

KENNICK
TOTTIFORD△
TRENCHFORD△
HARCOMBE HOUSE

B3212

△BURRATOR
Buckfastleigh
AVON DAM△

mouth

A38

A379

A384

A385

Totnes

A3022

A38

A380

A377

A376

HOME
FARM

Newton
Abbot

Exmouth

Torbay

A39

A396

A358

A361

A38

WESSEX

M5

OTTERHEAD△

A303

A30

Chard

A373

PAYHEMBURY

A30

A375

Honiton

A35

A3052

Lyme
Regis

A35

Exeter

M5

Miles

0   10   20   30

ARGAL and COLLEGE

nr Falmouth, Cornwall

Although these reservoirs are in same area — linked by short stream — Argal is best reached via B3291 from Penryn or Falmouth, turning right after 3m, and College from Penryn travelling 1m SW.

Controller: South West Water Authority (Div I).

Description: Argal (65 acres) is larger of these reservoirs — College covers 38 acres. They are situated in pleasant countryside within easy reach of Falmouth and Penryn.

Species/sizes: Brown and rainbow.

	Brown	Rainbow
Average	1lb 2oz	1lb 2oz
Record	6lb 6oz	6lb 5oz

Stocking: Argal stocked with brown and rainbow trout before season opens, then at intervals. College stocked periodically with rainbows only.

Rules: Fly only. Limit: 3 brace 10in and over. Fishing 9am to one hour after sunset.

Season: 1 April to 12 October. As an experiment the rainbow trout season was extended through the autumn. The experiment may be repeated.

Permits: st £40; wt £8; dt £1.50. Half price for OAPs, disabled and juniors. Boats: £2 day, £1 after 4pm.

Permits from: Self-service unit (wt and dt); st from warden — Bob Evans, Little Argal Farm, Budock, Penryn (tel. 72544) — or Information Office, South West WA, 3—5 Barnfield Road, Exeter, EX1 1RE. Boat bookings with warden.

Comments: College is comparatively shallow and the trout run bigger than they do in Argal. The reservoirs together produce some 3000 trout a season. Standard patterns — Black and Peacock Spider, Butcher, Peter Ross, sedges, Black Lure and Whisky Lure. Tackle for hire at £1 day, 50p half-day, excluding flies and leaders.

AVON DAM

nr South Brent, Devon

On A38 just N of South Brent and about 8m NE of Totnes. Final walk of 1½m is involved.

Controller: South West Water Authority (Div III)).

Description: 50-acre reservoir in picturesque Avon valley.

Species/sizes: Brown trout only. Reservoir not fully established as fishery; further details awaited.

Stocking: Some surplus fry introduced.

Rules: Fly only, no bag limit, size limit 7in. Fishing 9am to one hour after sunset.

Season: 16 March to 30 September.

Permits: st £7.50; wt £2; dt 50p. OAPs, disabled and juniors half-price. No boats.

Permits from:
Anchor Inn, South Brent.

Comments: This reservoir was not opened for fishing until 1973. Contact the warden, Ted Fowler (tel. South Brent 3268) for further details.

BURRATOR

nr Yelverton, Devon

A386 from Plymouth, then B3212 to Yelverton, about 11m.

Controller: South West Water Authority (Div II).

Description: 150-acre reservoir beautifully situated in Dartmoor National Park. Only half of water is open to South West WA permit-holders.

Species/sizes: Wild brown trout and stocked rainbows averaging 10oz.

Stocking:: Rainbows stocked as fry.

Rules: Zoned fly and spinning.

Season: 16 March to 30 September.

Permits: st £7.50; wt £2; dt 50p. Half-price for OAPs, disabled and juniors. Boats: £2 a day, £1 after 4pm.

Permits from: Self-service unit at Burrator Lodge or in advance from Watershed Foreman (at lodge, Sheepstor, Yelverton, Devon) who will also take bookings for boats.

Comments: This reservoir stays open from sunrise until midnight. Popular flies by day include March Brown, Blue Upright and Pheasant Tail and by night, Teal Blue and Silver, Stoat's Tail and Butcher. Boats are not available until 8.30 am.

COLLEGE
see Argal and College

CROWDY

nr Camelford, Cornwall

From Launceston take A395 to Camelford, then moorland road E for about 2m to reservoir.

Controller: South West Water Authority.

Description: 115-acre moorland reservoir in Camel Valley.

Species/sizes: Brown and rainbow.

	Brown	Rainbow
Average	1lb	1lb
Record	3lb 8oz	3lb 8oz

Stocking: Once, before season opens.

Rules: Fly only. Limit: 3 brace 10in and over. Fishing 9am to one hour after sunset.

Season: 1 April to 12 October.

Permits: st £20; wt £5; dt £1. Half-price for OAPs, disabled and juniors. No boats.

Permits from: Self-service unit at reservoir (dt and wt);
st from Information Office, South West WA, 3—5 Barnfield Road, Exeter, EX1 1RE.

Comments: Black and Peacock Spider, Buzzers and the dry fly later on are said to account for the larger fish.

DARRACOTT RESERVOIR
see under Gammaton and Jennetts

THE DRIFT

nr Penzance, Cornwall

Just N of main A30 Penzance to Land's End road, about 2m from Penzance.

Owners: South West Water Authority/ Chyandour Estate Office.

Description: Landscaped reservoir of 65 acres amid area of great natural beauty.

Species/sizes: Brown and rainbow.

	Brown	Rainbow
Average	12oz	12oz
Record	1lb 12oz	1lb 12oz

Stocking: Generally The Drift is restocked once, at the start of the season.

Rules: Fishing hours sunrise to 11pm; no trouser waders; water is fly only; double or treble hooks, and spinning, prohibited; fish under 8in to be returned to water. Limit: 4 rainbows. No limit brown trout.

Season: 1 April to 30 September.

Permits: Full st £16.40; wt £4; dt £1.40; evening fishing (after 6pm) 70p. No boats.

Permits from:
Chyandour Estate Office, Chyandour, Penzance (tel. 3021) during normal office hours, Mon to Fri.
T. B. Shorland (bailiff) at new bungalow 'Driftways', situated right beside dam (tel. Penzance 3869)
F. E. Weston, Anglers Shop, The Bridge, Newlyn.
Sports and Leisure, Fernlea Terrace, St. Ives.

Comments: The Drift Reservoir was formed in 1961 when a valley on part of Mrs Charles Williams' Trewidden Estate was flooded by the West Cornwall Water Board to create a reservoir supplying the Land's End Peninsula. A stock of brown trout were introduced to augment the population of native fish derived from the valley streams, and the water is now established as a lake of mainly natural free-rising brown trout. In the spring of 1969 rainbow trout were introduced. Advice on how to fish the water is available from Terry Shorland, the bailiff (address above). Mrs Charles Williams, who retains the sporting rights, appreciates the active support of anglers and other interested parties in conserving the natural beauty and wildlife.

EAST BATSWORTHY LAKES

Rackenford, nr Tiverton, Devon

About 10m NW of Tiverton and 2½m W of Rackenford, down a lane running S off the B3221 Tiverton to South Molton road.

Owner: C. H. Gardner.

Description: Man-made landscaped lake of 1½ acres.

Species: Rainbow only, averaging 2lb, biggest 4lb 8oz.

Stocking: At intervals through the season.

Rules: Fly only.

Season: 1 March to 30 September.

Permits: dt £1.50 plus £1.00 per fish, maximum 3 fish per ticket.

Permits from: Owner, at East Batsworthy, Rackenford, Tiverton, Devon.

EXE VALLEY FISHERY

Exebridge,
Dulverton, Somerset

Just off A396 7m N of Tiverton and 2m W of Bampton.

Owner: Hugh Geoffrey Maund.

Description: Two man-made ponds, natural banks, covering about three-quarters of an acre.

Species/sizes: Brown and rainbow.

	Brown	Rainbow
Average	2lb 8oz	2lb 8oz
	(approx)	(approx)
Record	3lb	13lb

Stocking: About once a fortnight, depending on angling pressure. Some 4000 fish introduced for 1976 season, including 1000 rainbows of 2—4lb and a small number of 8lb-plus fish.

Rules: Fly only. Limit: 2 brace. No fish to be returned to water.

Season: 15 April to 30 September.

Permits: £1 per half-day, plus 50p per lb of fish caught.

Permits from:
Exe Valley Fishery, Exebridge, Dulverton, Somerset (tel. Dulverton 328).

Comments: This fishery has built up a large following of anglers, who appreciate the friendly, informal atmosphere and the quality of the sport. The capture of a 13lb rainbow demonstrates its potential.
Black fly patterns are reported to be most popular (sizes 8—12), though a tiny dry fly can prove a successful and sporting way to catch these leviathans.

FERNWORTHY

nr Chagford, Devon

Lies off A382 about 3m SW of village of Chagford, or can be approached via B3212 from Moretonhampstead (6m).

Controller: South West Water Authority (Div III).

Description: Picturesque Dartmoor reservoir of 76 acres.

Species/sizes: Brown and rainbow averaging about 13oz.

Stocking: Pre-season stocking with browns and rainbows.

Rules: Fly only. Limit: 3 brace 10in and over. Fishing 9am to one hour after sunset.

Season: 1 April to 12 October.

Permits: st £20; wt £5; dt £1. Half-price for OAPs, disabled and juniors. Boats: £2 day, £1 after 4pm.

Permits from: Resident Warden, who will also deal with boat bookings. (Sid Potter, Fernworthy House, Chagford (tel. 2440)).

Comments: This reservoir produced 1403 trout in 1975. Popular flies include Black and Peacock Spider, Alder and Black Gnat.

GAMMATON and JENNETS RESERVOIRS

nr Bideford, Devon

Also Darracott Reservoir (nr Torrington). In Torridge valley to east and west of river. Brown and rainbow. Fly only. Waters controlled by Torridge Fly F.C. Tickets from hon sec: E. J. Blight, 128 Stucley Road, Bideford, Devon, or Petherick's Tackle Shop, High St, Bideford (st £15; wt £3.50; dt £1.25).

HARCOMBE HOUSE

Chudleigh, Devon

½m from A38 Exeter to Plymouth road.

Owner: S. R. Bridle.

Description: Three landscaped reservoirs covering 5 acres in all.

Species/sizes: Brown and rainbow.

	Brown	Rainbow
Average	1lb 7½oz	1lb 12oz
Record	5lb 2oz	5lb 9oz

Stocking: Stock replaced every week throughout season, plus 10 per cent.

Rules: Fly only, and only one fly. Limit: 2 brace. No fish to be returned to water. 12 rods a day only.

Season: 1 April to 30 September.

Permits: dt £5; part-day £3 (both +VAT). *Charges under review.*

Permits from:
Estate Office, Harcombe House, Chudleigh, Devon.

HOME FARM FISHERY

Kenton, nr Exeter, Devon

Small private water, a lake of 1 acre stocked with rainbow trout, open all year round. Fly only: dt £4.50 (limit: 2 brace), or £2.50 half day after 3pm (limit: 1 brace). Contact Mr F. Williams, Home Farm, Mamhead, Kenton, nr Exeter, Devon.

JENNETS RESERVOIR
see Gammaton and Jennets Reservoirs

KENNICK and TOTTIFORD

nr Bovey Tracey, Devon

Two of group of three reservoirs lying off A382 Bovey Tracey to Moreton-hampstead road about 8m NE of Newton Abbot. The third, Trenchford, is not now stocked with trout owing to presence of large numbers of pike — it may become general coarse fishery.

Controller: South West Water Authority (Div III).

Description: Covering 42 and 35 acres respectively, these reservoirs are beautifully located.

Species/sizes: Brown and rainbow.

	Brown	Rainbow
Average	15oz	15oz
Record	6lb 1oz	4lb

Stocking: At intervals. Rainbows only in Kennick, Mainly brown trout in Tottiford.

Rules: Fly only. Limit: 3 brace 10in and over. Fishing 9am to one hour after sunset.

Season: 1 April to 12 October. Experimental extension of rainbow season on Kennick until November 1975 may be repeated in 1976.

Permits: st £40; wt £8; dt £1.50. Half price for OAPs, disabled and juniors. No boats.

Permits from: Self-service unit between reservoirs (wt and dt). For st apply to Information Office, South West WA, 3—5 Barnfield Road, Exeter, EX1 1RE.

Comments: In 1975 these waters produced 4373 trout, the average daily catch being 1.2 fish per rod. Popular flies include Black and Peacock Spider, Butcher, Greenwell's Glory, Alexandra (dusk) sedges, chironimids and various lures.

LITTLE DART FISHERY

Witheridge, Devon

½m off A373 8m from Tiverton and 10m from South Molton.

Owner: G. C. Manning.

Description: Landscaped reservoir of two acres.

Species/sizes: Brown and rainbow.

	Brown	Rainbow
Average	1lb 8oz	1lb 8oz
Record	5lb 4oz	8lb 3oz

Stocking: Five 'plantings' of rainbows each season; heavy stock of native brown trout.

Rules: Fly only. Limited to 4 rods. Bag: 2 brace full-day, 1 brace half-day.

Season: 1 March to 30 October.

Permits: dt £5; half-day £3.

Permits from: Proprietor at 'Dart Raffe', Witheridge, Tiverton, Devon (tel. Witheridge 557).

Comments: A very small 'personal' fishery. The owner will be pleased to advise anglers on patterns and techniques at time of booking.

MELDON

nr Okehampton, Devon

South of A30 between Okehampton (3m) and Launceston.

Controller: South West Water Authority (Div II).

Description: 54-acre moorland reservoir.

Species/sizes: Wild brown trout and stocked rainbows averaging about 10oz.

Stocking: With fry surplus to outside requirements only.

Rules: Fly only. No bag limit. Fishing sunrise to one hour after sunset.

Season: 16 March to 30 September.

Permits: st £7.50; wt £2; dt 50p. Half price for OAPs, disabled and juniors. No boats.

Permits from: Self-service unit at reservoir (wt and dt); st from Information Office, South West WA, 3—5 Barnfield Road, Exeter, EX1 1RE.

Comments: A disappointing season in 1975 — only 49 fish taken at an average of 0.3 per rod.

PAYHEMBURY TROUT PONDS

Payhembury,
Honiton, Devon

Just S of A373, about 4m W of Honiton.

Description: Two ponds, of 1 and 1½ acres.

Species/sizes: Brown and rainbow trout averaging 2lb 4oz.

Rules: Fly only. Limit related to category of dt.

Permits: dt £2.50 (limit: 3 fish). after 6pm £1.50 (limit: 1 brace).

Permits from:
Mrs M. MacKenzie, Hoskins, Payhembury, Honiton.

PORTH

nr Newquay, Cornwall

Off A3059 about 4m E of Newquay.

Controller: South West Water Authority (Div I).

Description: 40-acre reservoir conveniently situated near popular seaside resort of Newquay in pleasant countryside.

Species/sizes: Brown and rainbow trout averaging just over 1lb.

Stocking: At intervals.

Rules: Fly only. Limit: 3 brace 10in and over. Fishing 9am to one hour after sunset.

Season: 1 April to 12 October.

Permits: st £40; wt £8; dt £1.50. OAPs, disabled and juniors half price.

Permits from: Self-service unit (wt and dt); st from warden on site or Information Office, South West WA, 3—5 Barnfield Road, Exeter, EX1 1RE.

Comments: This reservoir yields around 2500 trout a season. They include some good fish (a rainbow of 4lb 3oz was caught recently). Popular flies are Black and Peacock Spider, Peter Ross, Mallard and Claret and various lures. Tackle may be hired for £1 day and 50p half-day; no flies or leaders supplied.

SIBLYBACK LAKE

nr Liskeard, Cornwall

Lies off A38 about 5m N of Liskeard and about 1m N of village of St Cleer.

Controller: South West Water Authority (Div I).

Description: 140-acre reservoir attractively situated in Fowey Valley.

Species/sizes: Brown and rainbow averaging about 1lb 3oz.

Stocking: At intervals.

Rules: Fly only. Limit 3 brace 10in and over. Fishing 9am to one hour after sunset.

Season: 1 April to 12 October.

Permits: st £40; wt £8; dt £1.50. Half-price for OAPs, disabled and juniors. Boats: £2 day, £1 after 4pm; similar extra charges for outboard motors.

Permits from: Self-service unit (wt and dt); st from warden, also boat bookings.

Comments: Siblyback produces around 6000 fish a season — a rainbow of 4lb 12oz has been taken. Recommended flies: Black and Peacock Spider, Black Gnat, Alexandra, sedges and hawthorn patterns. Also Buzzers, Whisky and Sweeny Todd lures. Tackle for hire £1 day, 50p half-day, excluding flies and leaders. This is one of Cornwall's most rewarding waters, with an average catch of 1.5 fish per rod day.

Opportunities for holiday fishing in the far south west.

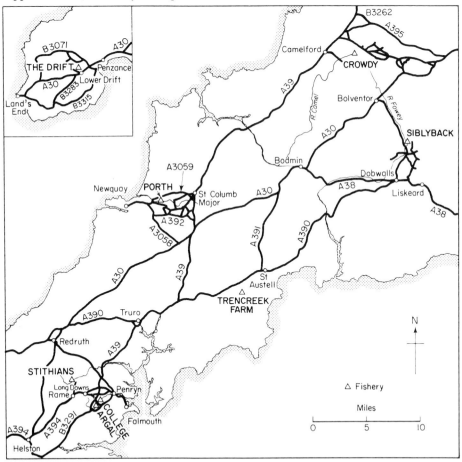

SLADE

nr Ilfracombe, Devon

B3231 from Ilfracombe; entrance about 1½m from town on left.

Controller: South West Water Authority (Div II).

Description: Two small reservoirs of 4 and 6 acres conveniently situated on outskirts of Ilfracombe.

Species/sizes: Brown and rainbow trout averaging just over 1lb.

Stocking: Pre-season.

Rules: Fly only. Limit: 3 brace 10in and over. Fishing sunrise to one hour after sunset.

Season: 1 April to 12 October.

Permits: st £20; wt £5; dt £1. Half-price for OAPs, disabled and juniors.

Permits from: Self-service unit (dt and wt); st from Information Office, South West WA, 3—5 Barnfield Road, Exeter, EX1 1RE.

Comments: Big fish are not to be expected from these small lakes — light tackle and small flies are recommended; Black Gnat, Butcher, Peter Ross, etc. Biggest recent catch was a 2lb rainbow.

STAFFORD MOOR

Dolton,
Winkleigh, N. Devon

From Bideford via A386 and B3220 to 3m N of Winkleigh.

Owner: A. C. D. Joynson.

Description: 14-acre man-made lake in attractive surroundings with large summer house overlooking lake for anglers' use.

Species/sizes: 95 per cent rainbow, 5 per cent brown trout.

	Brown	Rainbow
Average	2lb	1lb 13oz
Record	6lb	11lb 1oz

Stocking: Weekly on 'put and take' basis.

Rules: Fly only. Limit 2 brace (1 brace on evening ticket) 1lb and over. No fish to be returned to water. No wading.

Season: 10 April to 10 October.

Permits: dt £4.86; £2.97 after 5pm. No boats.

Permits from:
Stafford Moor Fishery, Dolton, Winkleigh, Devon (tel. Dolton 371).

Comments: Created in 1972 specifically as a trout fishery, this water has already acquired a considerable reputation, which may be measured by the fact that in 1975 no fewer than 27 fish were caught over the 7lb mark; best bag was two brace weighing 17lb 14oz. Average weight of fish caught has steadily improved as a result of careful management. Fly life is plentiful and includes midges, sedges, black gnats, pond olives and dragon fly nymphs, Representations of these generally do better than lures or attractors.

STITHIANS

nr Redruth, Cornwall

Lies N of A394 between Penryn and Helston.

Controller: South West Water Authority (Div I).

Description: Moorland reservoir covering 274 acres.

Species/sizes: Brown and rainbow averaging 12oz.

Stocking: Only with brown and rainbow trout fry not required elsewhere.

Rules: Fly only. Limit: none. Size limit: 7in. Fishing 9am until one hour after sunset.

Season: 16 March to 30 September.

Permits: st £7.50; wt £2; dt 50p. Half-price for OAPs, disabled and juniors. No boats.

Permits from:
F. Hollis Tackle Shop, Tresevern, Goonlaze, Stithians;
Golden Lion, Menherion;
Carnmenellis Post Office, Redruth.

Comments: As will be seen by the size limit, big fish are not to be expected from this water, though a 2lb brown trout has been taken. Flies should be on the small side also   Black and Peacock Spider, Butcher, Peter Ross and sedge patterns are recommended.

TAMAR LAKE (LOWER)

nr Kilkhampton,
Bude, Cornwall

Off A39 from Bude (5m).

Controller: South West Water Authority (Div II).

Description: 51-acre reservoir in lovely Tamar Valley not far from popular seaside resort of Bude.

Species/sizes: Mixed fishery containing rudd, carp, brown trout and stocked rainbows.

Stocking: Fish surplus to outside requirements only.

Rules: Fly and bait fishing allowed, single hooks only. Limit: 2 brace 10in and over. Fishing 9am to one hour after sunset.

Season: All year for rainbows. 16 March to 30 September for brown trout.

Permits: st £7.50; wt £2; dt 50p. OAPs, disabled and juniors half-price. No boats.

Permits from: Cottage by dam.

Comments: Marks a departure for waters in this area in being a mixed fishery. Usual fly patterns take fish.

TAMAR LAKE (UPPER)

nr Kilkhampton,
Bude, Cornwall

Controller: South West Water Authority (Div II).

Description: New reservoir opening for first time in 1976 — 81 acres.

Species/sizes: Brown and rainbow.

Stocking: This water was initially stocked with 1000 brown trout and 2000 rainbows, and further stocking will take place at intervals.

Rules: Fly only. Limit: 3 brace 10in and over. Fishing 9am to one hour after sunset.

Season: 1 April to 12 October.

Permits: st £40; wt £8; dt £1.50. Half price for OAPs, disabled and juniors. Boats: £2 day, £1 after 4pm.

Permits from: Self-service unit (wt and dt); st from Information Office, South West WA, 3—5 Barnfield Road, Exeter, EX1 1RE. Boats from warden on site.

TOTTIFORD
see Kennick and Tottiford

TRENCREEK FARM FISHERY

St Austell, Cornwall

Take A390 W from St Austell and after about 3m turn on to B3287 — lakes are 1m along on left.

Owner: Trencreek Farm Caravan and Chalet Park.

Description: Lakes covering 2½ acres.

Species/sizes: Brown and rainbow.

	Brown	Rainbow
Average	12oz	12oz
Record	—	3lb 1oz

Stocking: At start of season.

Rules: Fly only. Limit: one brace 9in and over.

Season: 15 March to 30 September (brown trout). Rainbows all year.

Permits: dt £1 (reductions for juveniles).

Permits from: Owners at Hewaswater, St. Austell, Cornwall PL26 7JG (tel. Grampound Road 882540).

WISTLANDPOUND

nr Barnstaple, Devon

Take A39 NE of Barnstaple, after 10m turn right on to B3226. Turn right again and reservoir is on left.

Controller: South West Water Authority (Div II).

Description: Attractive reservoir of some 41 acres, 7m NE of Barnstaple near Blackmore Gate.

Species/sizes: Brown and rainbow averaging 1lb.

Stocking: Pre-season with browns and rainbows.

Rules: Fly only. Limit: 3 brace 10in and over. Fishing sunrise to one hour after sunset.

Season: 1 April to 12 October.

Permits: st £20; wt £5; dt £1. Half-price for OAPs, disabled and juniors. No boats.

Permits from: Self-service unit (wt and dt); st from Information Office, South West WA, 3—5 Barnfield Road, Exeter EX1 1RE.

Comments: In 1975 this reservoir produced 733 trout averaging just over 1lb. Standard patterns are mostly used.

7 The Thames Region

THAMES WATER AUTHORITY
Reading Bridge House, Reading, Berks., RG1 8PR (tel. 0734-583583).
Director of Scientific Services: Hugh Fish, OBE.
Amenity and Fisheries Manager: D. Parton.
Regional Fisheries Officer: M. J. Bulleid (tel. as above, ext. 319).

Trout licences: Single combined licence for all rod and line fishing at £2 year, 50p a month and 25p a day. No licence required for juniors under 16. OAPs and disabled, 25p year.

Close seasons: It is anticipated that the new Thames Water byelaws will come into force in September 1976. Until such time, and where no byelaw exists to the contrary, the close season for brown trout is as laid down in Schedule 1 of the Salmon and Freshwater Fisheries Act 1975: between 30 September and 1 March. No close season for rainbows unless specified by byelaws. These dates cover all waters in the Thames area, except those in the Kent River Division: 1 October to 31 March (except Great Sanders and Darwell Reservoirs: 16 October to 31 March).

Metropolitan Water Division (for ex-MWB reservoirs)
Divisional Manager: L. O. Wild, New River Head Laboratories, 177 Rosebery Avenue, London, EC1R 4TP (tel. 01-278 3300).

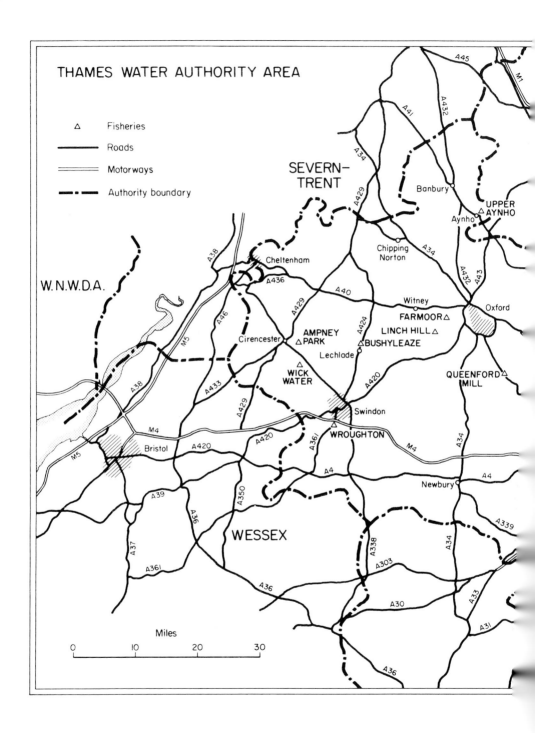

THAMES WATER AUTHORITY AREA

△   Fisheries

———   Roads

===   Motorways

—·—·   Authority boundary

SEVERN-TRENT

W.N.W.D.A.

WESSEX

Cheltenham
Cirencester
AMPNEY △ PARK
△ WICK WATER
Lechlade
Swindon
△ WROUGHTON
Bristol
Newbury
Banbury
Chipping Norton
Witney
FARMOOR △
LINCH HILL △
△ BUSHYLEAZE
Oxford
QUEENFORD △ MILL
UPPER △ AYNHO
Aynho

Miles
0   10   20   30

A45   M1   A41   A432   A34   A429   A38   A436   A40   A424   A34   A432   A43   A46   M5   A429   A38   A433   A429   A420   A34   M4   A420   A361   M4   A4   A4   A39   A350   A36   A37   A361   A36   A338   A303   A34   A339   A30   A33   A31   A36

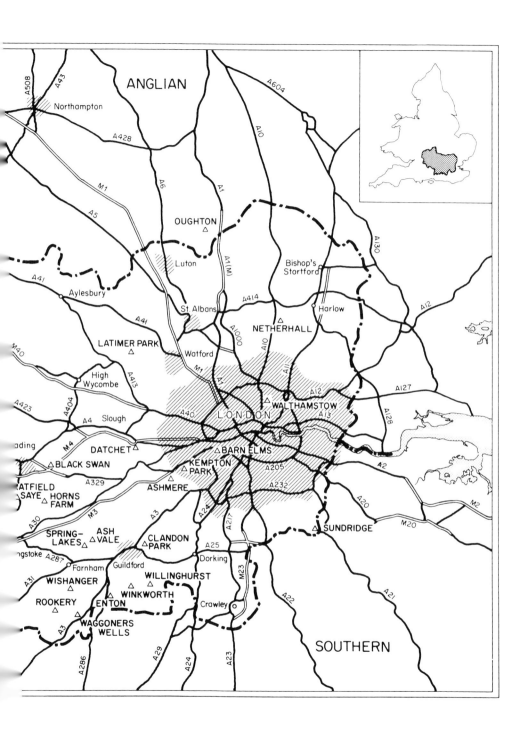

The Surge of Great Rainbows at Sundridge

reflections from GEOFFREY BUCKNALL

The three Sundridge lakes lie on the floor of the North Downs between Sevenoaks and Westerham. The River Darent, once a noted trout stream, flows through them and the general tone of the water is alkaline from the chalk hills. The lakes themselves are old greensand workings, having the characteristic changes of depth common to most worked-out pits turned into fisheries.

The recent history of the lakes is interesting. After the workings had flooded, the two lakes became a coarse fishery, eventually noted for the great carp. Many carp anglers avowed that these fish were second only to those of famous Redmire in size. Although many of them were washed away by the catastrophic Darent Valley floods some years ago, even now carp of enormous size flourish, apparently without bad effect on the trout fishing — though plans to transfer them to other waters are now in progress.

The floods moved fish populations right through the valley, and shortly afterwards the owner decided to let the water for trout fishing. My bid, on behalf of the Rod & Line shop, was accepted.

The first policy decision was made in favour of season ticket fishing as an extension of the retail service given by the shop. Being keen golfers, my partner and I were very conscious of the way in which that sport gives its followers facilities for tuition, choice of equipment and a place to use it as an all-in service. Season ticket fishing was favoured against day-permits because of the limited area of water available, so close to London. We did not want a crowded fishery; nor did we relish the thought of turning people away.

The next decision was to make Sundridge a 'big fish water'. Remember, we are talking about a time, several years ago, when intensive weight production was relatively unknown on trout farms, and perhaps only Two Lakes in Hampshire or Coldingham Loch in Scotland were noted for exceptionally large fish. Today, when we expect a few nine-pounders at Sundridge, a mere four-pounder is a nice, run-of-the-mill fish; whereas ten years ago such a rainbow was thought of as the catch of a lifetime, nowadays I expect to catch half-a-dozen four pounders each year.

When Sundridge opened, some eight years ago, it gained an immediate reputation for large trout and some anglers joined specifically for the chance to break the record for that species.

To take a closer look at the nature of the fishery is to understand its development and problems in the early days. Two lakes were fished, the large deep one for trout, the lower small one for coarse fish, notably carp. The trout lake covered some 20 acres with varying depths, having shallow bays where weed easily reached the surface and where, a few feet away, the lake floor suddenly fell away into 50-foot holes. This lake had lost a high proportion of its fish population in the floods. The insect life was very rich but an entomological survey revealed, alas, that this richness was predominately confined to bottom-living fauna — snails, shrimps, corixa, hoglouse and leech. We knew that early fishing would be directed towards the bottom with sunk line and that surface rises would be scarce until such time as the lake floor was cropped by the fish.

In those day you only had to place boot on bank to see hordes of corixa and the like scuttling for safety, but today, while the crustacea are there still, the effect of continuous trout feeding has been to clear the bottom extensively and to force trout to hunt on the surface for hatching nymphs and floating flies.

Intensive stocking was, therefore, a necessity, not so much to provide good sport — for a rate of 50 fish per acre will ensure that — as to increase eventually the amount of surface feeding so that true fly fishermen would have as much opportunity to enjoy their sport as the lure addict and his sinking line.

Even from the first summer there were sporadic rises to buzzer, lake olive and the occasional sparse hatches of sedge. A predominant fly was the Alder, the larvae of which feed extensively on sedge, and one of the pleasant consequences of intensive stocking was the removal of the Alder to such an extent that sedge flies are now fairly prolific, enabling our dry-fly purists to enjoy fine sport on summer evenings.

To this day we still stock at a rate in excess of 7000lb of trout per annum, though naturally this has to be on a replacement basis of several smaller stockings spread out over the season. To afford variety we introduce fish over a wide size range, from 1½lb to double-figure fish. We have had occasional inputs of brown trout, but the emphasis remains on the rainbow because the brown breeds naturally in the Darent system and there is always a vestigial population in the lake, sometimes of enormous bottom-loving brutes of pike-like behaviour.

Rainbows thrive in the water, the deeps furnishing retreat for summer heat and light. Their diet is varied once they have learned that they have to forage for their food, a process which can take up to a fortnight's hunger pangs from the last stew pellet. The learning, though, is slow, and at first many unlikely things are taken for food, including the unnatural lure.

I found a handful of catkins in the tummy of a fish, relating it to a place where branches swept the water and wave action moved the catkins sinuously. In Spring the tadpole and frog are hunted, in late summer the fry shoals are raided voraciously, especially along the shallow shelves of the lake.

A problem at Sundridge is that new fish plummet into deep holes for a few days after introduction where they are very easily raked by big lures on fast sinking lines. A sad factor we cannot guard against is that a high proportion of stock fish are taken before they have learned the craft of identifying natural food. This means that the imitative fly fisherman is fishing for the surviving remnant, or the older fish which have become acclimatized.

This problem remains with us, unsolved, and I know of few fishery managers who have solved it, except perhaps Alex Behrendt at Two Lakes, who fences off his stock in an area of his lake to allow them to learn the ways of the wild before he removes the chicken wire barrier between them and the angler. Commercially, it may be no problem; anglers generally like easy fish on the stripped lure, but most angler-managers, like myself, yearn to provide a 'quality of sport'. We ameliorate the trouble by strict, though fair, bag limits which allow one season's survivors to winter through as fairly wild stock for the following year. Fry stocking would be impossible at Sundridge due to the predation on small fish by larger ones and the small number of chub and perch, ever present.

Three years after opening it was decided to abandon the smaller, shallow lake as a coarse fishery and to switch it to trout. The main reason was that anglers simply will not pay a reasonable price for even fine carp fishing and poaching was far more of a problem there than on the trout lake. The characteristics of the two lakes were completely different, and in this smaller lake the fish became great surface feeders, favoured by our nymph and dry-fly men. We soon placed this lake under a floating-line rule, and we plan to extend this control to the size of hook and type of fly used there. A further small lake is being opened during the coming year and it is planned to keep this exclusively for dry-fly only. Thus the group of lakes will cater for every type of fly fisherman.

As the years went by the average weight of fish grew as bigger fish were being made available from the trout farms. I remember the very first opening day, when I walked up to the lake in swirling snow to see a boat angler stuck fast into a five-pounder, which was probably the biggest rainbow ever taken in Kent at that time — until Mr. Lyddon hooked out a 6½lb fish a few days later.

This past year we have recorded five fish, each over 9lb, and the four-pound-plus trout run into several dozen. We cannot expect these big fish to increase in weight before they are caught, but so rich is the food supply that they never go back in condition, and perhaps the most pleasing thing of all is that when a large trout is taken, no matter how long it has survived, it is always a spanking form. If a rainbow does live in the lake for many weeks, it grows into the 'Sundridge shape', very thick of body, brightly coloured and small of head, and such a fish fights with tremendous verve and power.

Our bailiff, Peter Leith, joined us about five years ago when we were having a poaching spree, and since then, by dint of catching and prosecuting them, the offenders are kept at bay. There will always be poachers on trout waters. There will always be a small minority of anglers who break the rules, mainly because they are poor fishermen. But while I can feel sympathetic to bad fishermen becoming rule benders, we owe it to our majority to take a stern view of those using bait or spinner which they know the rules forbid, so some, though very few, expulsions have taken place. Sundridge, being a big-fish water, offers a temptation, but Peter's high standard of bailiffing, aided by many of the members themselves, has reduced error to the minimum.

How does a typical Sundridge season go? The fishery work naturally starts long before opening day, on 1 April. During the winter, renovation of bank and boats take place, war is waged on the wild mink, a ferocious fish bandit in the Weald, but our two resident otters are spared and always will be. In a hard winter, Peter may feed surviving trout, knowing that modern trout food also contains anti-disease substances. We, the managers, plan our stocking programme and policy for the coming year, and the biggest change has been to convert the various grades of season ticket, one day, week-day, etc., into a single all-in permit, only 100 of which are issued to prevent over-fishing.

Early season fishing is mainly with the lure and sunk line in the cold water, though recently we have had fish taken on the surface with smaller flies. As the weather improves, our buzzers begin to appear, notably a small black fellow, and later on the large orange-silver variety, so named by John Goddard. I find the small Black and Peacock spider kills for the first, and a Grenadier is effective for the second.

Of the lures, perhaps the various Muddlers are the most effective patterns, and I favour yellow or orange varieties of this famous lure. A simple, black hairwing has always been successful at Sundridge, and while many exotic lures find favour, the skill and persistence of the angler is probably the thing that establishes firm favourites.

In early summer, surface rises come into their own, and while some anglers will fish lures right through the season, the more adaptable will now be switching to floating lines, some to fish with single nymphs, others, like former Welsh international teamster, Harry Jeffs, will work wet-flies with great expertise. One of the most exciting things at Sundridge is to see, perhaps to feel, one of the really great rainbows surging at a small fly, for the sheer improbability of that vast V-wave engulfing the tiny offering takes one by surprise until the fly-less cast springs back from the smash take.

I must end with some personal preferences, for I've learned from Two Lakes masters like Barry Welham or David Jacques that the best way to use a smaller fishery is to stalk individual fish with finesse. The cream of my fishing is on summer evenings or mornings, using a small hatching buzzer or sedge to attack rising fish. It is an art too complex to relate here, involving the choice of area, the ability to cast a size 5 line on a light rod, the anticipation of where the trout wants the fly, and how he wants to see it. The striking and holding of big fish on this ultra-light equipment involves some heart-stopping moments, some sad losses.

The lakes are beautiful enough to offer solace, when I gaze across the fields and woods to the high Downs beyond. By evening, flights of Canada geese swoop down in echelons and then, after dark, when perhaps everyone has gone, really great trout emerge from their holes to chase fry around the small islands. Perhaps I will sit for half-an-hour watching the fountains of spray go up from their charges, or the smacking rings of their surface whorls widening across the steel-like surface as it reflects the ever-darkening sky. May this go on for many years yet!

AMPNEY PARK

Ampney Crucis,
Cirencester, Glos.

2m E of Cirencester on A417.

Owner: T. C. Small.

Description: 2½-acre landscaped lake, with island, and half a mile of brook fishing.

Species/sizes: Brown and rainbow.

	Brown	Rainbow
Average	12oz	3lb
Record	1lb 12oz	5lb 4oz

Stocking: Weekly, depending on take.

Rules: Fly only, and only one fly; no hook bigger than No. 10. Limit: 2 brace; others must be paid for — all fish caught to be killed. Five rods only. Rod-sharing for members only, and by arrangement.

Season: 1 April to 15 October.

Permits: st (full) £120, (half, i.e. one agreed day per fortnight) £65; dt £6, evenings £3. Boat (one only) at nominal fee (about 50p). All charges exclusive of VAT.

Permits from:
Tim Small, Stable Cottage, Ampney Park, Cirencester (tel. Poulton 534); to be booked and paid for in advance.

Comments: This lake, which has been extensively deepened, fishes well throughout the season for most of the day. Fairly spectacular Mayfly hatch late May and June. There is a clubhouse.

ASH VALE LAKES

Ash Vale, Yateley, Hants.

Off Lakeside Road, Ash Vale, 2¾m NE of Aldershot.

Owner: Sir Cyril Hancock.

Description: Two secluded lakes, 7 and 4 acres.

Species/sizes: Brown and rainbow, former average about 1lb; no figures yet for rainbows.

Stocking: Every month.

Rules: Fly only. Limit: 4 fish per day, 60 per season. Members limited to 50.

Season: 1 April to 30 September.

Permits: £80 season. Each member allowed 4 paying guests per season. Boats: two at 50p/hr.

Permits from:
Stillwater Fisheries Ltd, Yateley, Hants., GU17 7NH (tel. Yateley (0252) 873240).

Comments: Anglers are separated into two divisions of their choice, to avoid overcrowding: either Mondays, Wednesdays and Saturdays, or Tuesdays, Thursdays and Sundays. Fridays are 'free for all'.

ASHMERE

Shepperton, Middx.

At Felix Lane, Shepperton, near start of M3, Sunbury Cross. About 18m from Central London.

Owner: Mrs Jean Howman.

Description: Two landscaped gravel pits 20—50 years old, covering 4½ and 15 acres respectively.

Species/sizes: Brown and rainbow.

	Brown	Rainbow
Average	1lb 8oz	1lb 8oz
Record	6lb 14oz	8lb
	(1975)	(1975)

Stocking: At intervals throughout season.

Rules: Fly only.

Season: 15 March to 30 September.

Permits: st only at varying rates;inquire of owner at Ashmere, Felix Lane, Shepperton, Middx. (tel. Walton 25445). Two boats on 15-acre lake at 25p/hr.

Comments: A useful water for London anglers, well stocked with brown and rainbow trout. As will be seen from the above figures, 1975 was a good season for the water, with records for both species being broken during one week in May.

BARN ELMS

Hammersmith,
West London

Access from Merthyr Terrace, Bridge Road, Hammersmith. London 5m.

Controller: Thames Water Authority.

Description: 20-acre partially landscaped reservoir (maximum depth 12ft).

Species/sizes: Rainbows.

Stocking: At intervals. 2000 rainbows put in for 1976 season.

Rules: Spinning and float fishing with worm allowed as well as fly fishing. No maggots, no ground-baiting.

Season: 15 March to 15 June.

Permits: dt (Mon-Fri) £2, £1.30 after 3pm. Weekends and Bank Holidays, £2.70, £1.80 after 3pm.

Permits from: Bailiff at Gate Hut.

Comments: A former coarse fishery now stocked experimentally with rainbows, but with spinning and worming still permitted — this represents (along with Walthamstow, Kempton Park, and, to a limited extent, Datchet) a lively response to the need for a variety of trout fishing in the London area.

BLACK SWAN LAKE

Dinton Pastures,
nr Reading

Located in Davis Street, Hurst, 3m N of Wokingham, which is on A329.

Owner: Peter Oldfield, OBE.

Description: Attractive landscaped reservoir of 68 acres providing 2m of bank with islands, bays and peninsulas.

Species/sizes: Brown and rainbow.

	Brown	Rainbow
Average	2lb	2lb 4oz
Record	3lb 10oz	9lb 8oz

Stocking: At regular intervals — monthly or fortnightly as required.

Rules: Fly only. Limit: 5 fish. All fish caught must be kept. No wading.

Season: 15 April to 31 October.

Permits: st £130, half-season £70.20;
also new st in 1976 entitling holder to
fish Mon to Fri for weekly limit of 10
fish, £216; dt £6.50 (includes VAT).
Father and son, one shared ticket. No
boats.

Permits from:
Jeremy Bisley, Dinton Pastures TF, Davis
Street, Hurst, Reading, Berks. For dt
phone Fishery Cottage (Reading 345480).

Comments: Although small lure fishing is
popular at the start and end of the season,
Black Swan primarily provides excellent
nymph and dry-fly fishing. Floating lines
are most popular. Shooting heads allowed
but of doubtful value. Season tickets
permit angler to fish on any one day during
the week — he is not tied to a specific day.

BUSHYLEAZE

nr Lechlade, Oxon.

Off Lechlade to Burford road (A361) ½m
N of Lechlade.

Owner: M. Pollard.

Description: 22-acre gravel pit.

Species/sizes: Brown and rainbow.

	Brown	Rainbow
Average	1lb	1lb 4oz
Record	1lb 2oz	3lb 14oz

Stocking: Fortnightly.

Rules: Fly only. No wading. Limit: 3 fish
per day or 2 fish half-day.

Season: 15 April to 15 October.

Permits: st £50; dt £3; £2 half-day (7am —
mid-day, mid-day to 1hr after sunset).

Permits from:
M. Pollard, Rainbows End, Linch Hill
Fishery, Stanton Harcourt, Oxon.
(tel. Standlake 774).

Comments: A new water for which a
definite pattern has not yet become
established. The lake fishes well all day as a
rule. Most fish are taken on dry fly as there
are very good hatches of Mayfly and olives.

CLANDON PARK

West Clandon, Guildford

½m from Clandon Village off A246
Guildford to Leatherhead road. London
30m. Waterloo (by train) 45 minutes.

Owner: Rt Hon the Earl of Onslow, c/o
Weller Eggar.

Description: Two carefully landscaped
man-made lakes, one 1½ acres and the
other 8 acres.

Species/sizes: Brown and rainbow.

	Brown	Rainbow
Average	—	1lb 8oz
Record	—	5lb 8oz

Stocking: At intervals throughout season,
from stock ponds with fish of 1 — 4lb.

Rules: Fly only. Small lake, dry fly only.
Limit: 5 brace in any week. 3 brace per
day.

Season: 1 April to 30 September.

Permits: st £147 (+ VAT). One boat, no
extra charge. No dt.

Permits from:
Weller Eggar, Cattle Market, Slyfield
Green, Guildford, Surrey (tel. Guildford
73386).

Comments: The fishery encompasses two
of three lakes in Clandon Park. The smaller
lake, fed by a chalk stream, is well stocked
with brown and rainbow trout, and is
reserved for dry-fly fishing. Below it is a
newly-formed eight-acre lake, fished for
the first time in 1975 — from April to July
these lakes produced over 700 trout.

DATCHET

Datchet,
nr Windsor, Berks.

Off A4 ¾m from Colnbrook. Access:
Horton Road, Colnbrook. London 16m E.

Controller: Thames Water Authority.

Description: New 475-acre concrete bowl
reservoir.

Stocking: Initially with brown trout.

Rules: Fly only. No bank fishing.

Season: 1 June to 30 September.

Permits: dt £6 to £8 per person. 20 boats.

Permits from: Fishing Lodge at reservoir.

Comments: Some disappointment has
been felt among anglers in the London
region that this vast new reservoir is not
to become more widely available. The
concrete slopes are considered to be too
dangerous for bank fishing and the boat
charges will be beyond the pockets of
many. However, there are prospects of
some extension of facilities once the
fishery becomes established.

ENTON LAKES

Witley, Surrey

Off A283 Milford to Petworth road, 40m
from London.

Owner: Enton Lakes Ltd.

Description: Four lakes in beautiful Surrey
scenery. Large Lake (23 acres), Upper Lake
(9 acres), Lower Lake (8 acres), and Enton
Little Lake (2½ acres). Lakes lie to east
and west of railway and are linked by
private footbridge.

Species/sizes: Brown and rainbow.

	Brown	Rainbow
Average	1lb 10oz	1lb 14oz
Record	4lb 12oz	7lb

Stocking: Heavy stocking at start of season
and at intervals throughout.

Rules: Fly only; dry fly on Little Lake.
Limit: 3½ brace/day, no size limit; all fish
caught to be killed.

Season: 15 April to first week in October.

Permits: None. Fishing for members of
Enton Fly Fishers Club only. (Limited to
60). Entrance fee £15.75, annual sub. £230
(plus VAT).
Boats: 12 available at no extra cost on
three lakes. Little Lake fished from bank
or casting platforms.

Comments: Enton Fly Fishers' Club,
established in 1912, provides some of the
best trout fishing near London. Fish over
4lb are by no means rare. Two comfortably
furnished lounge huts are available for
members' use and there are individual rod
and locker huts. All inquiries to company's
registered office — 62/64 Hartfield Road,
Wimbledon, SW19 3TB.

FARMOOR RESERVOIR

Oxford

Covering 120 acres, this water is owned by Oxford City Water Co. and leased to Farmoor F.F.C. Holds good stocks of heavy browns and rainbows but there is a long waiting list for membership and little chance for the visiting angler. F. Taylor, Tackle Shop, James Street, Oxford, can give latest data.

HORNS FARM

Eversley, Hants.

Off A327 about 4m SSW of Wokingham and 30m from London.

Owner: J. A. Pearce.

Description: Five-acre man-made lake.

Species/sizes: Brown and rainbow.

	Brown	Rainbow
Average	1lb 8oz	3lb
Record	2lb	6lb 8oz

Stocking: Rate of 100lb to the acre aimed at on 'put and take' basis with fish up to 6lb.

Rules: Fly only. Limit: 3 fish (further fish may be taken if paid for).

Season: 1 April to 30 September.

Permits: st £180 for one day per week per season (OAPs and juniors if accompanied by adults, £120); dt £8, evenings £3 (OAPs one-third off).

Permits from:
Horns Farm, Lower Common, Eversley, nr Basingstoke, Hants. (tel. Eversley 732076).

Comments: Another recently-created fishery accessible to London anglers who should not find it too difficult to take limit bags of large trout.

KEMPTON PARK

Hanworth, Middx.

Off Feltham Hill Road, about 4m W of Kingston on Thames. Entrance in Sunbury Way.

Controller: Thames Water Authority.

Description: 20-acre partially landscaped concrete reservoir.

Species/sizes: Brown and rainbow.

	Brown	Rainbow
Average	1lb 8oz	1lb 8oz
Record	6lb 12oz	7lb 8oz

Stocking: At regular intervals.

Rules: Fly only, no wading.

Season: 1 April to 30 September.

Permits: dt (weekday) £2; weekends and Bank Holidays £2.65; after 3pm (weekday) £1.30; weekends £1.80.

Permits from: Gatekeeper's Lodge. Advance booking from Head Office, Thames WA, New River Head, 177 Rosebery Avenue, London, EC1R 4TP. Mark letter 'Fish Permit' (tel. 01–837 3300).

Comments: A popular water with London anglers — good trout taken amid somewhat uninspiring surroundings. In 1975 3847 anglers caught 1830 trout.

LATIMER PARK LAKES

Latimer, Chesham, Bucks.

On B485 about 3m from Chesham and
27m from London.

Owner: C. W. Cansdale.

Description: Two natural lakes and stretch
of river covering 13 acres in all.

Species/sizes: Brown and rainbow.

	Brown	Rainbow
Average	1lb 12oz	1lb 15oz
Record	4lb	4lb 6oz

Stocking: Every 8 — 10 days from own
stew-ponds.

Rules: Fly only. Limit: 2½ brace.

Season: 2 April to 30 September.

Permits: st £140, half season £75; dt £7
(evenings £3.50). Boats (6) at £1 day.

Permits from:
Latimer Park Lakes Ltd., Latimer,
Chesham, Bucks. HP5 ITT (tel. Little
Chalfont 2396). Advance booking
essential.

Comments: An attractive fishery easily
accessible from London in the valley of the
River Chess, one of the few British streams
where rainbows breed naturally.

LINCH HILL FISHERY

*Stanton Harcourt,
nr Witney, Oxon.*

On B4449 4m S of Witney.

Owner: M. Pollard.

Description: 58-acre gravel pit.

Species/sizes: Brown and rainbow.

	Brown	Rainbow
Average	1lb 4oz	2lb 8oz
Record	1lb 12oz	8lb

Stocking: Weekly stocking of 12in-plus
fish.

Rules: Fly only. Limit: 4 brace, 1 brace
evening anglers. No wading.

Season: 1 April to 31 October..

Permits: st £42; dt £3.50, £1.50 evenings.
Boats (3) £2 day.

Permits from:
M. Pollard, Rainbow's End, Linch Hill
Fishery, Stanton Harcourt, Oxon. (tel.
Standlake 774).

Comments: Fish rise well throughout the
day except in hot weather, when the
evenings are most productive. Small dry-fly
and nymph patterns are effective, fast
sinking lines not recommended. Useful
patterns include: *Dry,* Grey Duster
(10—14), lake and pond olives (10—16).
Also, any green-coloured nymphs (10—16)
and black or white lures. The record
rainbow for the water was taken three
days after Christmas, 1975 — there being
no close season for rainbows in the area.
It fell to a Whisky Fly on a 4lb cast.
A specially successful pattern for this water
is the Grey Ghost with tying as follows.
Tail: yellow duck; *Body:* black floss; *Rib:*
medium silver; *Throat hackle:* yellow;
Wing: 4 pure white cock hackles. Black
varnish head may be eyed with advantage
and tied on long-shank hooks 6—12.
Another consistent fish producer is the
Green nymph, tied thus. *Body:* 4 strands
sea-green ostrich herl; *Rib:* silver wire.
Thorax: tied in centre of body with

fluorescent red wool. Best on long-shank thin wire hooks 12—14. Fished either greased in surface film or 3—4ft below surface, moved either in fast twitch or long, very slow draws.

NETHERHALL TROUT FISHERY

Hoddesdon, Herts.

In Dobb's Weir Road, Hoddesdon, less than 18m from central London.

Owner: A Harris.

Description: Semi-landscaped gravel pit of about 6 acres.

Species: Rainbow only, averaging 2lb, biggest around 6lb.

Stocking: Fortnightly through the season.

Rules: Fly only. Single fly. Limit: 2 brace. No boats, no wading.

Season: 1 April to 30 September.

Permits: st (one named day per week) £75; dt (Mon to Fri) £4, but £5 for Sat, Sun and Bank Holidays. All charges include VAT.

Permits from: Owner, at Crown Fishery, Carthagena Lock, Broxbourne, Herts. (tel. Hoddesdon 61048).

OUGHTON FISHERY

Ickleford, nr Hitchin, Herts.

Off A600 about 2m N of Hitchin.

Owner: Burford Trout Farm.

Description: Natural lake of about 2 acres, fed by River Oughton, a chalk stream.

Species/sizes: Brown and rainbow.

	Brown	Rainbow
Average	1lb 4oz	1lb 8oz
Record	2lb 4oz	4lb 8oz

Stocking: At rate of 150 fish per acre, restocked when this falls to 100 per acre based on catch record.

Rules: Fly only. Limit: 2 brace. No fish to be returned.

Season: 1 April to 30 September.

Permits: st £110; dt £5 (charges exclude VAT): Other permits by arrangement.

Permits from:
Burford Ray Lodge, Bedford Road, Hitchin, Herts. By telephone — Hitchin (0462) 4201 or 52855.

Comments: Recently opened for angling, this lake is well stocked with fish of good average size and there is an abundance of natural food, such as freshwater shrimp and snails. Anglers using imitations of these have been most successful.

QUEENFORD MILL

Dorchester on Thames, Oxon.

Off A423 10m due S of Oxford.

Owner: M. Pollard.

Description: 18-acre gravel pit.

Species/sizes: Rainbow trout only, averaging 3lb, biggest 6lb 6oz.

Stocking: Monthly.

Rules: Fly only. No wading.

Season: 1 April to 31 October.

Permits: st £75; dt £5 (one brace).

Permits from:
M. Pollard, Rainbow's End, Linch Hill Fishery, Stanton Harcourt, Oxon. (tel. Standlake 774).

Comments: One of a series of Home Counties fisheries offering the chance of a big rainbow for anglers based in the Oxford and London areas.

ROOKERY

nr Bordon, Hants.

Off B3004 Alton to Bordon road.

Controller: Oakhanger A.C.

Description: New 4-acre landscaped reservoir.

Species/sizes: Rainbows only averaging 12oz, biggest 2lb 8oz.

Stocking: No established pattern yet.

Rules: Fly only. Rods limited.

Season: 1 April to 15 June.

Permits: st £5; no dt.

Permits from: Hon sec: I. J. Cooke, 1 Chalcrafts, Alton, Hants., GU34 2HD.

Comments: Note the restricted number of rods and length of season on this new water.

SPRINGLAKES

Aldershot, Hants.

On A3013 between Farnborough and Ash, easily reached from London.

Owner: Mrs G. A. Homewood.

Description: Three spring-fed lakes covering 25 acres in all.

Species/sizes: Brown and rainbow.

	Brown	Rainbow
Average	1lb 4oz	1lb 4oz
Record	3lb 10oz	3lb 12oz

Stocking: Autumn and spring, and monthly intervals throughout season.

Rules: Fly only; all fish to be killed, weighed and recorded. Limit: 2 brace. Rods limited to 75. Permits not transferable. Wading prohibited.

Season: 1 April to 30 September.

Permits: Subscription only, £85 season approx. Three boats at 50p per person per day. Members may take four fishing guests over season at £3 day. Subscription payable in advance on or before 1 February from Springlakes Ltd., The Gold, Aldershot (tel. 20434).

Comments: This well-established and comfortable fishery is producing sport of consistent quality in pleasant, landscaped surroundings.

STRATFIELD SAYE LAKE

Stratfield Saye,
Basingstoke, Hants.

	Brown	Rainbow
Average	1lb 8oz	2lb
Record	7lb 4oz	9lb 13oz

On A32 between Reading and Basingstoke. London about 45m.

Owner: Stratfield Saye Estates Management Co. Ltd.

Description: Landscaped lake in Loddon Valley.

Species/sizes: Rainbows averaging 2lb; biggest 7lb 3oz.

Stocking: At intervals.

Rules: Fly only. Eight rods only on water.

Season: 1 April to 31 October.

Permits: st £120; dt £5 (+VAT). No boats.

Permits from:
Head River Keeper, The Fishery Bungalow, Stratfield Turgis, nr Basingstoke, Hants. (tel. Turgis Green 543).

SUNDRIDGE LAKES

Sundridge,
nr Sevenoaks, Kent

About 30m from London via Sevenoaks to Westerham road (A25).

Owner: Rod and Line Ltd., Lewisham (address below).

Description: Three lakes totalling about 20 acres in pleasantly-wooded Darent Valley.

Species/sizes: Brown and rainbow.

Stocking: About every two weeks.

Rules: Fly only.

Season: 1 April to 31 October.

Permits: Season permits only at £108. Boats available at no extra charge.

Permits from:
Rod and Line Ltd, 70/72 Loampit Vale, Lewisham, London, SE13. (tel. 01-852-1421).

Comments: A policy of stocking the lakes with large fish is reported to have been very successful. The total input for the 1975 season was 7422lb of trout. Stocking with grayling for winter fishing is contemplated.
For more information about Sundridge, see the article by Geoffrey Bucknall on page 136.

UPPER AYNHO FISHERY

Aynho, Banbury, Oxon.

Off A41, 1½m S of Aynho.

Owner: J. S. Lawrence, Upper Aynho Grounds, Aynho, Banbury, Oxon.

Description: Three attractive man-made lakes covering 5 acres, with stream, in peaceful setting.

Species/sizes: Brown and rainbow

	Brown	Rainbow
Average	1lb 8oz	2lb
Record	3lb 8oz	4lb 8oz

Stocking: At intervals.

Rules: Fly only.

Season: 19 April to 17 October.

Permits: st £140.40 (full rod), £81 half rod. All rods let by invitation only and only on a season's basis. Letting policy adjusted to ensure that no more than eight rods are on the water at any one time.

WAGGONERS WELLS

Grayshott,
nr Hindhead, Surrey

Just N of the A3, between Hindhead and Liphook, about 45m from London.

Owner: National Trust.

Description: Small lake in thickly wooded surroundings.

Species/sizes: Brown trout only (record 3lb).

Stocking: November and June.

Rules: Fly only. Limit: one brace 10in and over. Returns to be left with warden or in letter-box at Fisherman's Hut.

Permits: st £5; dt £1.

Permits from:
The Warden, Summerden, Waggoners Wells, nr Hindhead, Surrey. Warden visits lake daily.

Comments: Lake provides pleasant fishing for small number of anglers. Trees make casting difficult and restrict fishable area. There is a Mayfly hatch.

WALTHAMSTOW (LOW LEVEL ONE)

Ferry Lane,
Walthamstow, Essex

6m NE of Liverpool Street Station (London) and 1m from borough of Tottenham.

Controller: Thames Water Authority.

Description: 20-acre natural lake used as reservoir (maximum depth 10ft).

Species/sizes: Brown and rainbow in ratio 1:2.

	Brown	Rainbow
Average	1lb 8oz	1lb 8oz
Record	6lb 4oz	7lb 3oz

Stocking: At regular intervals.

Rules: Fly only, no wading. Limit 2 brace (3 fish evenings).

Season: 1 April to 30 September.

Permits: dt (weekday) £2; weekend £2.65; half-day (weekday) £1.30; weekend £1.80.

Permits from: Gatehouse (tel. 01-808 1527). Advance bookings from Head Office, Thames WA, New River Head, 117 Rosebery Avenue, London EC1R 4TP. Mark letter 'Fish Permit'.

Comments: A most useful water for London trout fishermen. Along with Kempton Park and the new trout fisheries at Barn Elms and Datchet (*see separate entries*) Walthamstow provides valuable sporting facilities a few minutes from the centre of London. Newcomers to the water — and old hands too — will find the register of returns kept in the gate-keeper's lodge a source of useful data on fly patterns, etc. In 1975 3262 anglers landed 1850 fish.

WICK WATER

South Cerney, Glos.

On Cotswold Water Park spine road at Wick Lane junction, about 4m SE of Cirencester.

Controller: South Cerney A. C.

Description:: Two lakes of 8 and 18 acres.

Species/sizes: Rainbows (large lake) and mixed brown and rainbow (small lake).

	Brown	Rainbow
Average	12oz	1lb 12oz
Record	—	6lb 5½oz

Stocking: Heavily stocked before season with fish of 1—3lb, thence fortnightly.

Rules: Fly only. Limit: 3 fish. Wading not permitted on small lake.

Season: 1 April to 15 October.

Permits: dt £3.50 (+VAT).

Permits from:
Central Garage, South Cerney (Mon-Sat during working hours), and
Membership Secretary, E. R. Harris, The Willows, Water Lane, Somerford Keynes, Cirencester, GL7 6DS.

Comments: Club membership usually taken up (1200 rods) but a waiting list is maintained. Visitors will be impressed with the larger lake particularly — it is old-established, weed and fly life are abundant and being on average about 7 feet deep, spring-fed and pure, it makes an ideal trout fishery. There is a good Mayfly season, and Mallard and Claret and Invicta do well. The rise on summer evenings is well worth waiting for — a large brown sedge (fished dry) and hatching nymph are successful then.

WILLINGHURST

*Shamley Green,
nr Guildford, Surrey*

Turn off B2128 from Guildford about 1½m S of Shamley Green at finger-post pointing east and reading 'Smithwood Common: Cranleigh School'. 600 yards along take left-hand fork to Winterfold. Turn left after 300 yards into Willinghurst Drive.

Owner: J. G. St. G. Syms.

Description: One lake of about 4 acres and smaller one covering one-third of an acre.

Species/sizes: Rainbow trout only averaging 1lb 12oz; biggest 5lb 13oz.

Stocking: Every ten days with fish up to 3lb.

Rules: Fly only, and only one fly until 30 June. Limit: 5 fish. Six rods only on water.

Season: 1 April to 30 October.

Permits: st £120; dt £7.

Permits from:
J. G. St. G. Syms, Willinghurst, Shamley Green, nr Guildford, Surrey, GU5 0SU (tel. Cranleigh 2828), and from
E. A. Groves, Stroud Lodge, Willinghurst (tel. Cranleigh 3739).

Comments: Best times in 1975 were between 10.30am and noon and from 4pm onwards. Over one-third of the lake is 16 feet deep and flies fished deep during hot weather proved successful.

WINKWORTH LAKES

*Hascombe,
nr Godalming, Surrey*

Off B2130 about 1m from Godalming.

Owner: National Trust.

Description: Two lakes formed about 1900 by damming small valley. Upper Lake 5½ acres, Lower Lake 4½ acres.

Species/sizes: Brown and rainbow.

	Brown	Rainbow
Average	1lb	1lb
Record	3lb 1oz	1lb 8oz
	(1975 returns)	

Stocking: Formerly only once, in December but extra stocking was planned for 1976 in July or August.

Rules: Fly only. No bank fishing. Limit: 3 brace of 12in and over. Ground baiting prohibited.

Season: 15 April to 30 September.

Permits: dt £2.50 (two rods). No reduction for one rod.

Permits from:
J. A. H. McKean, 'Thicketts', Hascombe, Godalming, Surrey. Apply by letter.

Comments: These lakes cannot be heavily stocked as the revenue won't permit it; nor can other costly improvements be undertaken; though voluntary help is always welcome. To avoid overfishing, a lake is never permitted to be booked for more than two successive days. Weekday bookings are advised on the Upper Lake as this is much frequented by bathers etc. on summer weekends. Bathing is prohibited on the Lower Lake.

WISHANGER TROUT LAKES

Churt, Farnham, Surrey

On west side of A287 Farnham to Hindhead Road, about ½m S of Frensham.

Owner: Wishanger Estate.

Description: Two lakes of just over 4 acres, of historic interest, peaceful and secluded, near River Wey.

Species/sizes: Rainbows only averaging about 1lb, biggest 2lb 3oz.

Stocking: Three times a season.

Rules: Fly only. All fish caught must be taken.

Season: 1 April to 30 September.

Permits: st £90; mt £30; ft £50; no dt.

Permits from:
Farm Manager (Tony Goodsell), Wishanger Farm, Wishanger Estate, Churt, Surrey (tel. Frensham 2408).

Comments: These lakes were originally monks' stewponds. They have been carefully landscaped and improved to form very attractive waters from which large numbers of rainbows are taken throughout the season.

WROUGHTON

*Wroughton,
Swindon, Wilts.*

Lies off A361 about 3m S of Swindon.

Controller: Thames Water Authority, Cotswold Division.

Description: Medium-sized reservoir covering just under 3 acres; maximum depth 20ft, minimum 2.5ft.

Species/sizes: Brown and rainbow.

	Brown	Rainbow
Average	1lb	1lb
Record	6lb	3lb 8oz

Rules: Fly only. Limit: 2 brace 13in and over.

Season: 1 April to 10 September.

Permits: dt £1.60; half-day £1. Punt (two anglers) 40p extra. Only four permits a day issued.

Permits from:
Thames WA, Cotswold Division, 17 Bath Road, Swindon, Wilts. (must be purchased in advance).

Comments: This water provides high-quality sport for a limited number of anglers. Several fish over 3lb are taken during the season. Further details from A. Knowler (tel. Swindon 24331, ext. 234).

REMINDER

Stocking policy depends on returns. Fishery managers have asked us to stress that whether you catch anything or not, please remember to fill in the form before leaving the water.

8 Wales

WELSH NATIONAL WATER DEVELOPMENT AUTHORITY
Cambrian Way, Brecon, Powys (tel. Brecon (0874) 3181)

Trout licences: As part of a new licence structure to replace the previous 67 different categories, the authority has specified a licence for trout which is valid throughout the area, as follows: season £3 (OAPs, juniors £1.50); week £1.80; day 60p (OAPs, juniors, same in each case).

Dee and Clwyd River Division
2 Vicar's Lane, Chester, CH1 1QT (tel. Chester (0244) 45004).
Fisheries Officer: David Cragg-Hine.
Trout close seasons: 30 Sept to 1 March, Bala Lake, 14 August to 15 January.

Glamorgan River Division
Tremains House, Coychurch Road, Bridgend, Glamorgan (tel. Bridgend (0656) 2217).
Fisheries Officer: Geoffrey Hopkins.
Trout close season: 30 September to 1 March.

Gwynedd River Division
Highfield, Priestley Road, Caernarvon, Gwynedd, LL55 1HR (tel. Caernarvon (0286) 2247).
Fisheries Officer: A. Neville Jones.
Trout close seasons: 30 September to 3 March; Trawsfynydd (browns) 31 August to 1 February, (rainbows) 30 September to 1 February; Tan-y-grisiau (rainbows) 31 October to 3 March.

South-West Wales River Division
Penyfai House, 19 Penyfai Lane, Furnace, Llanelli, Dyfed, SA15 4EL (tel. Llanelli (05542) 57031).
Fisheries Officer: Derek Lee.
Close season: 30 September to 10 March.

Usk River Division
The Croft, Goldcroft Common, Caerleon, Newport, Gwent (tel. Newport (0633) 420399).
Fisheries Officer: Ron Millichamp.
Trout close season: 31 Oct to 4 April.

Wye River Division
4 St John Street, Hereford, HR1 2NE (tel. Hereford (0432) 6313).
Fisheries Officer: Eric State.
Close season: 30 September to 1 March.

Note: Close season dates are exclusive. Trout licences cover brown and rainbow trout, and char. Sea trout (sewin) licences are based on given categories and vary from £4.80 to £21.60 season, £2.40 to £10.80 week and 90p to £3.60 day.

Where Trout may be Smaller but Fishermen Fewer

F. W. HOLIDAY surveys the Welsh scene

Statistics make dull reading. Anyone interested in stillwater fishing in the Principality, however, will want to know the sort of choice available. The Welsh Sports Council lists some 133 Welsh reservoirs with a total area of 11,843 acres, of which eight are of 500 acres and over. The council also lists 200 lakes covering 6,711 acres. A quarter of these are 25 acres and over. This is a lot of water by any count.

Not all Welsh lakes are available to the public; a number are still feudalistically in private hands although these tend to get less. Refreshingly, Wales is almost free of that angling non sequitur — the heavily-stocked stewpond in which declining Etonians can flop a languid fly after eating a sandwich wrapped in the *Financial Times*. Many prefer the wild trout of Welsh uplands even if they are only a quarter the size of fish elsewhere. Admittedly this could be sour grapes, although a similar outlook prevails among climbers who eschew the expanding piton and liken it to arriving on the summits of mountains via helicopter. If fishing is to be rigidly equated with the end result, then all of us had better buy some nets.

A fatuity besets most Welsh stillwater fisheries. With fascinated gaze the controlling officials of these fisheries have watched the price of tickets at English reservoirs rocket from a few shillings a day up to several pounds. A nod being as good as a wink to a blind donkey — especially when it knows nothing about biology — they moved in for the kill. Waters which had carried a modest price-tag for years were soon £1 a day and upwards. In many cases a nominal restocking was carried out to placate outraged natives who found no difference whatever between the water they had fished at the old and the new prices. But the reason for the change was not hard to discover.

The major reorganization which ushered out the old river authorities and gave birth to area water authorities was a bureaucrat's dream come true. Even junior engineers found themselves provided with a new Range Rover at public expense. Staffs proliferated and each area office became a sort of mini-Whitehall. Costs, of course, went through the roof — and were instantly passed down to everyone who so much as touched water, including the angler. Even farmers with excellent springs on their property had to pay a water rate. One official had a special number-plate fitted to his vehicle at a reported cost of a thousand pounds. Logic, restraint and good housekeeping had become quaint Victorian memories. To expect fair charges for fishing during this bureaucratic bonanza would have been unrealistic.

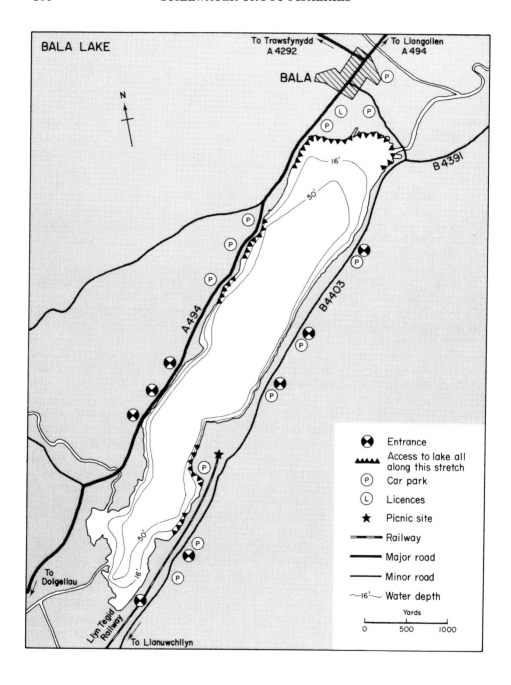

BALA LAKE

To Trawsfynydd
A 4292

To Llangollen
A 494

BALA

N

B 4391

16'

50'

A 494

B 4403

50'

16'

To Dolgellau

Llyn Tegid Railway

To Llanuwchllyn

⊗ Entrance

▲▲▲ Access to lake all along this stretch

Ⓟ Car park

Ⓛ Licences

★ Picnic site

▬ Railway

▬ Major road

▬ Minor road

~16'~ Water depth

Yards

0   500   1000

Compared to Ireland, Wales is geographically unlucky. The western half of Ireland, with its reefs and escarpments of limestone, provides a series of watersheds for shallow lakes with pH 7-plus values. Wales, on the other hand, with so many of its watersheds composed of ancient Silurian rocks, has to be content with pH 7-minus values. The difference, as we all know, means much less food and slower-growing fish. Instead of the burly four-pound youngish trout one so often encounters in the alkaline Shannon system, for instance, one finds that most Welsh stillwater trout range from four to the pound to the occasional pounder; fish bigger than this have usually adapted themselves to a feeding-routine almost pike-like in character.

The ph values attaching to stillwaters is, in fact, a good criterion upon which charges should be based. The lower the pH value the lower the overall quality of the fishing and therefore the lower the relative price that should be charged. Rapid growth (and big, well-shaped trout) is the result of good feeding, not the result of stock brought from the hatchery. Many water authorities seem totally ignorant of this well-known fact, if we are to judge by the restocking of acid upland waters which are already overstocked. But perhaps we are naive and it is really a political exercise to justify the absurd price increases in the annual balance-sheet.

A newcomer to Welsh stillwater fisheries, especially one with small children and a tight budget, could do worse than try his hand at Llyn Tegid (Bala Lake). Although it is readily accessible and a popular holiday resort the upper half is usually peaceful enough. Bala is about four miles long and covers 1100 acres. It contains coarse fish, such as pike and perch, and has a reputation for big trout. Trolling with a dead-bait has accounted for plenty of Bala trout up to about 8lb.

Vyrnwy is an example of a reservoir which has settled down to respectable old age (work was started on it in 1881 to supply Liverpool). The fishing is owned by the Lake Vyrnwy Hotel and the trout average a little over half a pound. It is interesting to compare the present catch of about 1000 fish a year to the palmy days of 1899 when a single basket from the lake yielded 43 fly-caught trout weighing 37½lb. The favourite fly for this period was reputed to be a Butcher 'dressed rather big'. Indeed the Butcher is still a good fly. I often use it as a top dropper on a two-fly leader as a change from those other useful flies, the Alexandra and the Coch-y-bonddhu. The Coch-y-bonddhu has been a favourite fly on Welsh stillwaters for at least 150 years. It used to be very popular with Welsh international contestants on Claerwen Reservoir near Rhayader. I have an 1844 third edition of Alfred Ronalds who calls it 'Marlow Buzz or Coch-a-bonddu'. Dressed on a size 14 hook, these flies simulate a small beetle.

The Elan Valley reservoir complex lying on the barren hills beyond Rhayader represents typical Welsh stillwater trout fishing in the slightly acid waters of the Principality. The fish average about herring-size — say three to the pound. Birmingham Water Department has done much to make the 1500 acres of upland water into an amenity centre with car parks, picnic sites, nature conservancy areas and so forth. Speaking personally, however, I have never found the Elan Valley very inspiring as a venue.

Usk Reservoir has long been a favourite with me. On arrival one enters a great natural amphitheatre in the hills with the 290-acre lake covering the floor. In this area of Wales there occur limestone ridges and these account for the River Usk's fame as a trout stream, since they neutralize the acid. Some of this limewater must get into the reservoir — it is built on the topmost reaches of the river — because the trout are better than average for Welsh stillwaters. A good basket will include fish of 1¼lb running up to 2lb and over.

Wales offers much scope for what could be called 'adventure fishing' in the many small glacial lakes high in the hills. Snowdonia is a good area for this sport, although such lakes occur all the way down Wales into the Carmarthen Vans. The lakes of Cader Idris — Llyn Cau, for example, at 1552ft — can produce a day of vivid sport if your luck carries the weather and the mood of the fish along with it. Looking down on Llyn Cau is like gazing into the inky crater of a volcano. The trout may be wildly on the feed or completely dour, according to the rapidly-changing atmospheric conditions. This is mountain fishing so you need suitable clothing and footwear even in summer.

The Edwardians rated this type of angling very highly. A favourite area with them used to be the Llyns of Ardudwy which lie in the wilderness of moorland bounded by the Vale of Ffestiniog and the River Mawddach. It is not very accessible fishing even nowadays. Walter Gallichan, writing in 1903, says blithely: 'The fisherman must be prepared to tramp 16 miles to and from his water, to say nothing of the exercise of casting as he moves along the rough shore of the lake.' A four-hour climb up and down a mountain for a few herring-size brown trout is not everybody's idea of fun. Many would prefer to drive up to a lake like Talyllyn in late spring to fish in what Welsh anglers used to believe was the finest natural trout lake in North Wales.

Few people realize that the centre of Wales is a desert nearly as barren as the Gobi. Paradoxically, the one form of riches it possesses is water. A glance at the map shows how this natural resource is being exploited. New reservoirs are springing up all down the backbone of the Principality in a great half-circle. Trawsfynydd in the north-west forms a chain with the old Vyrnwy Reservoir, followed by Clywedog, the Elan Valley, Llyn Brianne on the upper Towy and Llys-y-fran in Pembrokeshire. At the moment the new reservoirs look a trifle raw but in a few years they will be as beautiful as Vyrnwy and Usk. But they are (and always will be) what Tom Ivens taught us to call 'oligo-trophic' lakes — waters of little nourishment.

The angler coming to Welsh stillwaters, therefore, should be aware at the outset of the advantages as well as the limitations of these particular venues. The majority have great natural beauty, seclusion and are fairly lightly fished. But they do not — and never will — produce the crops of quick-growing trout found in the English and Irish alkaline lakes. To parody T. L. Peacock's *The War Song Of Dinas Fawr:*

> The mountain trout are sweeter,
> But the valley trout are fatter;
> We therefore deemed it meeter
> To carry off the latter.

The flat, tame landscapes of the English southern midlands will always attract anglers who are willing to queue for the big trout. The real attractions of this aspect of still-water fishing have to be weighed against the mountain landscapes where you will need to fish hard to creel half the weight of fish. But you can do it without having a crowd breathing down your neck.

As regards tackle for Welsh stillwater fishing, I am an avid exponent of the simple kit. Let others arrive with bulging rod-rack and 500 flies in the boot. If you want to stow a luxury then shove a fly-vice and some assorted plumage into a big plastic bag; and a second luxury could be a small smoker to cook your first wild Welsh trout. The visiting fisherman, if he tries hard enough, can do as well as the late Oliver Kite, whose fly-selection fitted into a matchbox.

The future for Welsh stillwater fisheries depends on how sane a policy is followed as regards usage. The Sports Council talks rather glibly of the multi-use of water and of the relative compatibility between sports. But water-skiing and power-boating are difficult to fit into any acceptable scheme no matter how much 'zoning' is done. Such sports, if they are not ruthlessly restricted, destroy all that is of value to others — particularly conservationists and anglers. With water-sport facilities it is not possible to please everyone in spite of what the politicians promise.

At the time of writing, so far as I am aware, no study in depth has ever been made of Welsh stillwater fisheries.*

The inquiring angler can only pick his way through works such as Gallichan's *Fishing In Wales* (Robinson: 1903) and W. H. Lawrie's *English And Welsh Trout Flies* (Muller: 1967) and supplement these with the fishing guide issued by the Welsh Tourist Board and the current issue of *Where To Fish*. The opportunities are wider than many might suppose.

*We hope this guide helps to fill the gap.—Editor.

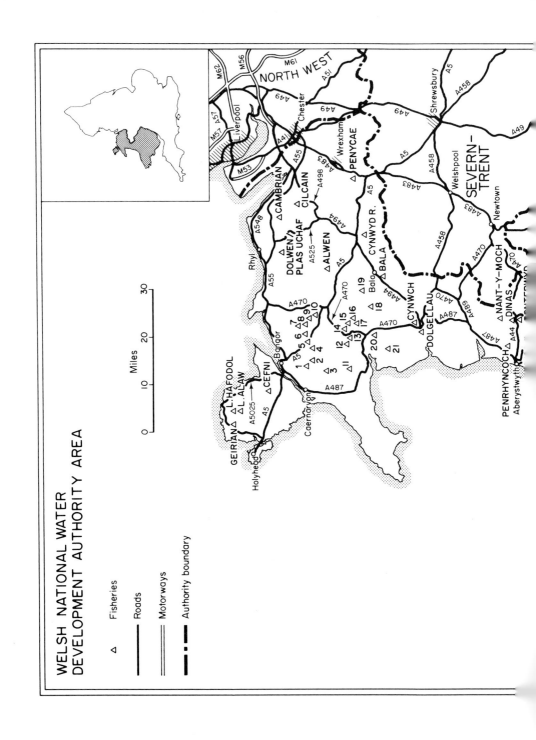

WELSH NATIONAL WATER
DEVELOPMENT AUTHORITY AREA

△ Fisheries

—— Roads

═══ Motorways

▬·▬· Authority boundary

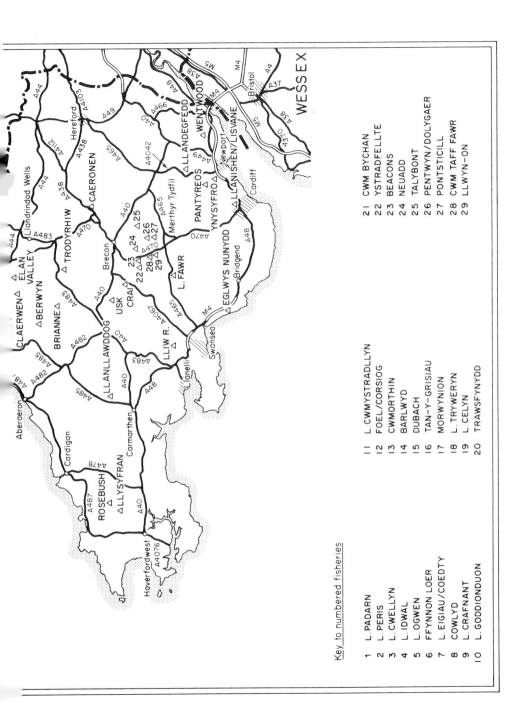

Key to numbered fisheries

1 L. PADARN
2 L. PERIS
3 L. CWELLYN
4 L. IDWAL
5 L. OGWEN
6 FFYNNON LOER
7 L. EIGIAU/COEDTY
8 COWLYD
9 L. CRAFNANT
10 L. GODDIONDUON

11 L. CWMYSTRADLLYN
12 FOEL/CORSIOG
13 CWMORTHIN
14 BARLWYD
15 DUBACH
16 TAN-Y-GRISIAU
17 MORWYNION
18 L. TRYWERYN
19 L. CELYN
20 TRAWSFYNYDD

21 CWM BYCHAN
22 YSTRADFELLTE
23 BEACONS
24 NEUADD
25 TALYBONT
26 PENTWYN/DOLYGAER
27 PONTSTICILL
28 CWM TAFF FAWR
29 LLWYN-ON

ABERYSTWYTH WATERS

Aberystwyth, Dyfed

Controller: Aberystwyth A.A.

Description: Series of lakes lying about 900ft above sea level, formed by damming during the last century to provide water power for lead mines in the valley below.

Species/sizes: Wild brown trout and stocked browns and rainbows.

	Brown	Rainbow
Average	12oz	12oz
Record	5lb 2oz*	3lb
	*from Llyn Glandwgan	

Stocking: Once a season.

Rules: Some waters fly only.

Season: 10 March to 30 September.

Permits: st £30; wt £12.50; dt £2.50 (all + VAT). Reductions for OAPs and juniors. Permit includes limited river fishing. Boats available, £3 season, 50p day (+ VAT).

Permits from: Sports Centre, North Parade, Aberystwyth, and Tackle Shop, Queen Street, Aberystwyth (tel. 7451). Boats by arrangement with Mr J. Rosser, Tackle Shop.

Comments: Lakes provide safe wading and all hold good stocks of wild brown trout (6—12oz) pink-fleshed and good eating. Many are also stocked annually with browns and rainbows; others by the addition of wild trout caught from mountain streams.

PENRHYNCOCH LAKES
Five lakes within 2m ENE of Aberystwyth.

Llyn Blaenmelindwr (OS 7183) is set in a conifer forest and its waters are very clear. Breeding of trout artificially restricted. Good baskets of 8—16oz fish have been taken from this lake, especially in the evening, and some very large trout are known to be present. Fly, spinning, worming.

Llyn Craig y Pistyll (OS 7285), the largest, is a public water supply source. Sound bank fishing all round. Trout average 6—8oz and some of a pound are recorded. Fly fishing or spinning.

Llyn Pendam (OS 7083), set among the trees, has a large population of small trout, but trout of one and two pounds are occasionally caught. Fly, spinning and worming.

Llyn Rhosgoch (OS 7183) lies above road from Blaenmelindwr and within short walk. Breeding occurs occasionally and trout are second to none in quality. The sedge hatches out here and this fly accounted for the 2½lb record fish for the lake. Fly only.

Llyn Syfydrin (OS 7284) has island inhabited by black-headed gulls. Some banks boggy but not dangerous. Trout of superb quality, averaging about 12oz but fish of 1½ to 2lb often taken. Boat is available and, in season, sedges hatch out in good numbers. Fly only.

PONTERWYD LAKES
Brays Pool (OS 7281). Otherwise known as Llyn Llywernog, lying alongside A44 2m from Ponterwyd. Eastern half is private. Trout tend to be small (6—8oz) but numerous enough to give good bags. Fly and spinning.

Eisteddfa Gurig Pool (OS 7985) holds good stock of small trout. Fly and spinning.

Llyn Llygad Rheidol (OS 7987) situated below summit of Plynlimon, is public water supply. Can be reached by following rough road branching off road running alongside eastern arm of Nant-y-moch. Climb is rewarded by some superb views — and chance of good bag of smallish brownies. Fly and spinning.

Llyn yr Oerfa (OS 7279). About 2m S of the Aberystwyth road (A44). Black-headed gulls nest on one shore area. Trout breeding subdued but restocking has given good head of handsome fish of up to 1lb or more, with a shy reputation, calling for cautious approach. Good hatch of sedge. Fly and spinning.

TRISANT LAKES

These three lakes are south of Aberystwyth to Devil's Bridge road (via Capel Seion), where one can often see red kites and ravens.

Llyn Eiddwen (OS 6067) SE of Aberystwyth, few miles from Llangwyryfon. Lake has island ruin at far end, which is rather boggy. Trout run up to 1lb. Fly or spinning.

Llyn Frongoch (OS 7275), alongside road, often yields more fish in 1lb and 2lb range than other lakes. Lake birds include grebes. Two six-berth caravans on shore, with electricity and flush toilets for hire (apply PRO, Aberystwyth Angling Association, PO Box 15, Aberystwyth, Dyfed, SY23 1AA). Fishing with two boats provided is reserved to caravan occupiers, except for Wednesdays, Saturdays and Sundays when permit holders may fish and also reserve the boats. Fly only.

Llyn Glandwgan (OS 7075) visible ¼m from Rhosrhydd Dam — lake is secluded and has good waterfowl population. May be fished all round except for marked sector towards dam end, which is private. Trout plentiful and ½lb fish common Larger fish include association's record of 5lb 2oz. Boat available. Fly, spinning and worming.

Llyn Rhosrhydd (OS 7075) is reached over farm road on which gates should be kept closed. Lake does not allow for breeding, thus size of fish is above normal — 1lb to 2lb. They are not easy to deceive. Boat available. Fly only.

ALWEN

*Cerrig-y-drudion,
Corwen, Clwyd*

Off B4501 3m N of Cerrig-y-drudion.

Controller: North West Water Authority, Wirral Unit.

Description: 368-acre reservoir, 3m long and about ½m wide, divided into three sections.

Species/sizes: Brown trout averaging 10oz (biggest 2lb 12oz); perch.

Stocking: At start of season.

Rules: Top section: fly only (rods limited). Middle section: fly and spinning. Lower section: spinning, minnow or worm. Ground-baiting and maggot fishing strictly prohibited on all sections. Limit: 3 brace 8in and over. Coarse fish caught to be killed.

Season: 1 March to 30 September.

Permits: st £3.24; dt 43p. No boats.

Permits from:
North West WA, Wirral Unit, 69 Allport
Road, Bromborough, Wirral, Cheshire
(st); dt at reservoir.

Comments: Aim is to make Alwen a
trout-only water.

BALA LAKE
see Llyn Tegid

BARLWYD LAKES
see under Blaenau Ffestiniog Waters

BEACONS
CWM TAFF FAWR
LLWYN-ON

Merthyr Tydfil,
Mid-Glam.

Off A470 between 3 and 9m N of Merthyr
Tydfil in Taff Valley.

Controller: Welsh National Water
Development Authority. Taff Water
Division, Cardiff Unit.

Description: Three landscaped reservoirs
— Beacons (53 acres), Cwm Taff (43
acres), Llwyn-On (144 acres).

Species/sizes: Brown and rainbow
averaging 12oz and running up to 2lb (4lb
brown trout taken from Llwyn-on).

Stocking: At intervals.

Rules: Fly only, but limited spinning
allowed at Llwyn-On.

Season: 1 April to 30 September.

Permits: st £12; dt £2 (reductions for
OAPs and juniors).

Permits from:
Llwyn-On Water Treatment Works,
Merthyr Tydfil (tel. 2849).
Cardiff Water Unit, Crwys House, Crwys
Road, Cardiff, CF2 4YF.

BERWYN LAKE

nr Tregaron, Dyfed

Off minor road 5m SE of Tregaron. Lake
lies ½m S of the road.

Controller: Tregaron AC.

Description: Natural lake of 10 acres.

Species/sizes: Brown trout only,
averaging around 10oz.

Stocking: Little or none.

Rules: Any legitimate methods.

Season: 10 March to 30 September.

Permits: st £10; dt £1.

Permits from:
Barclays Bank, Tregaron.

Comments: Typical peaty lake holding
brown trout on the small side.

BLAENAU FFESTINIOG WATERS

Blaenau Ffestiniog, Gwynedd

Blaenau Ffestiniog lies on A470 from
Dolgellau to Betws-y-Coed amid a
scenically beautiful area, and a most
interesting one from the fishing point of
view. The Cambrian Angling Association
has its headquarters here and controls the
sport on several excellent hill lakes. The

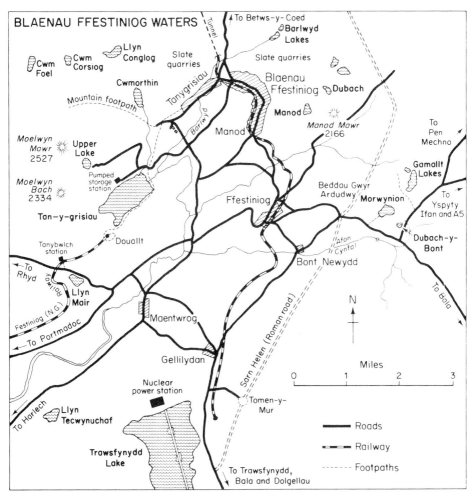

BLAENAU FFESTINIOG WATERS

To Betws-y-Coed

Barlwyd Lakes

Cwm Foel

Cwm Corsiog

Llyn Conglog

Slate quarries

Slate quarries

Blaenau Ffestiniog

Dubach

Cwmorthin

Mountain footpath

Tanygrisiau

Manod

Manod

Manod Mawr 2166

To Pen Mechno

Moelwyn Mawr 2527

Upper Lake

Moelwyn Bach 2334

Pumped storage station

Gamallt Lakes

Tan-y-grisiau

Ffestiniog

Beddau Gwyr Ardudwy

Morwynion

To Yspyty Ifan and A5

Tanybwlch station

Douallt

Afon Cynfal

Dubach-y-Bont

To Rhyd

Bont Newydd

N

Railway (N.G.)

Llyn Mair

To Bala

Festiniog (N.G.)

To Portmadoc

Maentwrog

Sarn Helen (Roman road)

Gellilydan

Miles

0 1 2 3

To Harlech

Llyn Tecwynuchaf

Nuclear power station

Tomen-y-Mur

Roads

Railway

Footpaths

Trawsfynydd Lake

To Trawsfynydd, Bala and Dolgellau

trout run small for the most part — a pounder is a good fish — though there is still a chance of contacting one of specimen proportions. And the views are often magnificent.

Although the lakes are not fly only, the fish rise well to fly when conditions are right. Ground-baiting is prohibited. Unless otherwise stated, the lakes are not stocked, though fertiliser has been added

to some in the hope of increasing the size of fish. Season: 3 March to 30 September.

All the lakes can be fished for a modest sum with permits obtainable from local tackleists — J. Davies, 1 Lord Street, Blaenau Ffestiniog and G. Payne, Ffestiniog; also G. Parry, newsagent, Ffestiniog. R. H. Williams, hon sec, Cambrian A.A. — Onfa, Heol yr Orsaf, Ffestiniog (tel. Ffestiniog 630) — will be pleased to advise anglers.

The area also takes in the noted Tan-y-grisiau Reservoir, on which fishing is controlled by the Central Electricity Generating Board.

Further details of individual waters are given below.

Barlwyd Lakes: Entails 25-minute walk from Betws-y-Coed road. Visitors are warned against soft peaty shore and floating islands. Well stocked with brown trout.

Cwmorthin: Take main road to Tan-y-grisiau, then westwards for short distance followed by 15 to 20-minute walk. Lake is 1330ft above sea level overlooking Tan-y-grisiau Reservoir. It is well stocked with fish around the half-pound mark which rise well to fly as a rule. It is reported to be especially good after dark.

Cwm Foel and Cwm Corsiog: Difficult to reach; west of town on Moelwyn Range. Trout up to 2lb have been taken and scenery makes a visit worth-while in itself.

Dubach: 1500ft above town centre — 30—40 minutes walk. Holds good stock of small trout. Not much use to fly fisher when wind is from north or north-east, as lake is well sheltered from that quarter. Eminently suitable for dry fly.

Dubach-y-Bont: On roadside leading to Ysbyty 200 yards to north-east of town above Morwynion. 2½ pounders reported but average around 3 to a pound.

Gamallt Lakes: Two lakes 1534ft above sea level, entailing 25 minutes walk along a track off Ffestiniog to Ysbyty Ifan road. Route marked with white quartz stones which help in misty weather. Excellent sport with fish well above average for area — about ¾lb; one of 2½lb taken. Lakes stocked yearly with

good-sized trout. Mid-June onwards gives best results, especially with evening and night fishing.

Manod: Between Manod Mawr and Manod Bach mountains above town to east — half an hour's walk. Rocky shores make fishing rather rough (night fishermen please note). Trout up to 2½lb taken, but average is about 3 to a pound.

Morwynion: 1500ft above sea level about 200yd off layby on Bala road near Ffestiniog. Most easily accessible of Blaenau lakes and holds good stock of fish averaging at least ½lb; one of 2lb taken.

BRAY'S POOL
see under Aberystwyth Waters

BRIANNE RESERVOIR

nr Tregaron, Dyfed

This 578-acre water provided excellent trout fishing for three seasons, with fish averaging around the 1lb mark, but was then closed by the Welsh Water Authority. Its future was under consideration as we went to press. Inquiries to the authority.

CABAN COCH
see Elan Valley Lakes

CAERONEN LAKE

Aberllynfi,
nr Brecon, Powys

On main Brecon to Hereford road (A470/ A438) at Three Cocks, Aberllynfi. Brecon 10m, Hereford 22m.

Owner: Vale Fisheries.

Description: Two-acre landscaped lake.

Species/sizes: Predominantly rainbows.

	Brown	Rainbow
Average	15oz	1lb 4oz
Record	1lb 6oz	1lb 14oz

Stocking: On 'put and take' basis. Early stocking of 1lb-plus fish; later, when growth rate is higher, trout of 12oz and some bigger fish are introduced.

Rules: Fly only. Limit: 2 brace. All fish caught to be killed.

Season: 1 March to 30 September.

Permits: £20 (+VAT) for seven visits. Guest tickets by prior arrangement. 4 rods per day only.

Permits from:
Vale Fisheries, Llandow Industrial Estate, Cowbridge, South Glamorgan, CF7 7VY (tel. Cowbridge 2061).

Comments: Caeronen was developed from a small natural lake in the winter of 1973. During 1975, the first fishing season, the average catch was 2.9 fish per visit. The lake fished very well in May and June, with trout rising all day and a very heavy evening rise some days. There were prolific midge hatches. The fish move best close to the trees in the middle and also alongside the trees on the north side. A floating line with small wet flies and weighted nymphs in summer do well. The management offer to help anglers in every possible way. *Note:* Two smaller lakes were being built on this site and were expected to become available for the 1976 season.
    Another small lake is to be opened near Llantwit Major and should provide good

sport for Cardiff fly fishermen. Future plans include the establishment of a hatchery and the creation of lakes in the Vale of Glamorgan.

CAMBRIAN FISHERY

*Afonwen,
nr Mold, Clwyd*

About ½m off A541 from Mold (8m) towards Trefnant.

Owner: J. Sutton.

Description: 17-acre man-made lake (built 1894) in beautiful surroundings. Fishing Lodge designed and built by Earl of Denbigh at turn of century; serves as lakeside restaurant.

Species/sizes: Brown and rainbow.

	Brown	Rainbow
Average	1lb 8oz	2lb
Record	4lb 12oz	8lb 8oz

Stocking: Several times per week during season.

Rules: Fly only. Limit: 3 brace.

Season: 15 March to 21 November.

Permits: st £70; dt (bank) £3. Boat dt; Mon-Fri single rod £4.50 day; 2 rods £6.50 day; Sat and Sun £7. Eight boats available, £2 deposit on booking.

Permits from:
Owner at Cambrian Fisheries, Afonwen, nr Mold, Clwyd (tel. Caerwys 589).

Comments: Lures fished on deep-sunk line do well early on; later a black nymph or dry fly (evenings) is successful.

CEFNI

*Llangefni,
Anglesey, Gwynedd*

A5 to Llangefni then N on B5109.

Controller: Welsh National Water Development Authority, Anglesey Water Unit.

Description: 172-acre landscaped reservoir.

Species/sizes: Brown and rainbow.

	Brown	Rainbow
Average	12oz	12oz
Record	2lb 7½oz	2lb 12oz

Stocking: Usually once, at start of season.

Rules: Fly only.

Season: 3 March to 30 September.

Permits: wt £2.50; dt £1. Boats: 75p day. 50p from 6pm to midnight.

Permits from:
Hugh Lewis, Gwendaven, Rhos Trehwfa, Llangefni.

Comments: Some expansion of canoeing on this reservoir is projected, though its long narrow shape and the fact that it is split in two by a roadway is deemed to make it unsuitable for sailing.

CILCAIN FISHERIES

*Cilcain,
nr Mold, Clwyd*

7m out of Mold on Denbigh road.

Controller: Cilcain F.F.A.

Description: Four small landscaped reservoirs covering 10 acres.

Species/sizes: Brown and rainbow.

	Brown	Rainbow
Average	1lb	1lb 4oz
Record	2lb 8oz	2lb

Stocking: At end of seasonn.

Rules: Fly only. Limit 3 brace, 10in and over.

Season: 1 March to 30 September.

Permits: wt £4; dt £1.25.

Permits from:
Hon sec, 9 Maes Cilan, Cilcain, Mold, Clwyd.

CLAERWEN
see Elan Valley Lakes

CLYWEDOG *see page 99.*

CLYWEDOG *see page 99.*

COWLYD

nr Llanwrst, Gwynedd

Trout reservoir free to licence holders. Apply Welsh NWDA, Gwynedd River Division, Highfield, Priestley Road, Caernarvon, Gwynedd, LL55 1HR.

CRAI

nr Trecastle, Brecon

Off A4067 about 10m WSW of Brecon.

Controller: Shared between Welsh National Water Development Authority (Glamorgan River Division) and CNWR Estate.

Description: 101-acre reservoir at about 1000ft above sea level.

Species/sizes: Brown trout only.

Stocking: None.

Rules: Fly only.

Season: 4 April to 31 October.

Permits: RWA dt at 66p (limited to 600yd of bank in NW corner; three rods only). CNWR Estate dt at £1.25 (50p after 6pm).

Permits from: Reservoir keeper, and Mr. D. Lloyd, CNWR Estate, Trecastle, Brecor

CRAIG-GOCH
see Elan Valley Lakes

CWM FOEL and CWM CORSIOG
see under Blaenau Ffestiniog Waters

CWM TAFF FAWR
see Beacons, Cwm Taff Fawr, Llwyn-On

CWMORTHIN
see under Blaenau Ffestiniog Waters

CYNWYD RESERVOIR

Cynwyd, Clwyd

Water of 5 acres leased to Corwen and District A.C., members only, long waiting list.

DINAS
see Nant-y-moch and Dinas

DOL-Y-MYNACH
see Elan Valley Lakes

DOLGELLAU LAKES

Merioneth, Gwynedd

Among trout-holding waters in this area is **Llyn Cynwch**, held by Dolgellau A.A. (hon sec: M. Salter, Cedris, Dolgellau, Merioneth). Permits from Celfi Diddan Tackle Shop, Eldon Square (wt £2; dt 50p). Several small glacial lakes among the hills provide free trouting for the energetic.
They include **Arran** (3m S) and **Gafr** (4m SW) also Llyns Cader, Cau, Cyri, and Gwernan. Some contain coarse fish as well. Celfi Diddan will give details.

DOLWEN and PLAS UCHAF

Llannefydd,
Denbigh, Clwyd

Turn off A525 from St Asaph (7m) or Trefnant (8m) and proceed on B5428 to Henllan and Llannefydd. Reservoirs are ¾m from village.

Controller: Welsh National Water Development Authority, Dee and Clwyd Water Division.

Description: Two landscaped reservoirs — Dolwen (19 acres) and Plas Uchaf (9 acres).

Species/sizes: Brown and rainbow averaging 10oz.

Stocking: Once, in February.

Rules: Fly and worm only. Limit: 2 brace, 8in and over.

Season: 1 March to 30 September.

Permits: £1 day (limited to 6 on Dolwen and 3 on Plas Uchaf). Boats (1 at each reservoir): 83p day.

Permits from:
Engineer's Department, PO Box No 2,
Plastirion, Russell Road, Rhyl (tel. 2254).
Phone bookings accepted provided
payment is received within 48 hours.

DUBACH and DUBACH-Y-BONT
see under Blaenau Ffestiniog Waters

DULYN

nr Bethesda, Gwynedd

Trout reservoir free to licence holders.
Apply Welsh NWDA, Gwynedd River
Division, Highfield, Priestley Road,
Caernarvon, LL55 1HR.

EGLWYS NUNYDD

Margam, West Glam.

Off A48 Cardiff to Port Talbot road,
about 1m from Margam and just west of
the junction of A44 and B4283 at
Cwrt-y-defaid.

Controller: British Steel Corporation.

Description: Works reservoir of 260 acres.

Species/sizes: Brown and rainbow.

	Brown	Rainbow
Average	1lb 8oz	1lb 4oz
Record	9lb 8oz	6lb 4oz
	(1969)	(1969)

Stocking: In close season and at intervals
during season.

Rules: Fly only. Limit: 2 brace.

Season: 1 March to 30 September.

Permits: st £20; wt £8; dt £2. No boats.

Permits from:
Sports and Social Club Office, Steel
Company of Wales, Groes, Margam, Port
Talbot, SA13 2NF. Tel. Port Talbot
3161, ext. 193.

Comments: Although not perhaps the
most beautiful of Welsh reservoirs,
Eglwys Nunydd makes up for what it
lacks in scenery by the quality of its
fishing, which is excellent by any
standards. Good prospects of something
for the glass case.

EIGIAU and COEDTY

Dolgarrog, Gwynedd

Dolgarrog F.C. water (st £6; wt £4; dt £1)
from hon sec: F. A. Corrie, 3 Taylor
Avenue, Dolgarrog, Conway, Gwynedd.

EISTEDDFA GURIG POOL
see under Aberystwyth Waters

ELAN VALLEY LAKES

nr Rhayader, Radnor, Powys
CABAN COCH, CLAERWEN, CRAIG-GOCH, DOL-Y-MYNACH GARREG-DDU, PEN-Y-GARREG

Take Elan Valley road (B4518) from
Rhayader, lakes lie to N and W 2—3m
along.

Owner: Elan Estate.

Description: This watershed includes
1200 acres of reservoir, 60 acres of
natural lakes and 50 miles of streams and
rivers. Lakes: Caban Coch (300 acres),
Claerwen (650), Craig-Goch (217),
Dol-y-Mynach (40), Garreg-ddu (200),
Pen-y-Garreg (124).

Species/sizes: Brown and rainbow (Claerwen, Craig-Goch and Dol-y-Mynach hold browns only).

	Brown	Rainbow
Average	8oz	8oz
Record	7lb	2lb 8oz

Stocking: Pen-y-Garreg, Garreg-ddu and Caban Coch are stocked at intervals throughout season. Other lakes contain abundance of brown trout and are not stocked.

Rules: Fly only on all except Craig-Goch, on which spinning is allowed. Bag: 6 brace per day, 10in and over.

Season: 16 April to 30 September (from 1 March on Claerwen, Craig Goch and Dol-y-Mynach).

Permits:
Caban Coch, Garreg-ddu, Pen-y-Garreg: st £20; wt £6.60; dt £1.80.
Others: st £20; wt £4.40; dt 90p.
One boat on each lake except Craig-Goch and Dol-y-Mynach: £1 oars, £2.50 outboard.

Permits from:
Bailiff at Kingsfield, nr Elan Valley Hotel; Estate Office, Elan Village, nr Rhayader, (tel. 449);
or Elan Valley Hotel (residents).

Comments: The construction of six dams across the valley of the rivers Elan and Claerwen has formed a series of large lakes with a capacity of 22,000 million gallons supplying water for Birmingham. The surroundings are impressive, the fishing variable. April to June is usually best; smallish flies preferred. The lakes are deep, but fish feed in the shallower water near the side. Anglers may find the trout rise more freely on the stocked waters, for which the charges are somewhat higher.

FFESTINIOG LAKE
see Tan-y-grisiau

FFYNON LOER
see Llyn Ogwen

GAMALLT LAKES
see under Blaenau Ffestiniog Waters

GARREG-DDU
see Elan Valley Lakes

GEIRIAN LAKES

Llanfechell
Anglesey, Gwynedd

8m N of A5 from Bangor to Holyhead.

Owner: E. G. Mounfield.

Description: Natural lakes covering 26 acres.

Species/sizes: Mostly brown trout ranging from about 1lb up to 4lb or so. Some rainbows.

Stocking: Has been stocked annually for over 50 years.

Rules: Fly only. Size limit: 16in.

Season: 3 March to 30 September.

Permits: dt £1.50 (includes use of boat).

Permits from:
Owner at Geirian Bungalow, Llanfechell, Anglesey.

Comments: May and September are usually the best months. More anglers fish wet fly, but in calm, warm weather dry fly seems best.

LLANBERIS LAKES

Llanberis, Gwynedd

A4086 from Caernarvon to Capel Curig runs parallel with lakes for 2m. Lakes easily accessible from Llanberis.

Controller: Gwynedd River Division, Welsh National Water Development Authority.

Description: Situated in heart of Snowdonia, lakes consist of Llyn Padarn, about 2m long, and Llyn Peris, joined to Padarn by a stream known as Rhyd y Bala. Lakes are over 100ft deep in places.

Species/sizes: Brown trout and char.

	Brown	Char
Average	6oz	6oz
Record	4lb	12oz

Stocking: At start of season.

Rules: Fly, spinning and bait fishing, but no ground baiting.

Season: 3 March to 30 September.

Permits: st £7.50; wt £2.50; dt £1. WNWDA licence required. Boats available for hire.

Permits from:
Gwynedd River Division, WNWDA; and Mr Evans, Castle Gift Shop, High Street, Llanberis.

Comments: Llyn Padarn is noted for its evening rises and sport can be excellent at these times. In May it pays to fish the deeper water, but as the season progresses the trout rise closer inshore. The best drifts run parallel to the shores; the water is shallower on the Llanberis side. Char are taken in the deeps and dawn is said to be the best time to try for them. They are caught on fly and spinner. Flies in sizes 13 or 14 are recommended.

For further details apply to hon sec, Seiont, Gwyrfai and Llyfni Angling Society: H. G. Williams, Pennant, Bontnewydd, Gwynedd.

LLANDEGFEDD

Pontypool, Gwent

Between Pontypool and Usk, 2m E of A4042 Newport to Pontypool road from village of New Inn and 7m from M4, Abergavenny exit.

Controller: Welsh National Water Development Authority, Taff Water Division.

Description: 435-acre landscaped reservoir.

Species/sizes: Brown and rainbow.

	Brown	Rainbow
Average	1lb 8oz	1lb 12oz
Record	5lb	4lb 12oz

Stocking: At intervals.

Rules: Fly only.

Season: 15 April to 14 October.

Permits: st £40; dt £2 (reductions for OAPs and juniors). Boats (16): £2 day, £1 half-day; motor extra.

Permits from:
Water Treatment Works, Sluvad, Panteg, Pontypool (st); dt from self-service kiosk at reservoir.

Comments: In 1968-9 the entire brown trout population of Llandegfedd was wiped out by UDN. Since then only rainbows have been stocked, with a few browns bred from diseased parents. However, the decline of UDN in the area has been quite marked in the last two years, so for the 1976 season the reservoir is being stocked with 10,000 rainbows and 11,000 browns. The stock fish will vary from 11in stewpond fish up to 2½ to 3lb rainbows from the reservoir's own farm. It is hoped that this will help to bring nymph fishing back into its own, as during the last two seasons the rainbows have become deep-water feeders with lures the most effective method. Boat fishing has been more productive than bank fishing during the day, with most fish being taken from the bank during the late evenings.

LLANISHEN AND LISVANE

Cardiff, S. Glamorgan

Both these reservoirs lie to N of Cardiff within the city boundary.

Controller: Welsh National Water Development Authority, Glamorgan River Division.

Description: Two concrete bowls of 20 and 19 acres respectively.

Species/sizes: Brown and rainbow trout averaging 12 oz and running up to 4lb.

Stocking: At intervals.

Rules: Fly only.

Season: 1 April to 30 September.

Permits: st £12; dt £2 (OAPs and juniors half-price).

Permits from: Reservoir keepers.

Comments: Being so accessible to Cardiff anglers, these reservoirs are subjected to considerable angling pressure.

LLANLLAWDDOG LAKE

Llanllawddog,
Carmarthen, Dyfed

6m N of Carmarthen on A485, 1m E along Llanllawddog marked road.

Controller/owner: R. and H. Alison.

Description: 2½ acre horseshoe-shaped landscaped lake.

Species/sizes: Rainbow trout only, averaging 1½lb, biggest 3½lb.

Stocking: Trout rearing farm on premises enables stocking to be done when necessary.

Rules: Fly only. No wading. Rods limited to 7, no bag limit.

Season: 10 March to 30 September.

Permits: dt £3 (+VAT).

Permits from: Mr and Mrs Richard Alison, Home Farm, Llanllawddog, Alltwalis Road, Carmarthen (tel. Llanpumpsaint 436).

Comments: The owners have found that 'the angler's frame of mind and attitude have far more to do with the number of fish he catches than the tackle he uses'.

LLIW RESERVOIRS (Upper and Lower)

In valley of R. Lliw, S of Crai Reservoir, Trecastle, Brecon. No fishing during 1976 season.

LLWYN-ON

see Beacons, Cwm Taff Fawr, Llwyn-On

LLYN ALAW

*Llanerchymedd,
Anglesey, Gwynedd*

Lies to N of Anglesey 3m SW of Amlwch. Turn N off B5109 Trefor to Bodedern road.

Controller: Welsh National Water Development Authority, Anglesey Water Unit.

Description: Among biggest of Welsh reservoirs, covering 777 acres. Average depth 7ft, maximum 35ft.

Species/sizes: Brown and rainbow.

	Brown	Rainbow
Average	1lb 14oz	1lb 14oz
Record	7lb 15oz	6lb

Stocking: New stocking programme for 1976 on 'put and take' basis.

Rules: Not fly only, but no ground-baiting or swim feeders.

Season: 3 March to 30 September.

Permits: st £20 (£16 Anglesey residents); wt £3.70; dt £1.50; evenings £1. OAPs and juniors half-price. Boats (10); £1.50 day; advance booking required.

Permits from: Fishing Office at reservoir (self-service), tel. Llanfaethlu 323

Comments: This formidable water provides good sport from boats and 9m of bank. Fish of more than 8lb have

been taken. The fly-only rule is being relaxed for an experimental period, with spinning and bait fishing allowed on the lake, except for the north bank.

LLYN BLAENMELINDWR

see under Aberystwyth Waters.

LLYN BYCHAN

nr Betws-y-Coed, Gwynedd

Off A5 from Betws-y-Coed, right over Pont-y-Pair Bridge or Ugly House farther along.

Controller: Betws-y-Coed Anglers' Club (for Forestry Commission).

Description: Five-acre lake lying beyond Llyn Goddionduon (separate entry) in forested area.

Species/sizes: Brown trout only averaging about 8oz, biggest 1lb 12oz.

Comments: Rules, permits, etc. as Llyn Goddionduon, with dt at £1. Although Bychan is a smaller water, much the same angling conditions obtain.

LLYN CELYN

nr Bala, Gwynedd

Controller: Welsh National Water Development Authority, Dee and Clwyd River Division.

Description: Natural lake of about 1000 acres when full, in valley of R. Tryweryn, Dee tributary, 900ft above sea level; used as reservoir to regulate flow of Dee and Clwyd river scheme.

Species/sizes: Brown and rainbow.

	Brown	Rainbow
Average	10oz	10oz
Record	1lb 8oz	1lb 4oz

Stocking: Twice, once at start of season and again in June/July.

Rules: Fly, spinning and worm fishing allowed, but no maggots, keep nets, gaffs or ground bait. Limit: 5 brace.

Season: 1 April to 30 September.

Permits: st £25; dt £1.50 (75p evenings). One boat available at £1.50 day.

Permits from:
Frongoch Post Office;
R. Evans, Bradford House or W. Pugh (tackleists, both Bala).

LLYN CORON

Bodorgan, Anglesey

B4422 from Llangefni towards Aberffraw — turn right at Bodorgan.

Controller: Trustees of Meyrick Estate.

Description: 80—90 acre natural lake.

Species/sizes: Brown trout, sea trout.

	Brown	Sea
Average	1lb 4oz	1lb 4oz
Record	3lb	2lb 12oz

Stocking: Not necessary so far, but careful watch is being kept on situation through anglers' returns.

Rules: Fly only. Anglers asked to keep to footpaths.

Season: 3 March to 30 September.

Permits: st £8; wt £3; dt 50p (OAPs £3 season, concessions to juniors also).

Permits from:
The Fishing Lodge (tel. Bodorgan 230), and
Estate Office, Bodorgan, Anglesey LL62 5LP.

Comments: An early lake (best up to June), but September can also be good. Algae growths can be troublesome in midsummer. Usual lake patterns do well.

LLYN CRAFNANT

Trefriw, Gwynedd

A55 from Chester to Colwyn Bay, then A496 to Llanwrst. Cross bridge for Trefriw then follow signs for Crafnant.

Owner: Crafnant Outdoor Recreation (H. A. Brown).

Description: 60 acre natural lake in tranquil Welsh valley, Snowdonia National Park.

Species/sizes: Brown and rainbow up to 3lb.

	Brown	Rainbow
Average	1lb	1lb
Record	3lb	2lb
	(approx)	(approx)

Stocking: Stocked for first time ever with rainbows for 1976 season.

Rules: Worm, spinner or fly fishing. No ground-baiting or maggot fishing. Limit (rainbows only), 1 brace.

Season: 3 March to 30 September

Permits: st £7.50; wt £3; dt 75p
(reductions for juveniles). Boats (11): £1
day, 50p half-day.

Permits from:
Lakeside Cafe, Llyn Crafnant, Cynllwyd,
Trefriw, Gwynedd, Ll27 0JZ (tel.
Llanwrst 640 818).

Comments: A fine centre for a family
fishing holiday. There are three cottages
and a large flat available for hire, plus
camping facilities, games room, cafe and
trout fishing from bank or boat. Fish
early and late in day for best results; try
reeded area at south-west end from boat.
Full details from above address.

LLYN CRAIG Y PISTYLL
see under Aberystwyth Waters.

LLYN CWELLYN

nr Caernarvon, Gwynedd

Off A4085 a few miles S of Caernarvon.
Holds salmon, sewin and brown trout.
Seiont, Gwyrfai and Llyfni A.S. have
fishing. Tickets: wt £5; dt £1.25; from
Huxley Jones Tackle Shop, Bangor Street,
Caernarvon, and from hon sec: H. G.
Williams, Pennant, Bontnewydd, Caernar-
von. The society also controls bank and
boat fishing on **Llyn Padarn** (*see
separate entry*) and on **Llyn Gadair**.

LLYN CWM PRYSOR

*Cwm Prysor,
nr Arenig, Gwynedd*

About 7m from Bala on A4212.

Owner: Blaen Cwm Farm and Major
Charlton, Banbury, fished by Bala A.A.

Description: Natural lake lying above
Llyn Celyn on River Tryweryn.

Species/Sizes: Brown trout only.

Stocking: None.

Rules: Fly only.

Season: 3 March to 30 September.

Permits: st £6 (local anglers £4), dt £1.

Permits from: W. E. Pugh, R. E. Evans
(tackleists, Bala); Blaen Cwm Farm and
Post Office, Frongoch, also club hon sec:
E. J. Leary, Sarnau, Mount Street, Bala.

Comments: An entomological survey was
conducted by Dr N. V. Jones, of Hull
University, which suggested that the
following artificials should take fish:
Footballer, Buzzers, Claret Dun,
Cinnamon Sedge, Brown Sedge, Mayfly
and nymph patterns to represent caddis
and yellow and black beetles.

LLYN CWMYSTRADLLYN

nr Portmadoc, Gwynedd

A487 from Portmadoc (4m S), turn off
between Penmorfa and Dolbenmaen.

Controller: Welsh National Water
Development Authority, Eyri Water Unit.

Description: 80-acre landscaped reservoir.

Species/sizes: Brown trout only averaging
5oz, up to 4lb.

Stocking: Under review.

Rules: Not fly only.

Season: 3 March to 30 September.

Permits: st £3.50; dt 50p.

Permits from: Treatment Works on access road.

LLYN CYNWCH

Dolgellau, Gwynedd

Dolgellau A.A. water, 23 acres, at 50p; wt £2. Inquiries to hon sec: M. Salter, Cedris, Dolgellau, Gwynedd.

LLYN EGNANT

see Teifi Pools

LLYN EIDDWEN

see under Aberystwyth Waters

LLYN FAWR

Treorchy, Mid-Glam.

¼m from Treherbert to Aberdare mountain road.

Controller: Upper Rhondda A.A.

Description: Natural landscaped reservoir of about 25 acres.

Species/sizes: Brown and rainbow.

	Brown	Rainbow
Average	12oz	12oz
Record	1lb 8oz	—

Stocking: Annually at start of season with 10—13in fish.

Rules: Fly only. Limit: 2 brace.

Season: 1 March to 30 September.

Permits: st £2; dt £1.

Permits from: Hon sec: D. Rossiter, 71 Miskin Street, Treherbert, Rhondda, CF42 5LR.

Comments: Upper Rhondda A.A. have stocked two pools with brown and rainbow trout with the aim of providing more fish for club waters. Eventually the association hope to be able to rear their own trout.

LLYN FRONGOCH
see under Aberystwyth Waters

LLYN GLANDWGAN
see under Aberystwyth Waters

LLYN GODDIONDUON

nr Betws-y-Coed, Gwynedd

Off A5 road from Betws-y-Coed (1½m) and across Pont-y-Pair Bridge to right — follow Red Fish signs from gate entrance.

Controller: Betws-y-Coed A.C. (for Forestry Commission)

Description: Natural lake in forest setting, covering 15 acres.

Species/sizes: Brown trout only averaging about 8oz; biggest 1lb 12oz.

Stocking: At intervals.

Rules: Fly only. Limit: 2 brace 8in and over. Fishing 9am to half-hour after sunset.

Season: 3 March to 30 September.

Permits: dt £1.

Permits from: Mr Parry, Tan Lan Cafe, Betws-y-Coed (next to Post Office).

Comments: Lake fishes best from end of March to end of July with fair breeze. Traditional patterns do well — March Brown, Mallard and Claret, Peter Ross, Alder, Bloody Butcher, Greenwell's Glory and Zulu, with Mayfly and silver sedge in season. Further details from club hon sec: Ernest Jones, 7 Brogethin, Betws-y-Coed, Gwynedd.

LLYN HAFODOL

Rhosgoch,
Anglesey, Gwynedd

S of Rhosgoch to Llanfechell road through farmyard ¼m from Sportsman's Hotel.

Owner: C. W. Grove-White.

Description: Natural bog lake of 3—4 acres according to weed growth.

Species/sizes: Wild brown trout, occasional sea trout. Browns average about 1lb; biggest 3½lb.

Stocking: Tried but abandoned. Wild trout only.

Rules: Fly only. Keep off land on Cae Coch Bank; proprietor will explain why.

Season: 1 April to 30 September.

Permits: dt £1.50 (limited to two rods). One punt available at 75p day.

Permits from: C. W. Grove-White, Brynddu, Llanfechell, Amlwch, Anglesey (tel. Cemaes Bay (040798) 245).

Comments: Lake is shallow and a reasonable caster can cover more than half the fishable water with thigh waders, though a staff is advisable. Some parts are only fishable from the punt and this involves hard work in negotiating reeds and rushes. The lake and adjoining bog are designated as a Site of Special Scientific Interest by the Nature Conservancy and the philosophy of management is to interfere with nature as little as possible — hence no restocking. The lake is unfishable during a drought and prolific weed growth makes wet fly fishing difficult during July and August even in a wet season. Algae bloom has also become a problem. Flies should be no larger than size 10 in a wind and most Anglesey patterns are successful — a Butcher in the spring and a dry small red sedge on a warm summer evening are the proprietor's favourites.

LLYN HIR
see Teifi Pools

LLYN IDWAL
see Llyn Ogwen

LLYN LLYGAD RHEIDOL
see under Aberystwyth Waters

LLYN OGWEN

Bangor, Gwynedd

Also Llyn Idwal and Ffynnon Loer: waters of Ogwen Valley A.A., containing small brown trout. Details and dt (£1) from hon sec: E. Parry, Llwyn y Gan, 2 Rhos y Nant, Bethesda, Gwynedd.

LLYN PADARN and LLYN PERIS
see Llanberis Lakes

LLYN PENDAM
see under Aberystwyth Waters

LLYN RHOSGOCH
see under Aberystwyth Waters

LLYN RHOSRHYD
see under Aberystwyth Waters

LLYN SYFYDRIN
see under Aberystwyth Waters

LLYN TARW

nr Newtown, Powys

Situated at Pontdolgoch on A470. Take
A492 W from Newtown and turn NW
on to A470 for Caersws and Pontdolgoch.

Controller: Montgomeryshire A.A.

Description: A small man-made lake
covering 17 acres, with island.

Species/sizes: Holds American brook
trout only, averaging 12oz; biggest
verified catch, 1lb 14oz.

Stocking: None. Wild fish present in large
numbers, descendants of stock first
introduced in Victorian times.

Rules: Fly only. No cars at lakeside.

Season: 18 March to 15 October.

Permits: st £6; wt £2.50; dt £1.

Permits from:
H. L. Bebb, Home Handicrafts, Newtown
Powys.

Comments: Notable as a haunt of
American brook trout, which give fine
sport on light tackle. Wet fly is said to
bring the best results, fished about 3ft
below the surface, size 12—14, black and
red patterns. July to September is the
best time, particularly fishing towards the
island.

Further details from club hon sec at 29
Rhoslan, Guilsfield, Welshpool, Powys.

LLYN TECWYNUCHAF

Maentwrog, Gwynedd

Also Llyn Tecwynisaf: waters of
Talsarnau A.A. containing small brown
trout. Apply to club hon sec: C. R. Jones,
4 Cilfor, Talsarnau, Gwynedd, for st, £1.50.

LLYN TEGID (BALA LAKE)

nr Bala, Gwynedd

A494 Bala to Dolgellau road runs along
whole of north bank.

Controller: National Park Committee on
behalf of Gwynedd County Council.

Description: Located in beautiful Dee
Valley, largest natural lake in Wales,
about 4m long and up to ¾m wide. In
places it is 150ft deep.

Species/sizes: Holds 13 species of fish,
including brown trout, averaging 2lb 8oz,
largest verified catch 11lb 2oz (1930s).

Stocking: None. Lake over-populated.

Rules: Most methods allowed, though
ground-baiting with maggots is forbidden.
Trout under 8in to be returned.

Season: 15 January to 14 August.

Permits: st £5.50; dt 60p. Boats (10): 50p/hr or £1.20 day.

Permits from: Lake Warden — office adjoining boathouse at Bala end of lake — at 24 Pensarn Road, Bala (tel. (office) Bala 626 (home) 491). Local tackleists also issue permits.

Comments: Bala is mainly a coarse fishery, but it does hold some excellent brown trout. A three-pounder is by no means rare and a Cheshire angler recently caught one of 8lb 14oz. They can be taken on fly. Sport is usually best early in the season.

LLYN TEIFI
see Teifi Pools

LLYN YR OERFA
see under Aberystwyth Waters

LLYNGWYN

nr Rhayader,
Radnor, Powys

1½m left of A44, 4m E of Rhayader.

Controller: Rhayader A.A.

Description: 16-acre natural lake.

Species/sizes: Brown and rainbow.

	Brown	Rainbow
Average	8oz	8oz
Record	2lb	2lb

Stocking: At intervals.

Rules: Fly only. Limit: 5 brace.

Season: 1 March to 30 September.

Permits: st £10; dt £1; Boats £1 day.

Permits from:
Nantymynach Farm, near lake.

Comments: Lake fishes best April to June on warm days with not too much wind. Smallish flies (size 12/14) are preferred.

LLYSYFRAN

Llysyfran,
nr Haverfordwest, Dyfed

Turn right off B4329 from Haverfordwest (10m).

Controller: Welsh National Water Development Authority, West Wales Water Division.

Description: 187-acre landscaped reservoir in Pembrokeshire country park.

Species/sizes: Brown and rainbow.

	Brown	Rainbow
Average	2lb	1lb
Record	7lb 2oz	—

Stocking: At intervals. (Rainbows first introduced in 1975.)

Rules: Worm fishing allowed. Limit: 3 brace, 9in and over.

Season: 1 April to 30 September.

Permits: st £18; dt £2.10 (reductions for OAPs, juniors). Boats (4) £2 day, £1 half-day, 50p evenings (after 5.30pm).

Permits from: site office (dt), and West Wales WD, Mayler House, St Thomas Green, Haverfordwest, Dyfed (st).

MANOD

see under Blaenau Ffestiniog Waters

MELYNLLYN

nr Bethesda, Gwynedd

Trout reservoir free to licence-holders. Apply Welsh NWDA, Gwynedd River Division, Highfield, Priestley Road, Caernarvon, LL55 1HR.

MORWYNION

see under Blaenau Ffestiniog Waters

NANT-Y-MOCH and DINAS

Rheidol,
nr Aberystwyth, Dyfed

North of A44 from Aberystwyth (10m). For Dinas turn north just before Ponterwyd. Reservoir is about 1m, on right. For Nant-y-Moch, turn north just past Ponterwyd for about 4m.

Controller: Central Electricity Generating Board.

Description: Two landscaped reservoirs in Rheidol Valley. Nant-y-Moch (680 acres) is easily larger — Dinas 60 acres.

Species/sizes: Brown and rainbow.

	Brown	Rainbow
Average	8oz	8oz
Record	2lb 3oz	4lb 6oz Nant-y-Moch
		4lb 8oz 8lb 12oz Dinas

Stocking: Both reservoirs stocked with two-year-old brown and rainbow trout throughout season from own rearing tanks on 'put and take' basis

Rules: Fly only on Nant-y-Moch; spinning, bait fishing allowed on Dinas, but fly only from boats.

Season: 13 March to 30 September.

Permits: Cover both reservoirs (separate ones not issued): dt £1.75; wt £8.75 (OAPs, juniors and disabled at reduced rates). Boats (2) for Dinas only, £3 day, £1.75 after 2pm and 75p after 6pm.

Permits from:
CEGB, Bron Heulog, Llandudno Junction, Gwynedd (tel. Deganwy 81397)
Evans Garage, Ponterwyd;
Hubbard's and Compton's (both tackleists), Borth.
Boat permits from Evans Garage.

Comments: As will be apparent from the figures, Dinas produces the bigger fish due to more regular stocking, but Nant-y-Moch holds larger stocks of wild brown trout. A notable recent capture was one of 2lb 8oz. Bailiffs are in daily attendance on both waters and will advise anglers on fly patterns, etc.
NB. Fishing on the nearby Cwm Rheidol Reservoir is let to Aberystwyth A.A. Inquiries to hon sec: Ian Sant, Hillside Cottage, Goginan, nr Aberystwyth, Dyfed.

PANTYREOS

nr Newport, Gwent

4m NW of Newport off Abertillery road (A467).

Controller: Welsh National Water Development Authority.

Description: Landscaped reservoir of 16 acres at height of 400ft.

Species/sizes: Brown and rainbow.

	Brown	Rainbow
Average	12oz	12oz
Record	3lb 11oz	2lb 6oz
	(1975 figures)	

Stocking: At intervals on 'put and take' basis.

Rules: Fly only, but spinning allowed in certain areas.

Season: 4 April to 14 October.

Permits: st £18; dt £1.50 (OAPs and juniors half-price).

Permits from: Reservoir superintendent on site.

Comments: Has not been a very productive fishery in recent years. However, the authority's proposed restocking on a 'put and take' basis should improve matters. The provision of boats is being considered.

PEN-Y-GARREG
see Elan Valley Lakes

PENRHYNCOCH LAKES
see under Aberystwyth Waters

PENYCAE

Penycae,
nr Ruabon, Clwyd

Off A483 at Ruabon near Parish Church, then 2m to Penycae; entrance opposite Penycae Vicarage.

Controller: Wrexham and East Denbighshire Water Co.

Description: Small landscaped reservoir covering about 11 acres.

Species/sizes: Brown and rainbow.

	Brown	Rainbow
Average	8oz	1lb
Record	4lb	2lb 8oz

Stocking: Twice a season.

Rules: Fly only (6 rods only). No ground baiting.

Season: 1 April to 30 September.

Permits: dt £1 (+VAT).

Permits from:
Reservoir Keeper, Reservoir House, Penycae (24 hours notice required by phone: Rhos 840116).

PLAS UCHAF
see Dolwen and Plas Uchaf

PONTERWYD LAKES
see under Aberystwyth Waters

ROSEBUSH (PRESCELLY)

Rosebush,
nr Haverfordwater, Dyfed

Turn right off B4329 about 12m from Haverfordwest and take B4313 for short distances — reservoir lies on left of this road.

Controller: Welsh National Water Development Authority, West Wales Division.

Description: Attractive and secluded 39-acre reservoir.

Species/sizes: Brown trout only averaging about 8oz, biggest 2lb (1974).

Stocking: None.

Rules: Fly only.

Season: 1 April to 30 September.

Permits: st £5; dt 50p (OAPs, juniors 25p). Boats available at no extra charge.

Permits from: Bailiff at Blaenpant, Rosebush (dt);
st from West Wales WD, Mayler House, St Thomas Green, Haverfordwest, Dyfed.

Comments: Although a pounder is a very good fish from this water, anglers may be attracted by the opportunity — becoming rarer these days — of pursuing wild trout in a peaceful setting.

SEVEN SPRINGS TROUT FARM

Caerwys, Mold, Clwyd

On site of Old Tannery Mill on B5122 in village of Caerwys. Approach from A5 (Holywell to St Asaph road) or A541 Mold to Denbigh road. B5122 joins these roads.

Owner: W. Forkings.

Description: Natural spring-fed lake of 1½ acres.

Species/sizes: Brown and rainbow, averaging more than 12oz.

Stocking: At intervals throughout season, depending on catch returns.

Rules: Dry fly, wet fly and nymph only.

Season: 15 March to 30 September.

Permits: st £40; dt £2.50.

Permits from:
Major J. W. Latham, 14 Londerw, Woodlands, Abergele, Clwyd LL22 7EA (tel. Abergele 823666) (st only);
dt from A. H. Fogerty, 29 Queens Street, Rhyl (tel. 54765), and
R. Gadd, 39 Market Street, Abergele (tel. 823083). Boat available at no extra charge.

TAF FECHAN WATERS

Mid-Glamorgan

The Taf Fechan group comprises Upper and Lower Neuadd, Pentwyn, Dolygaer and Pontsticill. These waters form part of the Brecon Beacons reservoir system. They lie opposite Beacons group to E of A470 Merthyr Tydfil to Brecon road, 6-8m N of Heads of the Valleys road (A465)

Controller: Welsh National Water Development Authority, Glamorgan River Division.

Description: Pontsticill, Pentwyn and Dolygaer are linked, covering about 349 acres in all. Upper and Lower Neuadd Reservoirs lie about 1m to N.

Species/sizes: Brown and rainbow. Pontsticill, Pentwyn and Lower Neuadd hold coarse fish as well.

	Brown	Rainbow
Average	12oz	12oz
Record	14lb	3lb
	(Pontsticill)	(Dolygaer)

Stocking: At intervals through season. Pentwyn stocked with 2500 12in brown and rainbow trout.

Rules: Dolygaer and Upper Neuadd fly only. Worm and spinning permitted on Lower Neuadd and Pontsticill. Pentwyn: fly and spinning.

Season: 21 March to 30 September.

Permits: Group permit covers all four waters: st £7; dt £1 (half-price for OAPs and juniors).

Permits from: Filter House at Pontsticill.

Comments: Popular flies for these waters are March Brown, Black Gnat, Black Spider, Coch-y-Bonddhu, Blue Upright, Greenwell's Glory and various nymph patterns.

TALYBONT

Talybont on Usk, nr Brecon

2m due W of Talybout off A40 Brecon to Abergavenny road.

Controller: Welsh National Water Development Authority, Gwent Water Division.

Description: 323-acre landscaped reservoir.

Species/sizes: Brown and rainbow.

	Brown	Rainbow
Average	1lb	1lb
Record	2lb 8oz	3lb

Stocking: By Usk River Division at intervals.

Rules: Fly only, but limited spinning one bank only, June onwards.

Season: 4 April to 31 October (including rainbows).

Permits: st £24, dt £2 (OAPs juniors half-price. Boats (2): £2 day.

Permits from:
Gwent WD at Station Bldgs, Newport Gwent (st); dt from reservoir superintendent.

TALYLLYN

Talyllyn,
Merioneth, Gwynedd

Turn off A487 Machynlleth to Dolgellau road on to B4405. Lake is about 2m from junction. Machynlleth 7m, Dolgellau 9m.

Controller: Tyn-y-cornel Hotel.

Description: Natural lake of 228 acres in beautiful Dysynni valley.

Species/sizes: Brown trout averaging 1lb; biggest 3lb 8oz (1975); some salmon and sea trout.

Stocking: Frequent introductions of trout reared in netted areas of lake.

Rules: Traditional lake flies only. No fishing around marked rearing area.

Season: 4 March to 30 September.

Permits: dt £2. Boats (10): £2 day.

Permits from:
Tyn-y-Cornel Hotel, Talyllyn, nr Towyn, Merioneth (when not taken up by hotel guests).

Comments: Late April and May, June and September are usually best for brown trout, and the last week in August and the whole of September for salmon and sea trout, depending on water conditions.

TAN-Y-GRISIAU (Ffestiniog Lake)

Blaenau Ffestiniog, Gwynedd

Lies to W of A496 about 2m south of Blaenau Ffestiniog.

Controller: Central Electricity Generating Board.

Description: Reservoir covering 95 acres, 1m long and ¼m wide.

Species/sizes: Rainbows only, averaging 1lb 8oz, biggest 10lb 7oz (caught April 1975 by Mr John Hughes and accepted as a record rainbow by the Welsh Record (Rod-caught) Fish Committee).

Stocking: On 'put and take' basis. Aim is 115 fish per acre.

Rules: All legal methods allowed. No wading. No fishing from dam or in front of power station.

Season: 3 March to October.

Permits: dt £1.75; wt £8.75 (reductions for OAPs, juniors and disabled).

Permits from:
Administrative Officer (Fisheries) CEGB, Bron Heulog, Conway Road, Llandudno Junction, Gwynedd (by post only); Reception Centre at lakeside; Royal Stores, Maelor Stores and John Davies, tackleist, all Blaenau Ffestiniog; Tackle Box, Seaview Rd, Colwyn Bay.

Comments: Recommended fly patterns include: Mallard and Claret, Peter Ross, York Special, Coch-y-Bonddhu, Greenwell's Glory, Black Spider and Dunkeld. Lures: Muddler Minnow, Black Lure, Polystickle and Sweeney Todd. Glyn Jones, the bailiff, a well-known international fly fisherman, is willing to give advice and free tuition during weekdays if other duties permit.

TEIFI POOLS

nr Strata Florida, Dyfed

Llyns Egnant, Hir and Teifi. 5m E of Pontrhydfendigaid (B4343). Access from Ffair Rhos crossroads.

Controller: Welsh National Water Development Authority, South-West Wales River Division.

Description: Reservoirs formed from natural lakes of 44, 61 and 13 acres. respectively.

Species/sizes: Brown and rainbow (browns only Llyn Hir).

	Brown	Rainbow	
Average	8oz	8oz	approx
Record	3lb	4lb	

Stocking: Staggered throughout season. 1750 9–14in browns introduced in 1975. Rainbows stocked 1972–74 in Egnant and Teifi.

Rules: Fly only. Limit: 3 brace, 9in and over.

Season: 1 April to 30 September.

Permits: st £10; dt £1 (OAPs and juniors half-price). These tickets cover all three lakes.

Permits from: Licence distributors in Tregaron (Arthur Morgan, Caron Stores) and Pontrhydfendigaid.

Comments: Two other lakes — Llyn Gorlan and Llyn Bach — belong to the Earl of Lisburne; inquire Talbot Hotel, Tregaron.

TRAWSFYNYDD LAKE

Trawsfynydd, Gwynedd

Off A487, 4m S of Ffestiniog.

Controller: Prysor A.A.

Description: Landscaped CEGB reservoir of 1180 acres.

Species/sizes: Brown and rainbow.

	Brown	Rainbow
Average	8oz	1lb 3oz
Record	—	7lb 6oz

Stocking: 800 fish per week throughout season.

Rules: Some areas fly only.

Season: 1 February to 31 August (rainbows to 30 September).

Permits: st £11.96; wt £5.83; dt £1.30. Boats (30): £1.95 day.

Permits from:
Hon sec: H. E. Lewis, Castle House, Trawsfynydd, and newsagents in Trawsfynydd.

Comments: Good conditions for top end of lake (main dam area) are cloudy, stiff breeze and warm. Best times morning (8—11.30 am) and evening (6—8.30 pm).

Flies fished about a foot below the surface take trout. Recommended patterns: Mallard and Claret, Invicta, Blae and Block, Black Pennel, Butcher, Zulu, Watson's Fancy, Dunkeld and York Special (local pattern).

TRISANT LAKES
see under Aberystwyth Waters

TROEDYRHIW LAKE

nr Llangammarch Wells, Powys

Off main Builth Wells to Llandovery road (A483) about 7m from Builth and 17m from Llandovery. Also via A470/483 from Brecon (23m).

Owner: Vale Fisheries.

Description: Landscaped reservoir of 1½ acres.

Species/sizes: Brown and rainbow, with some wild browns.

	Brown	Rainbow
Average	15oz	1lb 4oz
Record	1lb	2lb 14oz

Stocking: On 'put and take' basis. Early stocking of 1lb-plus fish; later, when growth rate is higher, trout of 12oz and some bigger fish are introduced.

Rules: Fly only. Limit: 2 brace. All fish taken to be killed.

Season: 1 March to 30 September.

Permits: £20 (+VAT) for seven visits. Guest tickets by prior arrangement. Three rods per day only.

Permits from:
Vale Fisheries, Llandow Industrial Estate, Cowbridge, South Glamorgan, CF7 7VY (tel. Cowbridge 2061).

Comments: This lake has been established for some 70 years and thus has a more varied fly hatch than Caeronen, which is under the same management—(*see separate entry*) — though the average catch was slightly less at 2.3 fish per visit. There was a hatch of Mayfly in early June of 1975 and also a hatch of very large sedge. A large bushy dry fly, e.g. Zulu or Coch-y-Bonddhu, is often successful. The presence of wild brown trout provides a formidable challenge. *Note:* A second lake has been created and was expected to be available for fishing during the 1976 season.

USK

Trecastle, Brecon, Powys

6m due W of Sennybridge, and N of Trecastle to Llandeusant mountain road.

Controller: Welsh National Water Development Authority.

Description: Landscaped reservoir of 290 acres at altitude of 1000ft.

Species/sizes: Brown and rainbow.

	Brown	Rainbow
Average	12oz	10oz
Record	5lb 6oz	2lb 8oz
	(1975 figures)	

Stocking: At intervals.

Rules: Fly-only rule under review. No wading.

Season: 4 April to 14 October.

Permits: st £30; wt £7; dt £2. Boats available.

Permits from: Reservoir superintendent on site and W. J. Davies (tackleist), Drug Stores, Sennybridge.

Comment: F. W. Holiday refers to this reservoir in his article on the Welsh scene on page 155.

VYRNWY *see page 103.*

WENTWOOD

Penhow, nr Newport, Gwent

7m NE of Newport, left off A48 Chepstow road.

Controller: Welsh National Water Development Authority.

Description: Landscaped reservoir of 41 acres at altitude of 450ft.

Species/sizes: Brown and rainbow.

	Brown	Rainbow
Average	12oz	12oz
Record	3lb 5oz	2lb 14oz
	(1975 figures)	

Stocking: At intervals.

Rules: Fly only, but spinning allowed in certain areas, including from dam.

Season: 4 April to 14 October.

Permits: st £24; dt £2 (OAPs and juniors half-price). One boat available.

Permits from: Reservoir Superintendent, Llanvaches, Penhow, Newport.

Comments: A reservoir very popular with anglers from the Newport area. The provision of more boats is being considered.

YNYSYFRO

nr Newport, Gwent

2m NW of Newport off M4. Turn right off A467 for ¾m.

Controller: Welsh National Water Development Authority.

Description: Two landscaped reservoirs of 16 and 10 acres.

Species/sizes: Brown and rainbow.

	Brown	Rainbow
Average	12oz	12oz
Record	3lb	2lb 8oz
	(1975 figures)	

Stocking: At intervals.

Rules: Fly only, but spinning allowed in certain areas.

Season: 4 April to 14 October.

Permits: st £18; dt £1.50 (OAPs and juniors half-price).

Permits from: Reservoir Superintendent on site.

YSTRADFELLTE

Ystradfellte, nr Merthyr Tydfil, Powys

Off A4059 10m NW of Merthyr Tydfil and 3m N of Ystradfellte village.

Controller: Welsh National Water Development Authority, Glamorgan Water Division.

Description: 59-acre moorland reservoir in Brecon Beacons National Park.

Species/sizes: Brown trout only, averaging 12oz and up to 2lb.

Stocking: None.

Rules: Fly only.

Season: 1 March to 30 September.

Permits: st £12 (also covers **Beacons, Cantref** and **Llwyn On**); dt £1.

Permits from: Llwyn On Filter House.

Comments: A useful water for those who like fishing for wild trout in surroundings to match.

REMINDER

We have not as a rule mentioned in the individual entries the need for a regional water authority licence as well as a permit, but this is usually necessary, except for the relatively few cases where the fishery holds a general licence.

9 Wessex

WESSEX WATER AUTHORITY
Techno House, Recliffe Way, Bristol, BSL 6NY (tel. Bristol (0272) 25491 or 25462).
Chief Fisheries and Recreations Officer: Kennedy S. Brown (tel. Bristol (0272) 25491).
Trout licences: season £3 (juniors £1.50), month £1.50 (juniors 75p), day 75p
(juniors 35p). No rod licence required for the authority's own reservoirs.

Avon and Dorset Rivers Division
Pollution and Fisheries Officer: A. S. Grater, County Gates House, 300 Poole Road,
Parkstone, Poole, Dorset (tel. Poole (02013) 763215).
Trout close season: 30 September to 1 April.

Bristol Avon Rivers Division
Divisional Fisheries Officer: M. J. Amey, Green Park, Bath, Avon
(tel. Bath (0225) 27541)
Trout close season: 15 October to 1 April.

Somerset Rivers Division
Divisional Fisheries and Recreations Officer: C. Arden, The Watergate, West Quay,
Bridgwater, Somerset (tel. Bridgwater (0278) 8271).
Trout close season: 15 October to 1 April.

Note: Licences cover brown, rainbow and sea trout.

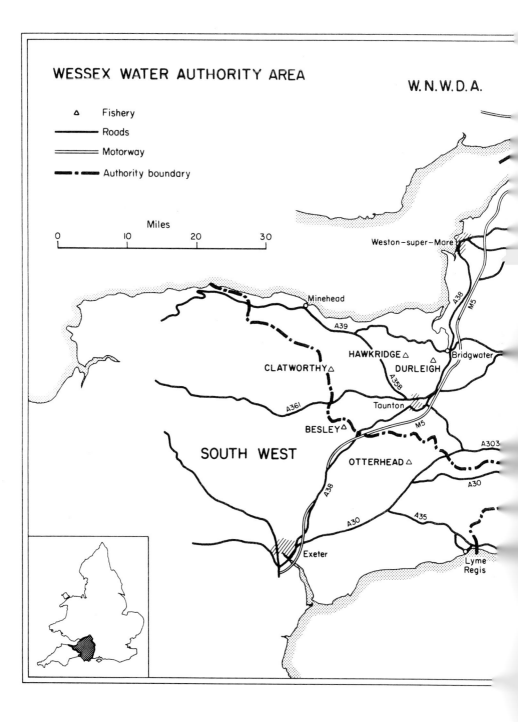

WESSEX WATER AUTHORITY AREA

W. N. W. D. A.

△   Fishery
────   Roads
══════   Motorway
▬·▬·▬   Authority boundary

Miles
0   10   20   30

Weston-super-Mare

Minehead

A39

HAWKRIDGE △

CLATWORTHY △

DURLEIGH △

Bridgwater

A358

A361

Taunton

BESLEY △

M5

SOUTH WEST

OTTERHEAD △

A303

A30

A38

A30

A35

Exeter

Lyme Regis

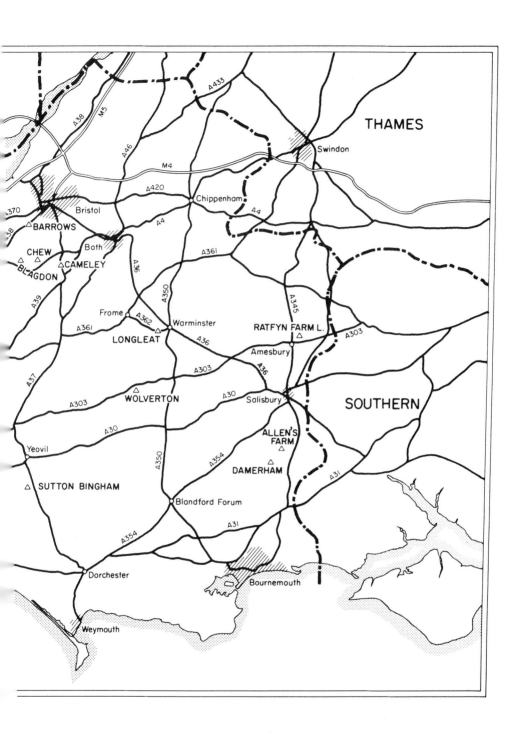

Tackling the Big Trout of Blagdon and Chew

Advice from JOHN GODDARD

The trout fishing reservoirs in the Bristol group are among the oldest in the country. They comprise Barrow No 2, Barrow No 3, Chew Valley Lake and Blagdon Lake. The first two are rather small concrete reservoirs and although from time to time they produce good trout, they are rather uninteresting to fish and will not be dealt with here. The remaining two waters are very famous and a lasting monument to the fine work and original research undertaken by the Bristol Waterworks Company under the guidance at the time of its very knowledgeable director, Mr Kennedy Brown.

Blagdon Lake

This great water was first opened for trout fishing in 1901 and for over half a century was the mecca for trout anglers in this country. Even today it is one of our top waters. Personally I have yet to fish a stillwater that can equal its charm and magic. Set in a most beautiful valley in the Mendips, the view from Orchard Bay on a bright sunny morning is without equal.

The lake is steeped in history. For many years it consistently produced the largest rainbow trout in the country, and without doubt proved initially responsible for the present sophisticated approach to stillwater trout fishing.

One of the greatest exponents of stillwater trout fishing between the wars was the famous Dr Bell of Blagdon. A very patient and observant fisherman, he quickly realized that there must be better patterns and techniques waiting to be discovered than the traditional loch-fishing style of his day, based as it was on attractor patterns fished in conjunction with a dropper. Admittedly on the right day — particularly from a boat — this is still a very killing method, but practised from the bank it left a lot to be desired. As a result of his methodical research he eventually produced two patterns which are still firm favourites at Blagdon to this day. They are the Buzzer nymph, or Black Buzzer, and the Amber nymph, which were the forerunners of the host of midge and sedge pupa dressings which are now two of the lifelines of the modern stillwater angler.

Despite the fact that this is a relatively large body of water, small flies, nymphs and special patterns tied to represent natural aquatic creatures seem to be more effective, whereas on other large waters such as Grafham, Draycote and even to some extent Chew, large lures and attractor patterns kill fish so well on certain occasions.

192

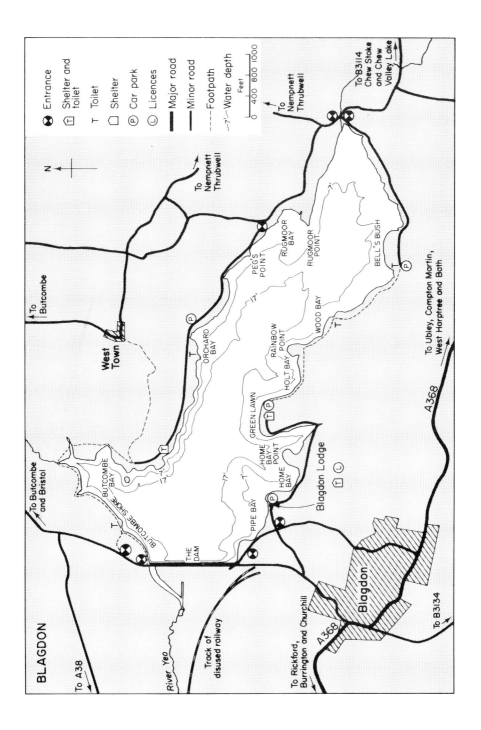

Although I have now been fishing Blagdon regularly for well over 20 years, I still experience that thrill of anticipation as I drive through the sleepy old-world village and down the steep hill through the winding narrow road to the fishing lodge for my ticket. In my opinion no dedicated lake fly-fisher has earned his spurs until he has netted one of the fine plump trout which inhabit these hallowed waters.

I have had some fabulous bags of trout from this superb water, but I would be the first to admit it is not an easy water to fish and on some days the trout can be infuriatingly difficult to take. This is no doubt due to the richness of its aquatic life and the consequent selectivity of its trout at times. Apart from this it is essential to know the water well, as not only do most of the trout seem to favour different areas of the lake as the summer progresses, but in these localities they also have their favourite spots. This is due to the uneven bed of the lake.

Like many of the more natural reservoirs, it was formed by building a dam at one end of a valley and then flooding it. Consequently the bed is riddled with old ditches, holes, hedgerows, footpaths and roads, and these underwater features seem to provide holding areas or lanes up which feeding trout travel. Most of these hot spots are known to me, and while I could show them to you if I were there, it is a little difficult on paper. However, I will endeavour to pin-point some of the better known places as I describe the lake shore.

Unfortunately I am unable to provide information as to where the trout are most likely to be found during the season, as this will to a large extent depend upon the direction of the wind and the temperature of the water. In this respect the best advice I can give is to ask one of the water rangers. They are on the water every day and will willingly advise you as to the most productive areas.

The lake lies roughly east to west, the latter end towards the dam being the deepest, while most of the eastern end, particularly along the southern bank, is very shallow. Starting at the dam on the southern bank near the lodge, the first notable spot we come to is a large inlet pipe about a hundred yards from the dam wall. This is an excellent location, particularly early in the year when the water is high, and over the years has consistently produced its quota of specimen-sized trout. When the water level drops, usually in the latter half of the season, it is impossible to fish successfully due to heavy weed beds that spring up in the vicinity.

A short distance to the lodge side of this pipe is a large rather shallow area called Pipe Bay. The water along the eastern edge of the bay is deeper, particularly on the point adjacent to a large tree, and unless the water is exceptionally low it always produces fish. Travelling eastwards towards the lodge, the shore here has little to offer except possibly very early in the season. Almost opposite the lodge you will find Home Bay Point, also a productive area early in the year.

Towards the end of the season, particularly when the water is very low, a point is formed to the right of the lodge out into Home Bay, and from here in the early morning I have had many limit bags of trout during August and early September on a Corixa pattern. Home Bay itself and the shore in front of Green Lawn always hold their quota of trout, but again fishing is usually better early in the year when the water is high.

On the other side of Home Bay we come to Long Bay and for about a hundred yards either side of the point of this bay is one of the most productive areas in the lake, no matter what the water level.

Still travelling eastwards, the next hot spot is Rainbow Point at the eastern end of Holt Bay. As its name implies, this area always seems to provide more than its quota of rainbow trout. The remainder of this southern shore from Wood Bay to the top end of the lake is mostly shallow and can only be fished early in the year. In hot, dry summers vast weed beds form along this stretch of shore and make fishing all but impossible.

However, before leaving this side of the lake it is worth noting that the area adjacent to Bell's Bush is often very productive during late May and June before the weed forms, as there are several deepish holes along here which always hold good trout particularly in the late evenings.

Let us now look at the North Bank. The main entrance is at the top or eastern end of the lake and brings you on to the water alongside Rugmoor Bay. Rather shallow, it is a little difficult to fish successfully from the bank, so most bank anglers prefer to fish the lake side of the long promontory called Rugmoor Point, which sticks out like a long finger into the main body of the lake. This is a most productive stretch of bank and seems to produce trout throughout the season, although June and July are probably the best months.

Moving along the bank we come to Peg's Point, a firm favourite with local anglers as there are one or two submerged ditches here where the shallow water of Rugmoor Bay deepens into the main lake.

The next stretch of bank between Peg's Point and Orchard Bay is rather flat and uninteresting, but it does provide good fishing on occasions. The point on the far side of Orchard Bay is a favoured hot spot as it is here that the water begins to deepen rapidly.

The rest of this north bank nearly as far as Butcombe Bay is very steep and the water deep. Probably the best area on the lake for consistency, it seems to provide good fishing throughout the season. Along this stretch of bank are several hedgerows and these are undoubtedly the real hot spots. Finally we come to Butcombe Bay and the Butcombe shore, both of which seem to produce better sport in the early part of the season.

As far as the boat fisherman is concerned, the above information should be of value, but it must be remembered that they should keep well clear of bank anglers. I have found that drift fishing from a boat on Blagdon is far more productive than the modern trend of fishing from an anchored boat. Particularly good drifts are as follows (providing of course the wind is favourable) . . .

Early in the season across the face of the dam or across the mouth of Butcombe Bay should be tried. There are also one or two interesting short drifts one can enjoy in the bay itself down into the mouths of two small streams which enter the lake. Another productive drift is across the mouth of Rugmoor Bay or from Rugmoor Point across to Rainbow Point. Later in the season my favourites are across the mouth of Orchard Bay or along the north shore itself between Orchard Bay and Peg's Point.

Recommended fly patterns

I have decided to restrict the number of patterns to a dozen or so which I have found to be consistently killing, used at the right time.

The Amber Nymph. Perfected by that superb angler, Dr Bell of Blagdon, this is best fished slowly on the dropper well below the surface during June, July and August.

The Butcher. Dressed on small hook (size 12 to 16) and fished on a dropper slowly beneath the surface, this is particularly effective during May and June either from bank or boat.

The Black Lure. A good imitation of the almost black leeches found in profusion in certain areas, this fly, fished on the point at a slow to medium pace on a sunk line near the bottom, is a consistent fish-taker throughout the season.

Black Palmer. I have found this pattern particularly effective fished on the top dropper from a boat on the drift in the early part of the year.

Corixa. An excellent pattern during August and early September when the trout are feeding on the naturals of the same name adjacent to weed in shallow water. In the early part of August I prefer a weighted pattern fished sink-and-draw style on the point, but later in the month I have found unweighted dressings fished fast just under the surface on point and dropper to be more killing.

Damosel Nymph. This large nymph can be a very killing pattern during late June, July and August when the naturals are about. Should be fished at a slow to medium pace on a floating line just under the surface on the point. Best fished from the bank in the morning or early afternoon.

Dunkeld. One of the time-honoured general attractor patterns, this has proved its effectiveness for me on many occasions. It should be fished from a dropper just under the surface and can be used from both bank and boat in the latter half of the season.

G & H Deer Hair Sedge. One of my own patterns, this is an exceptionally good floater which is the most important aspect of any dry sedge. From July onwards, fished on the drift on the top dropper, or from the bank on the point, it is a very killing fly.

Invicta. Fished on the dropper in the surface film, this old and well-tried pattern is an excellent imitation of a hatching sedge. It is best fished during July and August when the natural sedges are hatching in the late afternoon or early evening.

Midge Pupa. My own or similar dressings are tied in variety of colours and sizes to represent the many different naturals to be found on most stillwaters. There are exceptionally good hatches of these tiny flies on Blagdon in the early mornings and late evenings during the first half of the season, and a team of artificials fished very slowly right in the surface film are most effective.

Persuader. A general representative pattern of my own, this has proved to be an exceptionally good artificial at Blagdon throughout the season. Should be fished from boat or bank medium fast just under the surface, or slowly sink-and-draw style for big browns in deep water.

Pheasant Tail or PVC Nymph. Both of these nymphs fished slowly on the point sink-and-draw style can be very killing in the vicinity of weed when either pond or lake olives are hatching.

Polystickle. This or similar patterns tied to represent sticklebacks can sometimes be effective, particularly during August when these tiny fish are most in evidence.

Sedge Pupa. Also one of my own patterns, tied in different colours and sizes they are proven fish-takers from July onwards. Should be fished on the point slowly midwater or near the lake bed.

Chew Valley Lake

When this water was first opened in 1956 it was advertised as the greatest trout fishery in Europe, and before the first season drew to a close it was generally accepted by most authorities to be true. I was fortunate to fish it on several occasions during this first season and I can only describe the quality of the fishing as fantastic. To this day I can still recall most vividly the serried ranks of huge trout head-and-tailing far out in the reservoir as the evening rise began. If one were wading the excitement was so intense it was difficult to restrain oneself until the rising trout came within casting range. That first year I think the average weight was well over 2lb, but I am sure it seemed much higher at the time to most anglers as trout of 4 and 5lb were the order of the day and even fish of over 6lb were not uncommon.

There is no doubt that when Chew opened it heralded a new era of stillwater fishing and furthermore set a very high standard for others. Alas! the magnificent fishing experienced in the first two seasons has never been repeated, but over the years it has settled down very well and is still one of the top reservoirs in the country.

This is a much larger water than Blagdon and requires a slightly different technique. Small flies and nymphs are not so effective, no doubt due to the fact that in its early days coarse fish, namely roach, became established, a problem from which Blagdon never suffered. The presence of these roach in Chew has resulted in many of the trout becoming accustomed to feeding on their fry, which in some seasons often reach a length of 2—3in. Naturally the authorities have made intensive efforts over the years to contain this menace by netting and other means, and I am delighted to report they have been reasonably successful.

Due to the large size of these fry, larger flies and lures seem to be very much more effective at Chew, and in fact in some seasons by early August many of the trout have become so completely preoccupied with feeding on the fry that the only chance of attaining a good bag is to use fry-imitating lures.

Due to the sheer size of this water, it is not feasible in the space available to describe all the shoreline and hot spots, so I shall therefore restrict myself to providing information on certain sections of bank which over the years have become accepted as good holding areas.

Like Blagdon, or in fact more so, the bed of Chew is riddled with old roads, ditches and hedgerows, providing many fish-holding areas for anglers who know where to find them. Generally speaking, I prefer bank fishing, but I must admit that I find the boat fishing at Chew particularly interesting as the bed of the lake is extremely rugged and there are many banks, channels and holes.

The lake is roughly oblong, with the deeper water towards the dam at the northern end and the shallower water at the southern end up to Herriots Bridge. The fishing lodge stands on the high ground overlooking the Woodford bank, giving one a magnificent view of the reservoir. The water along this stretch of bank deepens very rapidly and while it fishes particularly well in the early part of the year, it also produces good results throughout the season. I seldom fish this stretch as it is rather featureless and uninteresting.

The same applies to Walley Bank, the other side of the lodge up to the dam. From the Woodford bank one can look across Villice Bay to Nunnery Point, without doubt one of the most favoured and productive areas on the reservoir. Around the point the water is fairly deep, except on the Villice Bay side. There are several ditches and holes and these are the hot spots if you know where they are, but I cannot pinpoint them as there are no obvious landmarks.

The Nunnery side of Villice Bay is good as there are two or three old hedgerows along this section of bank. Before the level of the lake drops too far, the top end of this bay is also very productive as there are several deep channels running along the bed of the lake formed by streams running into the bay. The other side of Nunnery never seems to fish as well, apart from a couple of spots where ditches are located. One of these is near the point which juts out into Herons Green Bay, but wading along this section of bank can be dangerous as there are numerous potholes.

On the other side of this bay is Moreton Point, which always seems to produce good trout throughout the season. Farther along the Moreton bank, near the car park, an old road enters the lake and this can be a real hot spot from the middle of June onwards. Towards Stratford Bay there are some very interesting old hedgerows or banks, and it is possible to wade out along the top of these for some distance into the lake. I have had some wonderful bags of trout from these in the past, usually during July and August.

Nearly opposite the lodge you can see the verdant green grass lining Wick Green. This is indeed an area of memories for me, as it has always been one of my favourites and has given up many a large trout. It fishes best with a south-west wind, and I have found the left-hand side of the green to be more productive than the right.

Another hot spot in this section is the old road that enters the water below the Wick Green car park. The east shore opposite Denny Island is a particularly interesting section as there are many channels and banks, some of which are exposed later in the year when the water drops. It is here that a small stream enters the lake under a bridge from the Denny Road and the long creek thus formed sometimes produces very big trout.

As I mentioned before, Chew is a very interesting sheet of water to fish from a boat. In the first few weeks of the season I have found the best area to fish is from Nunnery Point down to the dam, and between the dam and Denny Island, but from then on the trout are likely to be anywhere in the lake. When the wind is in the right direction, a very nice drift is across Nunnery Point and the mouth of Villice Bay. When the wind is from the west a drift right up the centre of Villice Bay always seems to produce fish.

From the middle of June onwards a most interesting drift is across an area called the Roman Shallows, midway between the Moreton bank and Wick Green. If you can find the edge of this bank and drift down it trout are almost assured.

From midsummer onwards one of my favourite areas is the shallows around Herriots Bridge. Depending on the wind, the best drifts to fish are either from Stratford Bay to the bridge keeping about 200yd offshore, or from Wick Green towards the bridge keeping as close to the shore as possible. On the former drift you will find isolated patches of old trees and bushes in the water, and trout are nearly always to be found around them. On the latter drift you will notice much of the bank is unfishable due to the very heavy growth of reedmace. In many places this growth has formed delightful little bays, and in the past I have had many a good trout out of these.

This is also a superb area in late summer for fishing a dry sedge, as clouds of naturals

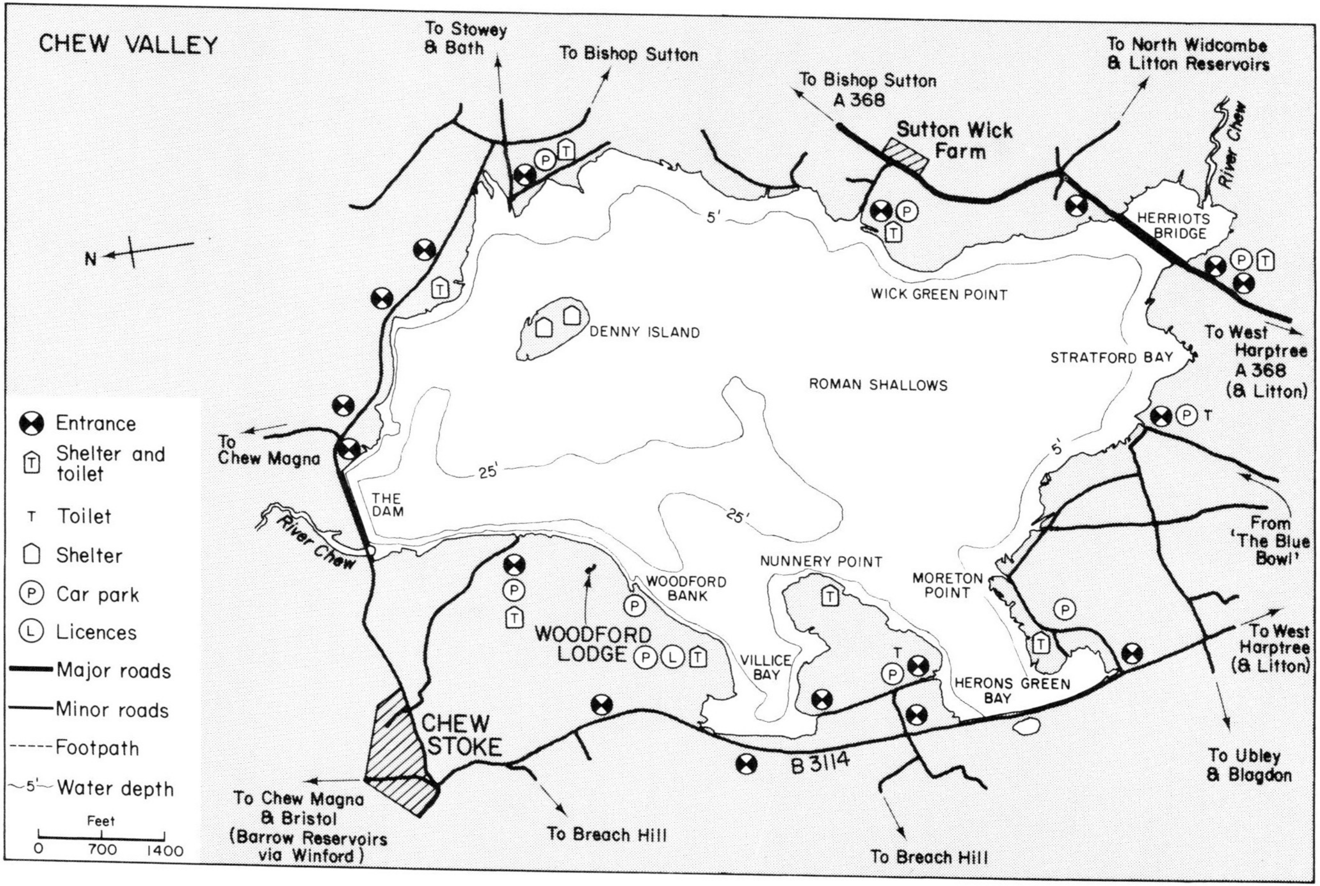

CHEW VALLEY
To Stowey & Bath
To Bishop Sutton
To Bishop Sutton A 368
Sutton Wick Farm
To North Widcombe & Litton Reservoirs
River Chew
HERRIOTS BRIDGE
N
5'
WICK GREEN POINT
DENNY ISLAND
STRATFORD BAY
To West Harptree A 368 (& Litton)
ROMAN SHALLOWS
To Chew Magna
25'
THE DAM
River Chew
25'
NUNNERY POINT
MORETON POINT
From 'The Blue Bowl'
WOODFORD BANK
WOODFORD LODGE
VILLICE BAY
HERONS GREEN BAY
To West Harptree (& Litton)
CHEW STOKE
B 3114
To Ubley & Blagdon
To Chew Magna & Bristol (Barrow Reservoirs via Winford)
To Breach Hill
To Breach Hill
Entrance
Shelter and toilet
Toilet
Shelter
Car park
Licences
Major roads
Minor roads
Footpath
Water depth
Feet
0 700 1400

are always to be found along the edge of the reedmace, and an artificial delicately presented as near to the reeds as possible as you drift quietly by will nearly always produce a few good trout. The deep channel up to the bridge itself is an excellent place to fish from an anchored boat, and as the bank on either side is now a nature reserve, peace and quiet is assured.

Two other good areas for boat fishing I must mention are 200 or 300yd south and slightly to the west of Denny Island, where there are some long narrow banks with deep water on the west side, and almost on the other side of the island opposite the Denny Road, as the bottom here is very rugged with many banks and potholes.

Recommended fly patterns

As for Blagdon I am restricting the number of patterns again to a dozen or so, and it will be noted that some of these are recommended for both waters.

Baby Doll. A relatively new fly designed by Bob Church, this is now a proved killer and seems to do well at Chew, especially for rainbows in the early part of the season.

Black Lure. Over the years this pattern has probably accounted for more large trout on this water than any other fly. Usually fished fairly fast on a sunken line, it will also take trout fished just under the surface on a floating or, better still, a sink-tip line. An early season pattern.

Church Fry. Another of Bob Church's patterns, this is an excellent fly to use at Chew during late July and August when the trout are on the roach fry.

Chomper Patterns. Designed by Richard Walker, these are tied in several different colours, usually with a weighted body, and should be fished on a floating line in the sink-and-draw style. In practice it will be found that many trout will take it as it is sinking. I have found the white pattern most effective at Chew, especially during July and August when a lot of corixa are present.

Damosel Nymph. This has always proved an excellent killing pattern during July and August. At this time of the year, when one experiences those terrible bright calm days, fished slowly just under the surface film it will often provide a good trout or two when all else fails.

Dunkeld. This pattern should always be fished from a dropper and is a useful fly either from a boat or the bank in the latter half of the season.

G & H Deer Hair Sedge. Fished from the bank on the point as a dry fly or dribbled over a good ripple on the top dropper from a boat, it is one of my own favourite dressings and has accounted for an astonishing number of trout when the natural sedges are about.

Midge Pupa. This best known of all stillwater patterns is tied in various colours and sizes, and is as indispensable on this water as it is elsewhere. An early morning or late evening fly, it is fished very slowly right in the surface film and is most effective in May and June.

Muddler Minnow. In recent years this famous American pattern has accounted for many trout at Chew. Best fished during July and August when fry or sedge pupa are about, as it is a fair representation of either.

Persuader. A relatively new general pattern of my own, this has now accounted for many big trout and I understand it is now becoming very popular at Chew as elsewhere. A good pattern throughout the year, it should always be fished on the point and is best retrieved at a medium to fast pace just under the surface.

Peter Ross. One of the old traditional general attractor patterns, it has always been a good fly on Chew at any time of the year and is equally effective from boat or bank.

Sedge Pupa. Another of my own dressings, this has accounted for many large trout over the years. It is tied in a variety of colours to represent the natural sedge pupa and may be retrieved at a medium to slow pace, just below the surface in midwater or near the bottom. The orange colour seems to be particularly effective later in the year.

Worm Fly. This well-known pattern has been a great favourite at Chew in the past and, fished on the point and retrieved slow or even quite fast, has accounted for many trout.

Zulu. An all-black fly with a red tag, it has proved a useful pattern fished from a boat on the dropper during the early part of the season.

ALLEN'S FARM

*Sandleheath,
Fordingbridge, Hants.*

Turn right from B3078 Fordingbridge to Damerham road at Sandleheath crossroads. Allen's Farm is on right (about ½m along).

Owner: Philip and Mary Read.

Description: Four landscaped lakes covering about 4 acres in all, and stretch of river in peaceful wooded valley.

Species/sizes: Rainbows in lakes, brown trout in river.

	Brown	Rainbow
Average	12oz	1lb 8oz
Record	2lb 8oz	3lb 9oz

Stocking: At least once a week.

Rules: Fly only. Limit (full day) 4 fish, (half day) 3 fish.

Season: 27 March to 17 October (extended for season rods only to 31 October).

Permits: Full st (one day per week) £77, other st at reduced rates; dt £3.35, half dt (up to or from 2pm) £2.55. Prices include Water Authority licence and VAT.

Permits from:
Allens Farm, Sandleheath,
Fordingbridge, Hants.
(tel. Rockbourne (07253) 313).

Comments: To keep charges down, this fishery is not stocked with very large trout, but it is claimed that the 12in fish stocked fight harder, pound for pound, than the bigger ones. Be that as it may, these lakes provide pleasant and rewarding sport in a secluded setting and are sure to improve

with time. They were not opened for fishing until 1974. A holiday flat is available — details will be sent on request.

BARROWS

*Barrow Gurney,
nr Bristol*

Off A38 about 5m S of Bristol.

Owner: Bristol Waterworks Company.

Description: Two concrete reservoirs of 26 and 39 acres respectively.

Species/sizes: Brown and rainbow.

	Brown	Rainbow
Average	1lb 13oz	1lb 14oz
Record	8lb 13oz	7lb 12oz

Stocking: Major planting in spring, then series of re-restockings during season.

Rules: Fly only. Limit 4 brace. No wading or standing in water, sloping banks dangerous.

Season: 16 April to 15 October.

Permits: st £46; dt £2 (OAPs, juniors and disabled half-price). Boats (2, pulling) £4.20 per rod; after 4 pm, £2 (min. two rods).

Permits from:
Woodford Lodge, Chew Stoke, Bristol BS18 8XH (st) (tel. Chew Magna 2339). or self-service unit at Barrow Filtration Works (dt) (6.40am to sunset 16—30 April, 24-hr service from 1 May).

Comments: These waters, somewhat overshadowed by their eminent brethren nearby, and nothing like so attractive, nevertheless hold some fine fish as the recorded captures show. Nymph patterns are reported to do well.

BESLEY LAKE

Holcombe Rogus,
Wellington, Somerset

On A38 between Tiverton and Wellington (3½m) 2½m from M5 motorway.

Owner: A. J. Wyatt.

Description: One acre natural lake on farmland.

Species/sizes: Brown and rainbow.

	Brown	Rainbow
Average	2lb	1lb 12oz
Record	2lb 12oz	3lb 4oz

Stocking: At intervals throughout season.

Rules: Fly only. No fish caught to be returned to lake. Limit: 5 fish on dt, 3 fish in an evening.

Season: 1 April to 15 October.

Permits: dt £2 (evenings £1.25), plus 50p per pound of fish caught, plus VAT.

Permits from: Owner at Lower Besley Farm, Holcombe Rogus, Wellington, Somerset (tel. Greenham 672474).

BLAGDON LAKE

Blagdon,
nr Bristol

Just north of A368 at Blagdon, about 4m E of A38/A368 junction at Churchill traffic lights.

Owner: Bristol Waterworks Company.

Description: Renowned 440-acre reservoir beneath the Mendips which, with its grassy banks, resembles a large natural lake.

Species/sizes: Brown and rainbow.

	Brown	Rainbow
Average	1lb 14oz	2lb 2oz
Record	10lb 4oz (1926)	8lb 8oz (1924)

Stocking: Major planting in early spring, then series of restockings during season.

Rules: Fly only. Limit 4 brace. No fishing from dam, bridge over by-wash or valve shaft.

Season: 16 April to 15 October.

Permits: st £90, dt £3 (Pensioners, juniors and disabled half-price). Boats (12 pulling) £5.50 per rod; after 4pm £2.75 (min. two rods).

Permits from:
Woodford Lodge, Chew Stoke, Bristol BS18 8XH (st) (tel. Chew Magna 2339). or self-service unit at Blagdon Lodge (6.40am to sunset) 16—30 April, 24-hr service from 1 May.

Comments: Always a trout fishery to rank with the greatest in the land, Blagdon has been scoring heavily in recent seasons and in 1974 all records were broken with a total catch of 9689. Lt Col Creagh-Scott's rainbow of 8lb 8oz, taken in 1924, held the British individual record for the species for many years until it was broken recently. Tackle is available for sale at the Anglers' Hut. *For recommended patterns see the entry for Chew Valley and for a comprehensive article on Blagdon fishing see John Goddard's contribution on page 192.*

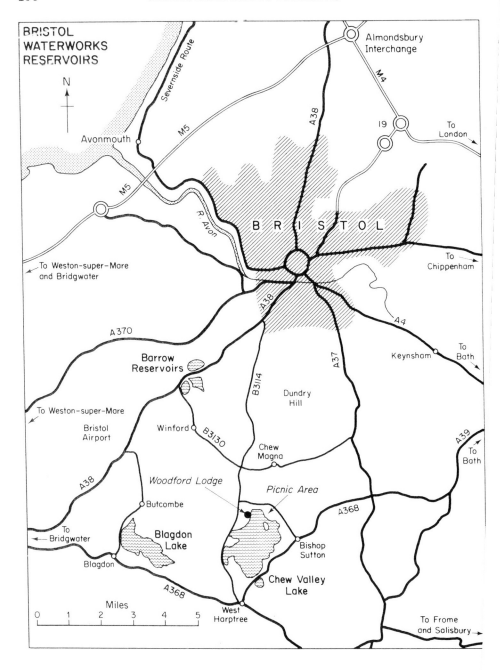

CAMELEY LAKES

*Temple Cloud,
nr Bristol*

About 10m S of Bristol off A37.

Controller: J. Harris.

Description: Two landscaped lakes covering about 4 acres.

Species/sizes: Brown and rainbow. Biggest brown 5lb, biggest rainbow 8lb 4oz (1975 figures).

Stocking: Larger lake with 12in browns and rainbows at regular intervals. Smaller lake with browns only.

Rules: Dry fly only. Limit: 2 brace.

Season: 1 April to 15 October.

Permits: Limited dt at £5. Full st (two days/week) £150, half st £80 (both +VAT).

Permits from:
Owner at Hillcrest Farm, Cameley, Temple Cloud, nr Bristol (tel. Temple Cloud 52423).

Comments: A second lake was opened for the 1976 season.

CHEW VALLEY

Chew Stoke, Bristol

Route from Bristol (10m) is S on A37 and then right onto B3130 for Chew Magna and Chew Stoke. From Bath (15m) route is W on A4/A39/A368 and watch for right turn (at Bishop Sutton) to Chew Stoke.

Owner: Bristol Waterworks Company.

Description: Landscaped reservoir covering 1200 acres in attractive fertile valley. Average depth 16ft, maximum 37ft.

Species/sizes: Brown and rainbow.

	Brown	Rainbow
Average	1lb 14oz	2lb 2oz
Record	10lb 12oz	7lb 9oz

Stocking: Major planting in early spring, series of re-stockings during season. Hatchery and three rearing stations produce 34,000 trout for Bristol reservoirs.

Rules: Fly only. Limit 4 brace. Fishing permitted from banks of summer sailing area, but not from fenced sailing club plateau near Woodford Lodge, nor from nature reserve, dame, valve tower or approach bridge.

Season: 14 April to 15 October.

Permits: st £90; dt £3 (half-price for pensioners, juniors and disabled). Boats (16, motor) £7 per rod; after 4pm £3.25 (min. two rods).

Permits from:
Bristol Waterworks Co., Recreations Department, Woodford Lodge, Chew Stoke, Bristol BS18 8XH (tel. Chew Magna 2339) (st)
or dt from self-service unit at lodge (6.40am to sunset 16—30 April, 24-hr service from 1 May).

Comments: A pioneer big-fish reservoir, Chew Valley has set a consistently high standard since it was opened in 1957. Total catches steadily rose to a peak of 18,841 in 1970, and 1974 produced its biggest-ever rainbow, captured on August 17 by Dick Neill of East Horsley, Surrey, from the Woodford Bank on a red-tagged worm fly. Fly-casting tuition is available free of charge for newcomers on weekdays by prior arrangement with the Recreations Officer. There is also a comprehensive stock of tackle at Woodford Lodge. Recommended fly patterns include: Amber Nymph, Butcher, Buzzer Nymph, Corixa, Dunkeld, Green Nymph, Grenadier, Invicta (standard or silver), Mallard and Claret, Peter Ross, Soldier Palmer, Alexandra Lure, Black Lure with jungle cock dressing, Dunkeld Lure, Water Leech, Worm Fly (double) (sizes 10—12 old scale). The Recreation Department staff will be pleased to answer inquiries. *For an appraisal of the water see John Goddard's article on page 192.*

CLATWORTHY

nr Wiveliscombe, Somerset

A361 W out of Taunton, then take Clatworthy road for about 4m.

Controller: Wessex Water Authority.

Description: Beautiful upland reservoir covering 130 acres on the fringe of Exmoor, about 15m NW of Taunton. Some 5m of shoreline; maximum water depth 100ft.

Species/sizes: Brown and rainbow.

	Brown	Rainbow
Average	15oz	1lb
Record	3lb 9oz	2lb 6oz

Stocking: Large injection in March then monthly.

Rules: Fly only. Limit 3 brace.

Season: 12 April to 15 October.

Permits: st £30; dt £2 (half price for OAPs and juveniles). Boats (6) at £3.50 per rod per day.

Permits from:
dt self-service unit at Fishing Lodge; st from Wessex WA, The Watergate, West Quay, Bridgwater, Somerset.

Comments: The ranger, Reg Deer, is always pleased to advise anglers on fishing this reservoir (tel Wiveliscombe 23549).

DAMERHAM TROUT LAKES

Damerham, nr Fordingbridge, Hants.

1m S of Damerham village off B3078 Fordingbridge to Cranborne road.

Owner: Colin Harms.

Description: Five man-made landscaped lakes covering 17 acres in all and now completely natural in appearance.

Species/sizes: Rainbows only averaging 2lb 5oz, biggest 8lb 8oz.

Stocking: Twice weekly throughout season.

Rules: Fly only, and only one fly. No fishing before 10am. Limit (day rods): 2 brace.

Season: 2 April to 31 October.

Permits: st £250 (any number of days per week), £175 (one day per week); dt £7.56.

Permits from:
Proprietor, Damerham Trout Lakes, Damerham South End, Fordingbridge, Hants, SP6 3HX (tel. Rockbourne (07253) 446).

Comments: This fishery has built up a reputation for the consistency of its catches regardless of the conditions. The lakes are long and narrow, and anglers may cast to seen fish in the gin-clear water. Imitative patterns fished carefully are more successful than lures or streamers. Although the fishery is no duffer's paradise, the average catch rate is two fish per rod per day to day visitors and rather higher to season ticket holders. In 1975 this water produced 44 fish over 6lb and 9 over 7lb.

DURLEIGH

Durleigh, Bridgwater, Somerset

On western outskirts of Bridgwater about 2m from town centre.

Controller: Wessex Water Authority.

Description: Landscaped reservoir of 80 acres.

Species/sizes: Brown and rainbow.

	Brown	Rainbow
Average	1lb 4oz	1lb 4oz
Record	5lb 8oz	6lb
	(1959)	(1954)

Stocking: Monthly.

Rules: Fly only. Limit: 3 brace.

Season: 1 April to 15 October.

Permits: st £30; dt £2 (OAPs and juveniles half-price). Boats (6) £3.50 per rod.

Permits from: dt self-service unit at angling lodge; st from Wessex WA, The Watergate, West Quay, Bridgwater, Somerset.

Comments: A popular lowland lake, Durleigh produces fish of good average size. The ranger, Bob Jones, is always willing to advise anglers (tel. Bridgwater 4786).

HAWKRIDGE

Spaxton, nr Bridgwater, Somerset

A39 W out of Bridgwater, then left on to Spaxton road. Reservoir is about 1m from village and 6m from Bridgwater.

Controller: Wessex Water Authority.

Description: 32-acre landscaped reservoir situated in a deep valley in the Quantock Hills. Maximum depth 65ft.

Species/sizes: Rainbows mostly, some brown trout.

	Brown	Rainbow
Average	1lb 6oz	1lb 3oz
Record	3lb 4oz	2lb 4oz

Stocking: Large injection in March then monthly.

Rules: Fly only. Limit 6 fish.

Season: 12 April to 15 October.

Permits: st £25; dt £2 (half price for OAPs and juveniles). No boats.

Permits from: dt self-service unit at reservoir; st from Wessex WA, The Watergate, West Quay, Bridgwater, Somerset.

Comments: Opened in 1964, this fishery was available only to season ticket holders until 1975, when day permits were issued for bank fishing. Recommended patterns include Peter Ross, Dunkeld (with jungle cock dressing), Silver Invicta and Worm Fly. Fluorescent nymphs and silver-bodied lures are also reported to have done well. The ranger at Durleigh, Bob Jones, also patrols this reservoir and will be pleased to advise anglers (tel. Bridgwater 4786).

LONGLEAT

Warminster, Wilts.

Off A362 at Longleat House, seat of Marquess of Bath, 2½m W of Warminster. Lake is adjacent to exit road S of house, nearest to lodge gates.

Owner: Marquess of Bath.

Description: Lake landscaped by Capability Brown, in grounds of historic country house.

Species/sizes: Brown trout averaging 6—7oz.

Stocking: Has been stocked in past, but no further stocking was contemplated for 1976.

Rules: Fly only.

Season: 15 April to 15 October.

Permits: dt £1.10.

Permits from: Bailiff on site or receptionist at Longleat House.

Comments: An opportunity to combine a family excursion to Longleat House with some not-too-serious fly-fishing.

OTTERHEAD LAKES

Churchingford, nr Taunton, Somerset

About 8m S of Taunton and 1m W of B3170 Taunton to Honiton road.

Controller: Wessex Water Authority.

Description: Two man-made lakes of 2 and 2¾ acres at head of River Otter, noted trout stream.

Species/sizes: Brown and rainbow.

	Brown	Rainbow
Average	12oz	15oz
Record	1lb 5oz	1lb 4oz

Stocking: Monthly.

Rules: Fly only. Limit: 3 brace.

Season: 5 April to 15 October.

Permits: st £25; dt £2 (OAPs and juveniles half price).

Permits from: dt self-service unit at The Lodge, Otterhead; st from Wessex WA, The Watergate, West Quay, Bridgwater, Somerset.

Comments: Two small lakes in an attractive setting in the Otter Valley just south of the Blackdown Hills. Small flies and light tackle are recommended.

RATFYN FARM LAKE

nr Amesbury, Wilts.

Off A303 about a mile E of Amesbury in Avon Valley.

Controller: Salisbury and District A. C.

Description: Natural lake of about 3 acres.

Species/sizes: Rainbow trout averaging 1½lb; biggest taken, 3lb 8oz.

Stocking: Four times a season.

Rules: Fly only. Limit: 1 brace.

Season: 14 April to 14 October.

Comments: The fishing on this lake is available only to members of Salisbury A. C., but there are vacancies — membership £9 season covers trout fishing in rivers and lakes. Inquiries to hon sec: G. W. Tedd, Yarmley Lane, Winterslow, Salisbury, Wilts.

SUTTON BINGHAM

nr Yeovil, Somerset

Take A37 out of Yeovil and proceed S for about 3m — reservoir lies about 1m W of road.

Controller: Wessex Water Authority.

Description: Mature landscaped reservoir (built in 1950s) covering 142 acres and with more than 5m of shoreline — generally shallow; maximum depth 40ft.

Species/sizes: Brown and rainbow.

	Brown	Rainbow
Average	1lb 4oz	1lb 3oz
Record	3lb 8oz	3lb 12oz

Stocking: Large injection in March then monthly.

Rules: Fly only. Limit: 3 brace. Boat fishing not permitted in sailing area on Thursdays, Saturdays and Sundays, though boats may pass through.

Season: 5 April to 15 October.

Permits: st £45; dt £2 (OAPs and juveniles half price). Boats (8) £3.50 per rod per day.

Permits from: dt self-service unit at Fishing Lodge; st from Wessex WA, The Watergate, West Quay, Bridgwater, Somerset. Boat bookings from Ranger, Des Delany.

Comments: Des Delany (tel. Yetminster 389) will be pleased to advise anglers on fishing the reservoir.

WOLVERTON FISHERY

nr Mere, Wilts.

2m W of Mere and ½m S of A303

Owner: Lt Col R. J. G. Heaven.

Description: 1-acre spring-fed man-made lake, lovely peaceful surroundings.

Species/sizes: Rainbow trout averaging 2lb; biggest taken, 6lb 11oz (1975).

Stocking: Stock of about 100 fish maintained throughout season.

Rules: Fly only. 4 rods only at any one time. Limit: 2½ brace daily or 1½ brace evenings.

Season: 1 April to 30 September.

Permits: st £100; dt £5 (evenings £3). Boat available by arrangement.

Permits from: Owner at Wolverton Fishery, Zeals, Warminster, Wilts.

Comments: This fishery forms part of the Samaaki Trout Farm. Built in 1971, it is well suited to the fisherman prepared to work for his bag, as there is so much natural food.

REMINDER

Stocking policy depends on returns. Fishery managers have
asked us to stress that whether you catch anything or not, please
remember to fill in the form before leaving the water.

10 Yorkshire

YORKSHIRE WATER AUTHORITY
West Riding House, 67 Albion Street, Leeds, LS1 5AA.
Fisheries Officer: S. Bailey (tel. 0532 448201 (ext. 239)).
Trout licences: season 80p (OAPs 40p); sea trout: weekly 30p (OAPs 15p).
Close seasons: 1 October to 31 March inclusive. Sea trout: 1 November to 5 April inclusive.

REMINDER

We have not as a rule mentioned in the individual entries the need for a regional water authority licence as well as a permit, but this is usually necessary, except for the relatively few cases where the fishery holds a general licence.

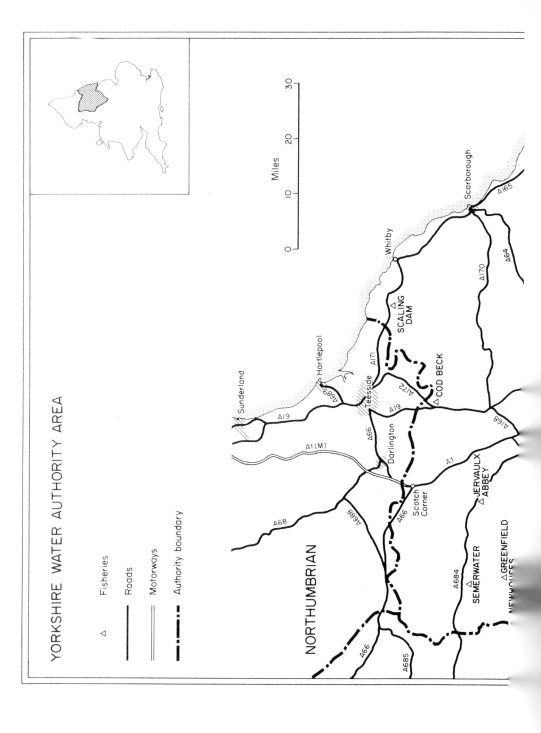

YORKSHIRE WATER AUTHORITY AREA

△   Fisheries

━━   Roads

══   Motorways

▬·▬·▬   Authority boundary

Miles

0   10   20   30

NORTHUMBRIAN

Sunderland

Hartlepool

Teesside

△ SCALING DAM

Whitby

Scarborough

△ COD BECK

Darlington

Scotch Corner

△ JERVAULX ABBEY

△ SEMERWATER

△ GREENFIELD

A19

A689

A171

A172

A170

A165

A64

A66

A1(M)

A1

A68

A688

A66

A684

A685

A19

A61

A168

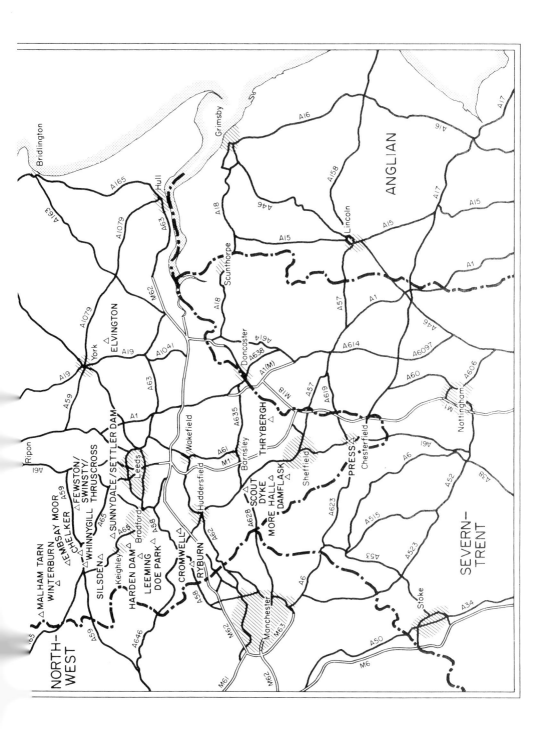

BOSHAW AND HOLMSTYES

Holmfirth, W. Yorks.

Strictly preserved by Huddersfield A.A. (75 members only). No dt.

CHELKER RESERVOIR

nr Skipton, N. Yorks.

A water of 57 acres, managed by the Bradford Waltonians club for members only, no day tickets. Reservoir is adjacent to A65 between Draughton and Addingham, about 4m from Skipton, and holds fair-sized trout. Club's hon sec is E. H. Weight, Crossfields, Old Lane, Hawksworth, Guiseley, Leeds.

COD BECK

Osmotherley,
nr Northallerton, N. Yorks.

A684 from Northallerton to Osmotherley (about 8m) or off A19 from Thirsk.

Controller: Yorkshire Water Authority.

Description: Reservoir in valley of Cod Beck. 1¼m of bank fishing; maximum depth 73ft.

Species/sizes: Brown trout averaging about 8oz.

Stocking: Annually.

Rules: Fly only. Limit: 3 brace 10in and over.

Season: 1 April to 30 September.

Permits: dt 25p. No boats.

Permits from:
Hambleton District Council Offices, 72 High Street, Northallerton; preference given to residents in Water Authority area. Permit holders may be accompanied by non-fishing companion at no extra charge.

CROMWELL LAKE

Brighouse, W. Yorks.

From Junction 25 on M62 proceed through Brighouse on Elland Road for 1½m.

Owner: Calder Gravel Ltd.

Description: 30-acre gravel pit.

Species/sizes: Rainbows averaging 1lb 3oz, biggest taken 5lb 15oz.

Stocking: Twice weekly during season on 'put and take' basis.

Rules: Limit: 3 fish. No wading.

Season: 1 April to 31 October.

Permits: st £80; mt £20; wt £10.50; dt £2.50; £1.50 evenings after 4pm. Boats (3) at £2 day, £1 after 4pm.

Permits from: Owner at Elland Road, Brighouse, W. Yorks, and from Grove Motel, also Elland Road.

DAMFLASK

nr Sheffield, S. Yorks

Situated about 3m to NW of Sheffield along minor road (B6077) towards village of Low Bradfield.

Controller: Yorkshire Water Authority, Southern Division.

Description: 115-acre reservoir in valley of River Loxley.

Species/sizes: Brown trout averaging about 12oz, and coarse fish.

Rules: All legal methods but no ground baiting.

Season: 1 April to 30 September.

Permits: dt 25p, half-day 15p.

Permits from: Fishing Attendant's Office at reservoir.

Comments: Damflask has yielded some good trout, but fly-fishermen may find coarse fish troublesome.
About 10m from Sheffield beyond Damflask near village of Stocksbridge lies Underbank Reservoir (103 acres), also stocked with trout and coarse fish, dt 20p, half-day 12½p. Tickets from attendant's office.

DOE PARK RESERVOIR

Denholme,
Keighley, W. Yorks.

A mixed fishery, including trout, managed by Bradford City A.A. for members only, no day tickets. Limit 10in. All legal methods allowed. The club's hon sec is A. J. Goggs, 6 Farringdon Grove, Buttershaw, Bradford 6. Subscription: £7.56.

ELVINGTON LAKE

Wheldrake,
nr York, N. Yorks.

A1079 from York for 4m, then right on to B1228 for Howden and Elvington, and right again at Jacques Garage for Wheldrake (2m).

Owner: S. Britton.

Description: 3¼-acre tree-fringed natural lake up to 32ft deep.

Species/sizes: Mixed fishery with brown and rainbow trout — fish up to 7lb taken, but mostly much smaller.

Stocking: Pre-season.

Rules: All legal methods allowed.

Season: 1 April to 30 September.

Permits: dt 75p. No boats.

Permits from:
S. Britton, Lake Cottage, Elvington.

Comments: Lake only occasionally fishes well to fly, and can then be very good; holds large coarse fish as well as trout.

EMBSAY MOOR

nr Skipton, N. Yorks.

A reservoir of 26 acres, 1½m off A59 Skipton to Harrogate road. Fishing restricted to members of Manchester A.A. Brown trout only, averaging 1lb, record 3lb 2oz. Stocked once only, before start of season. Rules as Whinnygill. Reservoir permit only issued (exclusively to members) at £4.50. Most fish taken on worm. Club's hon sec is P. J. Mellor, 2 Stansfield Drive, Rochdale, Lancs., OL11 5RK.

FEWSTON, SWINSTY and THRUSCROSS

nr Otley, N. Yorks.

These reservoirs are linked by a stream crossed by the A59 to Harrogate. Fewston and Swinsty adjoin each other nr Blubberhouses on the S side of the road and Thruscross lies to the N.

Controller: Yorkshire Water Authority, North Central Division.

Description: Long, narrow reservoirs in open country easily accessible from Harrogate or Leeds.

Species/sizes: Brown trout averaging 15oz.

Stocking: Annually, before start of season.

Rules: Thruscross fly only, others fly and minnow. Limit: 3 brace 9in and over. No wading. No Sunday fishing.

Season: 1 April to 29 September.

Permits: dt (Fewston and Swinsty) 40p, (Thruscross) £1. No boats.

Permits from: Vending machines at fishing lodges. Reservoir keeper's house at Thruscross.

GREENFIELD LAKE and PONDS

Buckden, nr Skipton, N. Yorks.

Turn off A684 from Leyburn or Hawes towards Buckden (B6160 best). At Buckden, with Buck Inn on right, fork left along lower road through

Hubberholme. Follow R. Wharfe to Beckermonds where Greenfield is signposted (1½m).

Owner: Langstroth Sevices Ltd.

Description: A partly natural lake, landscaped and extended by construction of dam: also ponds.

Species/sizes: Brown and rainbow.

	Brown	Rainbow
Average	9oz	12oz
Record	1lb 12oz	4lb
	(approx)	(approx)

Stocking: Stock of native brown trout, but restocking also takes place annually or at intervals, depending on catches.

Rules: Fly only. Limit: 2 brace 10in and over.

Season: 1 April to 30 September.

Permits: dt £3. One boat, £1 day. Maximum: eight bank and two boat anglers.

Permits from:
Langstroth Services Ltd, Greenfield, Buckden, Skipton, N. Yorks., BD23 5JN (tel. Kettlewell (075676) 832), and most local hotels.

Comments: Attractively located in Upper Wharfedale, the lake and ponds are well stocked with trout up to 3½lb in weight. The lake is secluded, has been dredged and landscaped, and is served by a quarry-bottomed road at the head of which cars may be parked. The feeder streams hold smaller trout and provide spawning grounds for indigenous fish.

HARDEN DAM

see Sunnydale.

JERVAULX ABBEY TROUT FISHERY

Jervaulx,
nr Middleham, N. Yorks.

Off A6108 Middleham to Ripon road 5m SE of Middleham and 16m NW of Ripon.

Owner: Jervaulx Abbey.

Description: Three landscaped lakes each of 1 acre in valley of River Ure (Yore).

Species/sizes: Brown and rainbow.

	Brown	Rainbow
Average	1lb 8oz	1lb 8oz
Record	3lb 2oz	2lb 5oz

Stocking: In February, with 200–300 11in fish. First stocking in 1974.

Rules: Fly only.

Season: 1 April to 30 September.

Permits: st £25; wt available only in special cases.

Permits from: Jervaulx Abbey, Ripon, N. Yorks.

Comments: Fishing on the River Ure is also available at £1 day — this is an 'all year' fishery, as grayling may be caught during the trout close season.

LEEMING RESERVOIR

Oxenhope,
Keighley, W. Yorks.

A trout water managed by Bradford City A.A. for members only, no day tickets Water is 20 acres plus, and contains brown trout only, averaging 8oz (record 6lb 8oz). Stocked once, in January. Bait fishing and spinning allowed. Season: 1 April to 30 September. The club's hon sec is A. J. Goggs, 6 Farringdon Grove, Buttershaw, Bradford 6. Subscription: £7.56.

LUMLEY MOOR

nr Ripon, Yorks.

Controller: Ripon Angling Club.

Description: Landscaped reservoir of about three acres.

Species/sizes: Brown and rainbow.

	Brown	Rainbow
Average	12oz	12oz
Record	3lb 4oz	2lb

Stocking: Once, at start of season.

Rules: Fly only.

Season: 1 April to 30 September.

Permits: Members and guests only (sub £22; limited to 40 members). Details from hon sec: A. R. Trees, 13 Skellfield Terrace, Ripon, Yorks.

MALHAM TARN

Settle, N. Yorks.

Off Langcliffe to Arncliffe Road, 5m NE of Settle.

Owner: National Trust.

Description: Natural lake set in open moorland.

Species/sizes: Brown trout only, averaging 1lb 2oz; biggest caught (Sept 1924) 5lb 14oz.

Stocking: Once yearly in March or April.

Rules: Fly only. Cars to be parked at Tarn House. Fishing from 10am only on Sundays. Yorkshire WA licence required.

Season: 1 May to 30 September.

Permits: dt £1; boats: weekdays £2, weekends £3.

Permits from:
The Warden, Malham Tarn Field Centre, Settle, N. Yorks., BD24 9PU (tel. Airton 331). A phone call is advisable.

Comments: Although the Tarn has provided some good catches in the past, it frequently proves a baffling water these days. Nevertheless, trout rise well to chironomid pupae in late May and June, and to emerging caddis in August and September, with sport most likely in the evenings. Weighted nymphs have proved successful on occasions and are always worth a try.

MORE HALL

Bolsterstone,
nr Sheffield, S. Yorks.

Lies between Damflask and Underbank Reservoirs in valley of Ewden Beck about 7m from Sheffield.

Controller: Yorkshire Water Authority, Southern Division.

Description: Landscaped reservoir.

Species: Brown trout.

Rules: Fly only. Wading and boat fishing prohibited. Limit: 1 brace 11in and over.

Season: 1 April to 30 September.

Permits: st £6; dt 50p. Yorkshire WA rod licence required.

Permits from:
Yorkshire WA Southern Division, Castle Market Building, Exchange Street, Sheffield, S1 1GB (to be obtained in advance).

NEWHOUSES TARN

Horton-in-Ribblesdale,
N. Yorks.

A small upland lake available only to members of Manchester A.A. Stocked each season. Trout over 3lb have been taken. Fly only. Club's hon sec is P. J. Mellor, 2 Stansfield Drive, Rochdale, Lancs., OL11 5RK.

RYBURN

Ripponden, W. Yorks.

A58 from Ripponden to Littleborough for half a mile; signpost on right-hand side of road.

Controller: Ripponden Fly-Fishers.

Description: Landscaped reservoir.

Species/sizes: Brown trout only, averaging 12oz; biggest caught, 1lb 7oz.

Stocking: At intervals of 3—4 years. Native fish have good spawning conditions.

Rules: Fly only.

Season: 1 April to 30 September.

Permits: st £65; dt to members' guests only.

Permits from: H. Hamer, The Hollies, Greetland, Halifax, Yorks.

Comments: Good sport with native brown trout. Patterns of lake olives kill at times, as do sedges and small dry patterns. Small wet flies are successful as well as larger attractors.

SCOUT DIKE

Penistone, nr Sheffield, S. Yorks.

Controller: Yorkshire Water Authority, Southern Division.

Description: Landscaped reservoir; maximum depth 40ft.

Species: Brown trout.

Rules: Any legal method permitted.

Season: 1 April to 30 September.

Permits: dt 40p.

Permits from:
Reservoir (Mon to Fri only) or Yorkshire WA, Southern Division, Jordan Hill, Gawber Road, Barnsley; also Castle Building, Exchange Street, Sheffield, S1 1GB. No tickets sold at weekends or Bank Holidays, but they may be purchased in advance.

SEMERWATER LAKE

Bainbridge, N. Yorks.

Lies in Ure (Yure) Valley off A684 from Leyburn near village of Bainbridge.

Controller: Bradford City AA/Wensleydale AA.

Description: Large natural lake in Wensleydale — ¾m by ½m, maximum depth 45ft.

Species: Brown trout, coarse fish.

Rules: Fly only before June 16. Limit 10in.

Season: 1 April to 30 September.

Permits: dt 40p.

Permits from:
J. Fawcett, Low Blean Farm (Bradford City A.A. water on south and south-west sides).
For west side (Wensleydale A.A.) contact Rose and Crown, Bainbridge.

Comments: Fly-fishermen are advised to avoid weekends if possible, as water skiing severely interferes with sport. Lake has yielded some good fish in the past, especially early on.

SETTLER DAM
see Sunnydale

SILSDEN RESERVOIR

nr Keighley, N. Yorks.

A 25-acre water, with good trout stocks
Available only to members of Bradford
Waltonians club. No day tickets. Club's
hon sec is E. H. Weight, Crossfields, Old
Lane, Hawksworth, Guiseley, Leeds.

SUNNYDALE

East Morton,
nr Bingley, Yorks.

Turn N off the A650 Bradford to
Keighley road to the village of East
Morton. From Green Bank Road at top of
East Morton turn left on to farm-type
road.

Controller: Bingley A.C.

Description: Landscaped reservoir
covering about three acres fed by stream.
Here water is shallowest (about 4ft). Rest
up to 20ft deep.

Species/sizes: Brown and rainbow.

	Brown	Rainbow
Average	12oz	1lb 8oz
Record	6lb 4oz	3lb 8oz

Stocking: Yearly with 2—3 year olds,
usually in close season. Rainbows
first introduced in 1974.

Rules: Fly and bait fishing; no spinning.
Limit: 1 brace 11in and over.

Season: 1 April to 30 September.

Permits: st £1.90 (proposed); dt 40p
(juniors, OAPs, etc. 90p full season).

Permits from:
Cullimore's, Bingley.
Richmond's, Morley Street, Bradford.
Carters Sports, Bridge Street, Bradford.
Also hon sec: B. Howard, 26 Spring Park
Road, Wilsden, Bradford, BD15 0EA.
Note: tickets for Sunday fishing must be
obtained in advance.

Comments: During April most anglers use
bait to take the best fish from the deepest
water towards the centre of the reservoir.
Fly will catch them late evenings. As the
water temperature rises from May onwards
they can be taken on slow-sinking fly
along the margins. The water fishes
especially well when clearing after heavy
rain.
Other stillwater trout fisheries held by
the club but reserved for members only
are:
Harden Dam, Harden, nr Bingley ($\frac{2}{3}$ acre;
brown trout up to 6lb);
Settler Dam, East Morton, nr Bingley (1
acre; brown trout up to 7lb; 2lb rainbows
introduced 1975).
These can be fished if full season book
(£1.90) is obtained.

SWINSTY
see Fewston, Swinsty and Thruscross

THRUSCROSS
see Fewston, Swinsty and Thruscross

THRYBERGH

Thrybergh,
nr Rotherham, S. Yorks.

Lies E of A630 about 3m NE of
Rotherham and 8m SW of Doncaster.

Controller: Yorkshire Water Authority, South-Eastern Division.

Description: Landscaped reservoir, maximum depth 30ft.

Species: Brown trout averaging 1lb 2oz, rainbows averaging 14oz.

Rules: Fly only. Limit: one brace 12in and over. No wading. No Sunday fishing.

Season: 1 April to 30 September.

Permits: st only. Holders limited to maximum of 50 half-day visits (i.e. before or after 3pm): Class A, Mon to Sat incl, £11. Class B, Mon to Fri incl, £8.50. Dt 80p may be issued on recommendation of st holder (limited to 3 per member).

Permits from:
Engineer and Manager, Doncaster and District Water Supply Unit, Copley House, Waterdale, Doncaster (apply in January); dt only issued on recommendation of st holder.

UNDERBANK
see Damflask.

WHINNYGILL RESERVOIR

nr Skipton, N. Yorks.

A club water belonging to Skipton A.A., for members only. A 10-acre reservoir, stone bowl, about 1m off Skipton to Ilkley road, on outskirts of Skipton. Brown trout averaging 1lb; record 4lb 12oz. Stocked once, about two months before start of season (1 April to 30 September). No boats. Fly, spinning and bait fishing allowed. Hon sec of Skipton A.A. is J. W. Preston, 18 Beech Hill Road, Carleton, Skipton; subscription £8 approx.

WINTERBURN RESERVOIR

nr Keighley, N. Yorks.

A 36-acre water, with good trout stocks, available only to members of Bradford Waltonians club. No day tickets. Club's hon sec is E. H. Wright, Crossfields, Old Lane, Hawksworth, Guiseley, Leeds.

Index

Set by Cold Composition Ltd., Tonbridge, Kent
and printed by William Brendon & Son, Tiptree, Essex